The
Cleveland Browns
A 50-Year Tradition

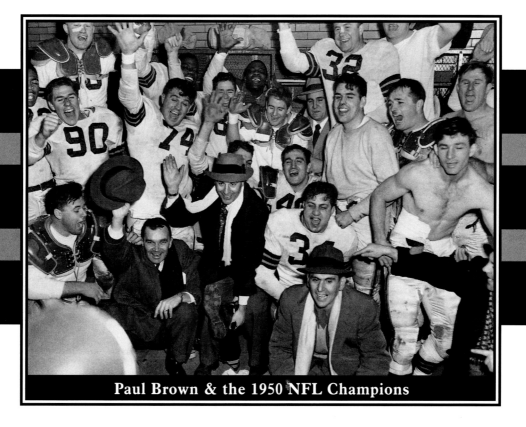

Paul Brown & the 1950 NFL Champions

EDITED, DESIGNED & PRODUCED BY
Bob Moon, SporTradition Publications,
Columbus, Ohio

WRITTEN BY
Steve Byrne, Jim Campbell & Mark Craig

PUBLISHED BY
Sagamore Publishing, Champaign, Ill.

TO: John Martello

FROM: Don Mack

Merry Christmas, December 25, 1995

Contents

Edited, Designed & Produced by Bob Moon
SporTradition Publications
798 Linworth Rd. East Columbus, Ohio 43235

Published by
Sagamore Publishing
302 West Hill St. Champaign, Ill. 61820

Library of Congress Catalog Card Number: 95-719-22

ISBN: 1-57167-020-3

Printed in the United States

Foreword

The Cleveland Browns remain the only National Football League team without a logo on their helmets. After 50 years, their uniforms display little change from the familiar brown and orange. Why mention such trivial facts about a football team? Because they are symbols of what this franchise is all about. Tradition is THE benchmark of the Cleveland Browns.

The Browns are a storied franchise, rich in a tradition that has made them one of the elite clubs in a league that boasts some of greatest legendary teams in professional sports history. When you think of sports tradition, you equate it to a team's level of success, and unquestionably, success is the tradition of the Cleveland Browns.

From the day the Browns first stepped on the field in 1946 as a member of the All-America Football Conference and then as an upstart entry in the NFL four years later, they won so often that through 1955 they were hailed as a sports dynasty, winning league championships every year in the AAFC and making championship game appearances in their first six campaigns in the NFL. Those glorious 10 seasons became the foundation of this proud franchise that ranks No. 5 in winning percentage and is at the top of the list with 23 playoff seasons in its 45-year history in the National Football League.

Despite some bumps in the road, it has been a thrilling ride through the first 50 years, and this commemorative book chronicles the journey — from Paul Brown fathering the club, to the dynasty years, through its stunning 1964 NFL championship victory over Johnny Unitas and the Baltimore Colts. It continues through the merger-motivated move to the American Football Conference, to the breathtaking Kardiac Kids days, which this observer saw up close as the beat writer for the *Akron Beacon Journal*, and through the exciting Dawg Pound Era of the Bernie Kosar-led team that knocked on the Super Bowl door three times in four years.

This journalistic trip next brings you to the present, a period of recovery and a return to Super Bowl contention, and then looks at the 10 greatest victories representing the various eras in Browns history.

The book continues with a chapter about those eagerly-awaited bitter rivalries over 50 years such as the Browns-Giants, Browns-Steelers and Browns-Bengals. Next comes a look at the major trades that have altered the course of franchise history and a profile of Browns fans. Finally, there is an interesting look at the people who have contributed to the great tradition of the Browns: Owner Art Modell, the head coaches and the players.

So lean back, relax, start turning the pages and enjoy this memorable and exciting journey through sports history.

Ray Yannucci
Publisher
Browns News/Illustrated

The History of the Browns

The Cleveland Browns: a tradition of winning, a tradition of excellence and a tradition of no-frills, no-glamour, basic football. A throwback to the old days. A team in plain brown uniforms, playing on grass, dirt and mud in one of the league's oldest stadiums. Intensely loyal fans appreciating substance over style, hard work over hype.

It all began with Mickey McBride, the entrepreneur, and Paul Brown, the innovator, taskmaster and teacher. Then came the great dynasty: 10 straight title games and seven championships led by Otto Graham and seven other Hall of Famers.

Next came the Jim Brown era, when the NFL entered the television age and Brown showcased the game at its professional best. The 1960s brought four more title games and a 27-0 crushing championship victory over the Baltimore Colts.

The 1970s brought a new conference and exciting new rivalries. Then in 1979 and '80, Brian Sipe and the Kardiac Kids won, and fluttered, the hearts of Browns fans everywhere. Next came Bernie Kosar, the "Dawg Defense" and five more playoff trips.

In 1995, their 50th season, the rebuilt and revitalized Cleveland Browns are once again reaching for the top.

Bernie Kosar

McBride's New Enterprise

T he man was a radical. We can use that word in the most positive way when describing Arthur B. McBride, the millionaire businessman from Cleveland who wanted to own a football team. The time was the early 1940s, when owning a professional sports franchise was considered nothing more than a rich man's hobby, as most pro sports teams failed to make money. McBride, known to all in Cleveland as Mickey, wasn't looking for another hobby. This man was all business and his football team was going to be a business venture as well, albeit a fun one. How different that attitude was to the rest of the professional football owners' fraternity. Most franchises operated in the red, and attendance was not much better than the average baseball game today. College football was still No. 1 in the hearts of American sports fans and most people accepted that.

Marion Motley

By Steve Byrne

Not McBride. Although the National Football League owners were, for the most part, as wealthy as he was, they were content to see their other businesses make up for revenue lost on football. But McBride was never content with losing. He saw no reason why one business should be allowed to lag behind simply because the others were successful. If Mickey were to own a team, the operation would be first class all the way.

McBride had worked his way up from the streets of Chicago, where he sold newspapers as a boy. He made additional money on the side when his regular customers would give him the free transfers they had just received from the street car conductor. In exchange for the transfers, McBride would give them newspapers. He then sold the transfers for three cents to people who would normally have to pay five cents, thus showing early evidence of his business acumen. Later, at age 23, McBride was a circulation director of William Randolph Hearst's *Chicago American*. He held that position with the *Cleveland News* from 1913-31 before going into business for himself.

Everything he touched turned to gold. He owned the Yellow-Zone Cab Co., Cleveland's only taxi fleet. He owned real estate in Ohio, Florida and Illinois, a radio station, a printing company and a horse race wire syndicate.

Ironically, it was college football that put the idea of owning an NFL franchise in his head. McBride had never been a football fan, or even a sports fan. He liked baseball and boxing, but could hardly be described as a big-time follower. But when his son, Arthur Jr., went off to Notre Dame in the fall of 1940, McBride made the pilgrimages to see the Irish play every Saturday, and not just in South Bend, Ind. He followed the Fighting Irish wherever they played. The love of football so prevalent at Notre Dame infected McBride in a big way.

Returning to Cleveland on the day after he watched his first Notre Dame game, McBride took in a Cleveland Rams game, his first NFL contest. A man who had never been to a football game in his life was now a familiar sight both at college and NFL affairs.

Unlike Notre Dame, the Rams were fodder for the Bears, Redskins and other successful clubs. They hadn't had a winning record over their first five seasons after their inception in 1937. The Rams had been sold in 1941 to Daniel F. Reeves, and the rumors that the team would eventually leave Cleveland were now flying. McBride was nonetheless convinced that with the right promotion, professional football could sell in Cleveland. He offered to purchase the Rams, but Reeves declined the offer.

Reeves' rebuff led McBride to the office of *Chicago Tribune* sports editor Arch Ward almost two years later, in the winter of 1944. He had heard Ward, who had already started the Major League baseball All-Star game and the all-star football game between top college seniors and the NFL champion, was looking to launch a second pro football league. The Rams had suspended operations in 1943, and McBride wanted to secure a team for Cleveland in the event of the NFL pulling out of town.

Two upstart leagues had already failed in recent years. Ward was determined it wouldn't

happen with his. He would have no problem with McBride in that regard. Money was not an issue with McBride, who wanted the best and was willing to pay for it. The two men hit it off as they each understood what the other wanted.

Representatives from six cities met with Ward in a St. Louis hotel room on June 4, 1944, to form the All-America Football Conference. Two more franchises would be added that summer and, on Sept. 4, it was announced the league had formed. The Cleveland Browns would join the Brooklyn Dodgers, Buffalo Bisons, Chicago Rockets, Los Angeles Dons, Miami Seahawks, New York Yankees and San Francisco 49ers.

McBride was not a very happy man when Reeves, despite the Rams having won the NFL championship in 1945, announced on January 12, 1946, the club was moving to Los Angeles. McBride thrived on competition and, even

SUCCESS STORY: *Mickey McBride (left) and Paul Brown share a moment of satisfaction after the Browns won their third straight AAFC championship in 1948. McBride's earlier investment in the team and the league had paid off: the Browns were a major success artistically and financially.*

BROWN'S BUCKEYES: *At Ohio State, Paul Brown (above) coached for three seasons (1941-43), winning a national championship in '42. When he joined Cleveland's new AAFC franchise, he signed some of his former Buckeyes, including middle guard Bill Willis (above right) and end Dante Lavelli (opposite page).*

though the Browns had yet to play a game, was winning the publicity war against the club in the established league.

McBride had hired Paul Brown, who had coached Ohio State University to a national championship in 1942, to coach the team. He had many OSU and Big Ten alumni and native Ohioans under contract. He held a name-the-team contest during the 1945 season when the Rams were on their way to a 9-1 record and an NFL championship. "The Cleveland Browns, who have never played a football game, are

already receiving more publicity than the Cleveland Rams, who have just won the world football championship," *Cleveland Plain Dealer* sports columnist James Doyle said.

Despite their success on the field, the Rams drew only 73,000 fans to four home games and 32,178 to the championship in Cleveland Stadium against a team with the biggest name in the game — the Washington Redskins and quarterback Sammy Baugh.

Hiring Brown was McBride's master stroke. The Norwalk, Ohio, native was already a legend in his home state. A graduate of Massillon High School and Miami University, Brown started his marvelous career at 21 when he was hired in 1930 as head coach of Severn Prep, a private school run by the Navy. Two years later, after compiling a 16-1-1 record at Severn, he returned to his alma mater.

Brown rang up an 80-8-2 record in nine seasons at Massillon. During his final six years the Tigers had a 58-1-1 record and were regarded as the finest high school program in the nation. When Ohio State lost Head Coach Francis Schmidt after the 1940 season, Brown was the

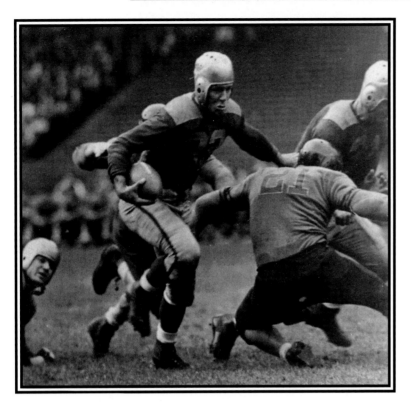

HALL'S FAME: *"Bullet" Parker Hall (32) was the Cleveland Rams' most famous name in the pre-World War II years. Hall was a classic tailback who could run, pass and kick. The Rams played in Cleveland from 1937-42 and 1944-45, dropping from the NFL in the war year of '43. They won the '45 championship, beating the Washington Redskins, before moving to Los Angeles in '46.*

logical choice to replace him. Brown didn't even have to apply for the job. It was done for him by sportswriters, OSU alumni and the Ohio Football Coaches Association. When he left Massillon he departed with not only an enviable record, but a 21,000-seat stadium (up from 5,000 when he arrived) named for him.

Brown compiled an 18-8-1 record in three seasons at Ohio State. His record might have been better had World War II not called away most of the younger members of the '43 team, which ended with a losing record (the only one Brown would suffer in his first 26 years of coaching). In the Navy himself in 1944, Lt. Paul Brown coached the Great Lakes Naval Training Center club to a combined 15-5-2 record over two seasons.

Brown, oddly enough, wasn't McBride's first choice to be head coach. As a Notre Dame

zealot, McBride wanted the Irish's dynamic taskmaster, Frank Leahy, who had posted a 24-3-3 record from 1941-43. Notre Dame officials, however, talked him out of it.

McBride then sought the advice of *Plain Dealer* football writer John Dietrich, who didn't hesitate to tell him Paul Brown was the man he wanted. Brown, Dietrich said, was young, a winner and popular in the part of the world where the Browns would be drawing fans.

Arch Ward concurred. Saying Brown would "be as good as anyone you could get," Ward offered to make the short trip to Great Lakes Naval Center to solicit him.

Brown signed a five-year contract on Feb. 8, 1945, in Ward's office at the *Tribune*. His annual salary was $25,000 per year. He was only 36 years old.

"Paul was the easiest person I ever hired," McBride said at the time. "I could've signed him for $15,000, but I wanted to make a splash for publicity. I wanted to say my team had the highest-paid coach in America."

The Rams announced their move to Los Angeles less than a month after their finest moment — a 15-14 victory in the NFL championship game of Dec. 16, 1945. The Browns reportedly would refrain from luring Rams players to stay in Cleveland, but five players and a coach decided not to make the trip west. The decision of one of the players, tackle Chet Adams, caused the Rams to bring a breach of contract suit against the Browns.

The Rams requested U.S. Federal Court Judge Emerich Freed to grant an injunction forbidding Adams to play for the Browns. The Browns, in return, dismissed back Ted Fritsch from training camp. Fritsch had played for the Green Bay Packers since 1942, and the Browns believed cutting him might make the Rams drop their suit. Fritsch rejoined the Packers and stayed with them through 1950.

Freed ruled on Aug. 29, 1946, that Adams could play for the Browns, citing the fact the Cleveland Rams ceased to exist after Jan. 12 and that Adams and the others were free agents. Adams said his having been signed by

Rams assistant coach Red Conkright, the coach who opted to remain in Cleveland, was a factor in his decision to jump leagues.

Adams and the other ex-Rams — backs Don Greenwood and Gaylon Smith, punter-safety Tom Colella and lineman Mike Scarry — were among the few players not hand-picked by Paul Brown. The football world had gotten a glimpse of the Brown method of building a team, and it was something of a shocker.

Brown stuck to people, both players and coaches, with whom he was familiar. Such a method might have smacked of cronyism, but Brown had an uncanny eye for talent, and was determined not to take a man simply because he was a "name" player. The fact that a man had NFL experience made little difference to Brown. He was looking for one specific type of man and was determined to stock the Browns with those people.

Lin Houston, a guard, played for Brown at Massillon and Ohio State. Others who played for Brown at OSU included guards Bill Willis and George Cheroke, tackles Lou Groza and Jim Daniell, fullback Gene Fekete and end Dante Lavelli. Playing for Brown at Great Lakes were fullback Marion Motley and defensive end George Young.

Brown also had an excellent memory for opponents. He remembered from his Ohio State years a halfback named Edgar "Special Delivery" Jones from the University of Pittsburgh. He made a mental note on a big end from Utah named Mac Speedie, who played for the Fort Warren team against Brown's Great Lakes squad.

The most important opponent Brown would recall was Otto Graham, a multi-sport star at Northwestern University. Recruited primarily for his prowess as a high school basketball player, Graham was not even invited to try out for the football team as a freshman. He got a shot the next year only because rumors had reached the varsity that a guy playing in the intramural league could really throw the ball.

Graham's football career progressed slowly, but by 1943 he was as renowned as a gridder as

BUILDING BLOCKS: *Paul Brown built the Browns with players and opponents from his past college and service coaching experience. It resulted in scenes such as this after the Browns won the 1948 AAFC title. From left to right are Edgar Jones (Pittsburgh), Lou Saban (Indiana), Otto Graham (Northwestern) and Marion Motley (Great Lakes Naval Training Center).*

he was as a basketball player. He led the Wildcats to an 8-2 record that year, second in the Big Ten, and was chosen All-America. When he left Northwestern, he had received three letters each in football and basketball and two letters in baseball.

If Brown's desire to bring Graham on board surprised anyone, it was possibly because Brown had made it known he would run the offense out of the T formation. Graham had only learned that offense in the service, with the North Carolina Pre-Flight. But Graham had all that Paul Brown wanted in a player, both athletically and personally. He became the Browns' first, and highest-paid, player, earning $7,500 in 1946.

"The two things I insisted on were that I would be in charge of the football end of the business and that I would have an absolute free hand in selecting my players," Brown once said. "I wanted them all to be high class, and I picked them on the basis of personality as well as ability. I'd always lived by the rule that you don't win with dogs and, to me, it's a rule that never has changed."

SPEEDIE MOVES: *Mac Speedie snares a pass near the sideline against the Dodgers in Ebbets Field in 1948. The sideline pass, innovative for its time, allowed Speedie or Dante Lavelli to run what appeared to be a deep route, only to "hook in" to the sideline, leaving defenders such as Harry Burrus (54) too deep to cover.*

The Rise & Fall of the AAFC

When the Cleveland Browns opened their first training camp on July 28, 1946, at Bowling Green State University in northwest Ohio, an experiment within an experiment was launched. First, there was the experiment of whether another professional league could make a go of it beside the established National Football League, in operation more than 25 years. But within the experiment that was the All-America Football Conference, there was the question of whether Paul Brown's novel way of running a team, with the head coach in complete control of all football operations, would succeed. Preparation was a Brown trademark. As was his style, he had been meticulous in his personnel selections for the Browns' first team. Not only did he choose his new players based on personal experiences with them, but he selected his coaches the same way.

The new staff included familiar names from many eras in Brown's coaching career: Fritz Heisler played for Brown at Massillon High School and was a member of Brown's staff at Massillon and Ohio State. John L. Brickels played against Brown as a student at Wittenberg College and coached against him at New Philadelphia (Ohio) High School when Brown was at Massillon. Blanton Collier, a highly successful high school football and basketball coach from Paris, Ky., was on Brown's staff at Great Lakes and helped develop the T formation there. Bob Voigts was an assistant at Great Lakes under coach Tony Hinkle, who preceded Brown.

As with his players, Brown insisted the coaches were people who knew what he wanted. What Brown wanted most of all was perfection. Mental discipline was as important as physical conditioning. The coach didn't want, as he said "just a bunch of tough guys who can take it." To that end he instituted the use of film clips to study an opponent's tendencies as well as grade his own players, notebooks and classroom sessions. He was the first head coach to keep his players

Lou Rymkus

By Steve Byrne

CAMP CONFERENCE: *Paul Brown gives instructions at Bowling Green State University, site of the Browns' training camp from 1946-51. Players lived in a sorority house and practiced next to a local cemetery (above), but the relaxed campus atmosphere was favored by Brown, who later moved the site to Hiram College. The Browns' seal brown and burnt orange uniform colors were adapted by Brown from BGSU's color scheme.*

sequestered in a hotel on the night before a game. He developed a passing game designed to locate holes in the defense, and a defensive strategy to counter opponents' passing attacks. Brown was the first coach to use intelligence tests to determine a player's coach-ability.

"Somewhere along the line the dumb guy will get your football team in trouble, probably on the field, maybe off," Brown said in a 1953 interview. "We can't afford to fool around with him."

Brown's men, he said, would love playing football for the game itself first and the paycheck second. He spoke with great pride when declaring he had "the most amateurish professional football team in the country" and "nothing more than a glorified college team." The Cleveland Browns were amateurs in spirit, but hardly in reality.

Perhaps the greatest testament to Brown's system was the number of men who became successful head coaches after playing or coaching for Brown. Chuck Noll, Bill Walsh, Don Shula and Weeb Ewbank won Super Bowls. Blanton Collier coached the Browns to the '64 NFL title. Lou Saban coached Buffalo to two AFL crowns. Ara Parseghian coached Notre Dame to two NCAA national championships. Otto Graham, Walt Michaels, Abe Gibron, Mike McCormack, Mac Speedie, Paul Wiggin and Lou Rymkus were also players under Brown who became NFL or AFL head coaches.

Brown also insisted everyone who worked for him display a decorum in practice and in public. Players were expected to come to practice in clean T-shirts and be as well groomed when they arrived as when they left. In public, the Browns had to wear jackets, slacks and polished shoes. Drunkenness and brawling were, naturally, forbidden. The practice, while possibly new to pro football, might have been an idea Brown borrowed from Joe McCarthy, the New York Yankees manager from 1931-46, who made his players wear jackets and ties while staying at the team's hotel during spring training. Both teams dominated their respective professional sports.

One illustrative story concerns a talented young college lineman in whom the Browns were interested. But when the player arrived at the team's training camp uncombed, unshaven and dressed like a laborer, Brown told him a mistake had been made and the man should visit the business manager, who would give him money for transportation home. Brown didn't even give the player a chance to right his own ship. The coach wasn't there to teach you to be a gentleman. You either came to him as one or didn't come at all.

But while Brown demanded that his players be gentlemen, the coach himself engaged in practices that in 1946 were hardly considered gentlemanly. He refused to agree not to raid the NFL or to pursue NFL veterans who had yet to be discharged from the armed services. While there was no rule barring black players from the league, Brown would have no part of any gentleman's agreement keeping blacks out of the AAFC.

The latter decision led Brown to offer tryouts to Bill Willis and Marion Motley a few days after the first training camp opened. It forced the NFL's hand, as the senior league anticipated the hiring of black players. The Rams had signed Kenny Washington and Woody Strode, the first black men in the league in 13 years, in the spring prior to the '46 season.

Brown's decision to court players with remaining college eligibility was even more controversial, and caused a rift between him and his former employer, Ohio State University, which was the main pool of his talent. Brown, however, insisted he only went after

players who had no plans of returning to school. "We're not trying to snatch athletes who want to return to college," Brown once said. "We are going to run our business aggressively — that means to win."

Such was the case of Lou Groza, who had only one season of college football experience when he joined the Browns. Groza lettered for the Buckeyes as a freshman in 1942 before entering the Army, but played no football during his time in the service. OSU Head Coach Carroll Widdoes accused Brown of raiding the Buckeyes, although Groza and Jim Daniell, who also had remaining eligibility, had said they would return as students only.

If Groza was a risk for lack of experience, so too was Dante Lavelli, who suffered a season-ending injury in his second year at Ohio State (1942), then joined the Army in 1943 and, like Groza, played no football while a serviceman. But Brown knew a football player when he saw one, and Lavelli caught 386 passes over his 11 seasons with 6,488 yards and 62 touchdowns.

GLAD GROZA: *After three years in World War II, Lou Groza was happy to be with the Browns in 1946. Ohio State coach Carroll Widdoes, however, was unhappy with Paul Brown for recruiting former Buckeyes such as Groza, who still had college eligibility remaining.*

Lavelli did not start in the first exhibition game of the first AAFC season on Aug. 30, 1946. Nor did Mac Speedie, the end who would join Lavelli as one of the most prolific receivers in Browns history with 349 combined AAFC-NFL receptions from 1946-52.

Cliff Lewis, a local product (Lakewood) and star at Duke University, was the starting

FIRST FOES: *The Miami Seahawks were the Browns' first regular-season opponent in 1946. Cleveland won, 44-0, a positive omen for the Browns, but a bad sign for the Seahawks. They finished the season at 3-11, then were expelled from the All-America Football Conference for "failing to meet contractual obligations."*

quarterback, as Otto Graham was just joining the Browns after leading the College All-Stars to a 16-0 win over the Rams on Aug. 24. Gene Fekete started at fullback over Marion Motley, who had only been in camp since Aug. 9.

The game was played in the Akron Rubber Bowl, against the Brooklyn Dodgers, in front of 35,964. The Browns won, 35-20, after overcoming a 13-0 deficit. Fred "Dippy" Evans, a star halfback for Notre Dame's unbeaten 1941 team, scored the first touchdown on a pass from Lewis. Evans also scored on an interception return, while Speedie and George Young caught touchdown passes from Graham. John Rokisky returned a fumble for a TD.

It was the only exhibition game of the inaugural season. One week later the Browns hosted the Miami Seahawks before a crowd that was only about 13,000 below what the Rams drew for four home dates in 1945 and almost double the size of the crowd that saw them beat the Redskins in Cleveland Stadium for the title. The legwork McBride did to drum up interest in the Browns worked beyond anybody's dreams, as 60,135 witnessed the first-ever regular-season Browns game.

Mac Speedie and Alton Coppage replaced Rokisky and John Yonakor as starting ends. The rest of the first string was a repeat of their exhibition game, with Jim Daniell and Chet Adams at tackles, Bill Willis and Ed Ulinski at guards, Mike Scarry at center, Edgar Jones and Don Greenwood at halfbacks, Gene Fekete at fullback and Cliff Lewis at quarterback.

The game was a sign of things to come in the future. It was simply no contest, just as the AAFC would be for the Browns for four seasons. Speedie scored the first touchdown on a 19-yard pass from Lewis. Graham and Lavelli combined on a TD pass and Tom Colella and Greenwood scored on runs. Ray Terrell added a TD on a 76-yard interception return and Groza kicked three field goals. The final score was Browns 44, Seahawks 0.

Motley started ahead of Fekete at fullback for the second game, played before 51,962 at Soldier Field in Chicago, a record for a professional game there. It was in this one that the Browns may have established themselves as the class of the league. Motley's 122 yards rushing, Greenwood's 41-yard touchdown gallop and a defense that held Elroy "Crazy Legs" Hirsch, the Rockets' star halfback, to minus-one yard rushing lifted the Browns to a 20-6 win. The Browns scored another shutout, 28-0, against the Buffalo Bisons, in Week 3, and rolled through the first half of the schedule unbeaten, outscoring opponents by a combined 180-34. Four home games averaged 58,000 fans.

Next, the San Francisco 49ers, behind quarterback Frankie Albert and his favorite target, Alyn Beals, handed the Browns their first loss, 34-20, before 70,385 in Cleveland Stadium. Albert, an All-America at Stanford and a master of the T-formation, was surprisingly hot-

Brown. After the Browns whipped the Yankees, 24-7, on Sept. 29, Flaherty verbally attacked his players for losing to a team "from podunk led by a high school coach."

The Yankees were a talented club, especially on defense, where Flaherty assembled two lines that alternated quarters. Bruce Alford, Bruiser Kinard, Darrell Palmer and Perry Schwartz were its stars. On offense, halfback Spec Sanders led the league in rushing (709

and-cold in his first professional season. But he was hot on that Oct. 27 day and so was the defense, as the Browns rushed for just 34 yards. The Los Angeles Dons beat the Browns the following week on a late field goal.

That was it for losing for one year. The Browns avenged the loss to the Niners, 14-7, on Nov. 10, and averaged 48 points a game over the last four contests. They finished the season with a 12-2 record and had outscored their rivals by an average of 30-10.

FAN APPROVAL: *Large crowds were the norm for the AAFC's first season in 1946, including this Browns-49ers game in Kezar Stadium, which drew 41,061. Gaylon Smith tackles Earle Parsons while Otto Graham (60) and Lin Houston (32), both on defense in the days of one-platoon football, approach the play. The Browns won, 14-7, their eighth victory of the season.*

T he championship game was Dec. 22 against the New York Yankees, who outclassed the Eastern Division via a 10-3-1 record, a seven-game lead over the other three clubs in the circuit. New York was coached by Ray Flaherty, who had coached the Washington Redskins to two NFL titles and a seven-year record of 56-23-3. Flaherty never hid his disdain for Paul

yards, six TDs). Quarterback Ace Parker was considered the equal of Graham and Albert.

Brown made the most controversial move of his coaching career just as the Browns were preparing for the biggest battle of the campaign. Jim Daniell, a starting tackle and team captain who played for Brown at Ohio State, was involved in an altercation with Cleveland police and charged with public intoxication. Daniell's companions, Mac Speedie and Lou Rymkus, were charged with disorderly conduct. Brown shocked the team and the community by firing Daniell before the next day's practice, while allowing Speedie and Rymkus

AAFC CHAMPS: *Tired but proud, Otto Graham, Dante Lavelli, Paul Brown and Mac Speedie (l-r) relax in the locker room after defeating the Yankees, 14-9, for the 1946 AAFC championship. Browns players received $931.57 apiece as their hard-fought winners share, considerably less than the value of a Super Bowl ring in the '90s.*

to stay with the club. Brown insisted he was not playing favorites. Daniell had specifically violated Brown's ironclad rule against drinking during the football season.

"It is up to the players to observe the rules or take the consequences," Brown said. "Daniell is not being made an example. He's simply getting what's coming to him."

Daniell was later cleared of the intoxication charge, but Brown did not invite him to return. He gave the rights to Daniell to the Chicago Rockets, but Daniell never played another professional football game.

As for the game, Motley, who gained 98 yards on 13 carries, gave the Browns a 7-3 lead on a one-yard touchdown run. The Yankees went up 9-7 as Sanders capped an 80-yard drive with a two-yard TD run. The Browns regained the lead in the fourth quarter and won, 14-9.

The winning drive started at their own 24-yard line. Graham passed to Edgar Jones, who made a diving catch at the Yankees' 42-yard line. Jones took a lateral from Graham and passed to Lavelli to the 28. Lavelli scored the go-ahead TD when he got behind Jack Russell at the seven-yard line, caught Graham's pass and stumbled the rest of the way to the end zone. Graham, who engineered the winning score, sealed the victory when he intercepted a Parker pass at the Cleveland 30-yard line. The "high school coach" had been vindicated.

"My satisfaction was proving my principles," Brown said afterward, "proving that the same ideals that won in high school and college could win in professional ball."

The Browns had defeated the Yankees three times and even Flaherty conceded, saying the Browns were just as good as the NFL-champion Chicago Bears. It wasn't long before others were copying the Browns' trap plays, on which Motley used his incredible starting speed to get through a hole in the middle of the line and then use his 230 pounds to plow over defenders; and their sideline passing routes that took advantage of the speed and cutting abilities of Speedie and Lavelli, and Graham's knack for reading defenses.

The AAFC was a rousing success in 1946. Only the Miami Seahawks and the Brooklyn Dodgers did not draw healthy crowds. The average AAFC game outdrew the average NFL affair by about 1,000. It appeared as if the dream of Arch Ward, to have two leagues operating separately, with a world-championship game at the end of the campaign, would come true.

But the league was victim of its own success. Salaries, especially for rookies, were esca-

KEY PLAY: *With snowflakes falling, Browns back Don Greenwood dives to intercept a pass intended for New York's Jack Russell in the 1946 championship game. It was Greenwood's second straight title game in Cleveland Stadium. He played for the '45 Cleveland Rams who beat Washington for the NFL crown.*

STREAKING: *The Browns' Ara Parseghian tackles New York's Spec Sanders in Cleveland's 34-21 win on Nov. 21, 1948 in Yankee Stadium. It was the 11th victory of the Browns' undefeated season. Cleveland defensive end John Yonakor approaches on the left.*

lating beyond some teams' ability to pay. The ongoing raiding of the rival league's rosters only upped the ante. The expense of air travel, something the AAFC did from the beginning, was a huge drain on budgets.

The league was also a victim of the Browns' success. The Browns put up a record of 52-4-3 in the four years of the AAFC's existence. They lost to only two of the seven other teams (Los Angeles and San Francisco each beat the Browns twice). They were the only champion the AAFC ever had. Included in the Browns' incomparable record were a 16-game regular-season winning streak and a 29-game streak without a loss.

The Browns went from Oct. 12, 1947, to Oct. 9, 1949 without experiencing defeat. Their

14-0 record and 49-7 victory over Buffalo in the 1948 championship game was the first of only two times a major-league football team ever went through a season unbeaten and untied. (The 1972 Miami Dolphins are the other.)

Although Paul Brown's coaching methods were never predictable, the results were, and predictability led to a lack of fan interest. The Browns were simply too good, so good that attendance was steadily backsliding. The home crowds that had averaged 57,000 in 1946 were 31,000 in '49.

The Browns were a bigger draw away from Cleveland Stadium in the final season of the AAFC, averaging 37,000 on the road (but only 5,000 showed up for the season finale against the Chicago Hornets, formerly the Rockets, in Chicago).

Oddly enough, it was the most humiliating defeat the Browns experienced in their AAFC years that resulted in the only decent crowd in Cleveland Stadium in 1949. The Browns had been embarrassed by the 49ers, 56-28, in San Francisco on Oct. 9. It was the end of their two-year unbeaten streak. It would be another 41 years before the record for opponents' points in one game would be broken.

Brown, while seemingly unperturbed at the end of the game, boiled over when the team got to its hotel in Los Angeles for the Oct. 14 game versus the Dons. Brown berated his club in no uncertain terms, saying he would break up the team if certain people stopped playing to their abilities. The Dons paid the price: the Browns returned to Cleveland with a 61-14 victory.

There were 72,189 on hand in Cleveland Stadium 16 days later when the 49ers came to town for the second meeting with the Browns that season. Albert passed to Len Eshmont for the first scoring of the contest, but the Browns led 30-21 when the 49ers scored their last TD with just 15 seconds to go. San Francisco half-back Joe "the Jet" Perry, who gained 156 yards on 16 carries on Oct. 9, was held to 28 yards on 10 carries.

The beating the Browns took in the first contest against the Niners might have been a

PLUNGING AHEAD: *Otto Graham (60) watches Edgar Jones plow through for the first TD in the Browns' 49-7 1948 AAFC title-game win over Buffalo in Cleveland Stadium. The victory capped the Browns' undefeated season. Blocking for Jones are Eddie Ulinski (36), Lou Groza (46) and Frank Gatski (22).*

case of overconfidence. They had been down 28-7 to the Bills in the opening game of the season, but rallied in the fourth quarter on three Graham TD passes, one to Horace Gillom and two to Mac Speedie, to escape with a 28-28 tie.

The rest of the season was anti-climactic, even though the Browns and 49ers would meet again in Cleveland for the AAFC title. A mere 16,506 attended the Nov. 6 game against Chicago, a record low for a Browns game in Cleveland. Only 22,550 fans paid to attend the 1949 championship game, a 21-7 Browns victory.

Mickey McBride was determined to see the AAFC survive. The Browns were profitable and McBride offered financial help to the struggling franchises. It was really to no avail. Most teams in both leagues were in the red as the bidding war for talent escalated. There also were rumors that Paul Brown would accept a college coaching position. After he signed a new seven-year contract on Jan. 1, 1949, those rumors were quashed.

But the Browns-49ers rivalry was fierce. Their matchups drew an average of 64,164. No NFL teams could make that claim. It wasn't

lost on the NFL. When merger talks were held in Chicago in January of 1949, the senior league agreed to take Cleveland and San Francisco, and let the other AAFC franchises fall by the wayside. McBride rebelled. He would not see his new friends "thrown to the vultures" as he put it. McBride had become close to Ben Lindheimer of the Dons and Jim Breuil of the Bills in particular, and balked at the idea that five of the seven AAFC teams should simply fold their tents. But the handwriting was on the wall. As long as the Cleveland Browns continued to remain unchallenged for supremacy, things could only get worse for the league.

It was clear the Browns were in need of a new challenge. Brown, as always, anticipated it would come. Two days before the Browns beat the 49ers, the leagues announced an end to the war. The National Football League would take

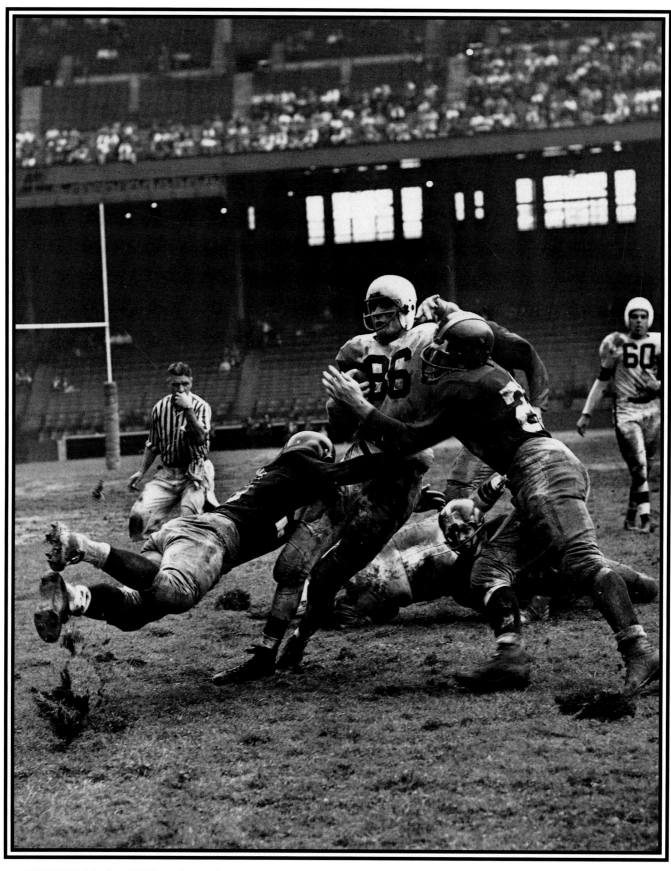

WINNING GAMES, LOSING APPEAL: *Empty seats are the backdrop as Dub Jones runs into two Brooklyn-New York Yankees defenders in a 14-3 victory at Cleveland Stadium in 1949. The Browns' domi-nation of the AAFC saw fan interest drop dramatically as the league headed toward extinction.*

in the champion Browns, the 49ers and the Baltimore Colts. Remaining players from the four defunct teams (the Dodgers had merged with the Yankees, making the AAFC a seven-team league in 1949) would be put in a pool from which all other NFL clubs could choose.

Brown and McBride made sure the truce wasn't a victory for the NFL. The two demanded the AAFC receive fair treatment, or the NFL could do without the Browns. Bert Bell was on the Browns' side and stated the Browns should be treated as members of the NFL, not losers in a war. No doubt, Bell saw the entry of the Browns into the older league as a great drawing card. "[The] merger is a victory for the public," Bell said, "and we'll treat it that way."

Brown insisted his club be put in a division with other eastern teams and fully expected to see the Browns take on the Eagles, the two-time defending NFL champion, in their first game in their new league.

There was nothing more for the Browns to prove except whether they could compete in the NFL, which was considered by most to be where the superior talent lay. Despite what the Browns and the entire AAFC had accomplished, there was still a prevailing attitude among a few that any NFL team could beat any AAFC team, and that the Browns were no exception. Many believed they'd get their comeuppance against the big-leaguers.

END OF THE LINE: *The bench was full, but the stands were not when the Browns beat Buffalo (top) in a December 1949 playoff game in Cleveland Stadium. Only 17,270 showed up, the Browns' second smallest home crowd in their four-year AAFC existence. A week later (above), Paul Brown and his players celebrated their last AAFC championship, a 21-7 victory over the San Francisco 49ers.*

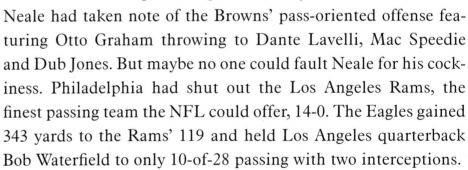
Making Believers of the NFL

Earle "Greasy" Neale might have been the only one with a right to scoff at the Cleveland Browns and the All-America Football Conference, and he did so, right after his Philadelphia Eagles won the National Football League championship on Dec. 18, 1949. "[The Browns] are a basketball team," Neale told a reporter after declaring there was no one left to challenge his Eagles. "All they do is throw the ball."

Neale had taken note of the Browns' pass-oriented offense featuring Otto Graham throwing to Dante Lavelli, Mac Speedie and Dub Jones. But maybe no one could fault Neale for his cockiness. Philadelphia had shut out the Los Angeles Rams, the finest passing team the NFL could offer, 14-0. The Eagles gained 343 yards to the Rams' 119 and held Los Angeles quarterback Bob Waterfield to only 10-of-28 passing with two interceptions.

Dub Jones

By Steve Byrne

Philadelphia could do a little passing itself. Quarterback Tommy Thompson completed 54 percent of his throws that year with 16 touchdowns and only 11 interceptions. He'd had a couple of great receivers with whom to work in Pete Pihos and Jack Ferrante.

But it was Steve Van Buren, the NFL's leading rusher four of the previous five seasons, who made Philadelphia what it was. He continued to prove it in the title game with 196 yards on 31 carries on a rain-drenched Los Angeles Coliseum field.

To the surprise of almost no one, least of all Paul Brown, the first game of the 1950 season would pit the two champions — Saturday, Sept. 16 in Philadelphia.

Rumors were Neale was secretly worried about the Browns' passing game. The Browns had sailed unbeaten through five exhibition games against their new NFL opponents, averaging 35 points a game. Mort Berry, a sports reporter for the *Philadelphia Inquirer*, was sent to follow the Browns throughout the preseason. He spoke in glowing terms of Cleveland's talent, but most dismissed his assertions as nothing

more than an attempt to spur on ticket sales for the upcoming opener.

If the Eagles' coach was indeed worried about the champions of the All-America Football Conference, it wasn't enough to make him scout them. Scouting was considered unnecessary in the NFL of the 1940s. The teams all played each other, twice a year in most cases, and were usually familiar with the opponents' various offensive and defensive tendencies.

But the Browns had never played a game in the NFL. While everyone expected the Clevelanders to get a strong lesson in reality from the Eagles, Paul Brown was busy making sure they wouldn't. When the Eagles and Rams were sloshing through the mud in the 1949 title game, Browns assistant coaches Fritz Heisler and Blanton Collier were somewhere in the crowd, taking note of every nuance of these division champions. The Browns had film of the Eagles and had nine months to study the club they knew they would play in Game No. 1.

Neale's pride and joy was the defense he had invented, an alignment of five linemen, four defensive backs and two linebackers who made contact with the receivers just beyond the line of scrimmage. Almost every other team copied it to the point it became known as the "Eagle" defense. Brown, however, saw serious flaws in the fact the defense had no middle linebacker. The Eagles stopped the run by clogging the line of scrimmage while the outside men swooped onto the quarterback.

Brown and his staff decided that if their offensive linemen could be spaced farther apart on the line of scrimmage, the Eagles' defenders would follow them when they moved out. The defense would, unwittingly, open wide holes for

READY TO GO: *The Browns' offense lines up in Philadelphia's Municipal Stadium, site of the Army-Navy game, prior to the 1950 opener versus the Eagles. Standing in the backfield are (left to right): HB Dub Jones, FB Marion Motley, QB Otto Graham and HB Rex Bumgardner. On the line are RE Dante Lavelli, RT Lou Rymkus, RG Lin Houston, C Frank Gatski, LG Weldon Humble, LT Lou Groza and LE Mac Speedie.*

the Browns' ball carriers, Marion Motley, Dub Jones and Rex Bumgardner.

Such a plan was all well and good, provided a team had the talent on a par with the Eagles. Brown made sure the Browns did, and secured some much-needed players for the 1950 season. There were holes to fill when three key members of the club that dominated the AAFC — halfback Edgar "Special Delivery" Jones, linebacker Lou Saban and guard Ed Ulinski — retired after the '49 campaign. Brown also decided that the play of John Yonakor, a starting defensive end since 1946, wasn't what it once was and traded him to the NFL's New York Yanks.

A separate deal with the Buffalo Bills brought the Browns three players exempt from the AAFC draft pool: defensive tackle John Kissell, halfback Rex Bumgardner and guard Abe Gibron. Bumgardner offset the loss of Jones and Gibron replaced Ulinski. To take Yonakor's spot, the Browns acquired Len Ford, who had been with the Los Angeles Dons since '48, in the pool. Ford went on to become All-Pro four times, one of the best defensive ends ever and a Pro Football Hall of Famer.

As well as the Browns did in the off-season before their maiden trip through the NFL, the conference-rival New York Giants did even better. In a deal with the Brooklyn-New York Yankees, the Giants took four players, all defensive starters, for Head Coach Steve Owen's Umbrella Defense. The Giants were the only team to consistently give Paul Brown's offense trouble in Cleveland's early years in the NFL.

That was because the core of the Browns' point-scoring machine was still around from Day One. Eight offensive starters on the 1950 team had been at the Browns' first training camp in '46. Quarterback Otto Graham, fullback Marion Motley, ends Mac Speedie and Dante Lavelli, center Frank Gatski, tackles Lou Groza and Lou Rymkus and guard Lin Houston were original Browns, as were three defensive stars — end George Young, middle guard Bill Willis and safety Cliff Lewis.

A new offensive standout had joined the Browns in 1948. Dub Jones had been with the AAFC's Brooklyn Dodgers, where he was a star in the defensive backfield. Brown was willing to trade the draft rights to Michigan's All-America halfback Bob Chappuis to acquire Jones to bolster the Browns' defensive backfield. But it became apparent that Jones' strength was as a runner-receiver. At 6-foot-4 he was, obviously, much larger than defensive backs who tried to cover him. Paul Brown would one day refer to him as the team's best all-around offensive player.

Jones started slowly. He had only nine catches and 33 carries in 1948. That increased to 12 receptions and 77 carries in 1949. In Cleveland's first season in the NFL, Jones blossomed — 83 carries, 31 catches and a team-leading 11 touchdowns.

The Browns roared through their five 1950 preseason games, with only the Chicago Bears, who would post a 9-3 record after a 9-3 mark the year before, giving them any trouble. That, perhaps, made the regular-season opening that much more of a draw, and 71,237 piled into Philadelphia's Municipal Stadium to see the four-time champions of a "Humpty Dumpty" league get a lesson from the two-time kings of the real professional league.

"We've been taunted and disparaged for playing in an inferior league" Brown told his team before its first preseason game, against Green Bay in Toledo. "There's not only this season at stake, but four years of achievement. I'm asking you to dedicate yourselves to preserving the reputation the Browns have made."

The Browns gained a new reputation on that humid Saturday night in Philadelphia. They pummeled the Eagles, 35-10. Granted, the Eagles were without fullback Steve Van Buren and starting halfback Bosh Pritchard, but the famed "Eagle Defense" couldn't handle the Browns' halfback-in-motion offense and was left vulnerable to the speed of Cleveland's receivers in one-on-one coverage.

Graham tossed touchdown passes to Jones, Lavelli and Speedie, and ran one in himself.

FORWARD PROGRESS:
Otto Graham dives goal-ward during a 20-14 victory over the Redskins on Nov. 20, 1950. It was Cleveland's fourth straight win en route to six straight to close out the regular season. Other Browns pictured are Weldon Humble (38), Frank Gatski (22) and Mac Speedie (58).

Bumgardner scored the final touchdown, on a run and at a meaningless time late in the fourth quarter. The rout had been thorough and complete.

The Eagles were not a power that year. After posting a 31-8-1 mark over the previous three seasons and winning NFL championships in 1948 and '49, Philadelphia slipped to 6-6 in 1950. The Giants were the only team owning a winning record the Browns would play that year and the New Yorkers defeated them two times. It wouldn't be until post-season action that the Browns would finally make believers of almost everyone.

The Giants had won 6-0 in Cleveland and 17-13 in New York. The first meeting spoiled the Browns' home opener and NFL debut in the Stadium. New York's Umbrella Defense permitted the ends in a six-man front to drop back and cover receivers, thus allowing seven men (two ends, a middle linebacker and four defensive backs) to defend against the pass.

Graham & Co. was stifled in the first half of the first game against the Giants but moved the ball at times in the second half. It simply could

PERFECT TOE: *Lou Groza kicks a field goal to put the Browns in front, 3-0, in the 1950 playoff game against the New York Giants. Sneaker-clad Forrest "Chubby" Grigg (48) loses his helmet on the frozen field in Cleveland Stadium.*

The conference title game was played in Cleveland Stadium in 10-degree weather, with a wind-chill factor well below zero. The Browns wore rubber-soled shoes except for Groza, who wore a rubber-soled shoe on his left foot and a football shoe with cleats removed on his right (kicking) foot. That idea must have worked. Groza kicked a field goal in the first half and another one with 58 seconds left to snap a 3-3 tie.

The hero of the game, however, was Bill Willis. The star middle guard chased down Gene "Choo Choo" Roberts, who had broken off the line of scrimmage and into the clear 47 yards from the Browns' goal line in the fourth period. Willis made up 20 yards and caught Roberts from behind at the Cleveland four-yard stripe. The defense held and the Giants were denied what probably would have been the game-winning TD. A safety made the final score 8-3, Cleveland.

The 1950 NFL championship game might have marked the beginning of an era in pro football history. The league's most sophisticated passing teams, the Browns and the Los Angeles Rams, were to meet in the title game. Like the Browns, the Rams had finished in a tie in their conference and beat a team in a playoff, the Chicago Bears, that had defeated them twice in the regular season. The game would mark the first time the Rams would play in Cleveland Stadium since they beat the Washington Redskins for the title in 1945, before abandoning Cleveland for the West Coast.

The Rams' offense could certainly match the Browns' attack, and do it with more people. Los Angeles had two outstanding quarterbacks, Bob Waterfield and young Norm Van Brocklin. They could match the Browns' Jones, Speedie

not get the ball in the end zone against Owen's umbrella. They got to the New York 10-yard line during one series, but Graham and Motley collided on a hand-off attempt, fumbled and the Giants then recovered. The Browns were shut out for the first time in their existence, and would not suffer another for 22 years.

Perhaps the Giants prepared for the Browns at the expense of other duties. They followed their victories over Cleveland with losses to decidedly inferior clubs, the Steelers and Cardinals. But both the Giants and Browns rolled through the second half of the season undefeated, creating a tie for the American Conference title, each with 10-2 records.

UNMATCHED SUCCESS: *Wearing a football shoe on his right kicking foot and a sneaker on his left, Lou Groza is carried off the Cleveland Stadium field after booting two field goals to beat the Giants in the 1950 playoff game. Carrying "the Toe" are (left to right) Marion Motley, Tony Adamle and John Kissell.*

and Lavelli with Elroy "Crazy Legs" Hirsch, Tom Fears, V.T. Smith and Glenn Davis. The Rams' running game was powered by Dick Hoerner, Paul "Tank" Younger and Dan Towler. Logically, the experts predicted a high-scoring game and they were right. Graham and Waterfield combined for 64 passes, 40 completions and five touchdown passes (four by Graham). The Browns won it in the last minute, 30-28, on a 16-yard field goal by Groza.

Paul Brown, although he never used such language, figuratively told the NFL what it could do with its superior-league theory in

1950. It would be hard to figure, then, why Brown would have considered any other job after becoming master of all he surveyed.

Whether he actually considered leaving the Browns is still unknown. Brown himself was typically close-mouthed about whether he'd said he wanted another job. Nevertheless, he

CAPTURED CARDINAL: *Running back Elmer Angsman is tackled by Tommy Thompson and Bill Willis in Cleveland Stadium in December 1951. Chicago scored 28 points on the Browns' defense that afternoon, the most by a regular-season opponent in the Browns' brief NFL history. Cleveland prevailed, 49-28, part of an 11-game win streak after an opening-game loss to the 49ers.*

was asked by the University of Southern California and interviewed by his former employer, Ohio State University, for their head coaching positions.

Brown turned down the USC job, citing the fact he couldn't share in the profits the way he could as a professional coach. As far as Ohio State was concerned, however, a powerful "Bring Back Brown" movement was said to have raised a huge sum for a signing bonus.

But Brown still had his enemies at OSU. He told Gordon Cobbledick, *Plain Dealer* sports editor, that he didn't ask nor was he offered a job at the interview he had in the winter of 1951 and that he knew many people at Ohio State still held a grudge against him for taking Lou Groza and Dante Lavelli to the AAFC when they still had college eligibility remaining.

In any event, the OSU Athletic Board recommended Miami University coach Woody Hayes for the position. A fight was expected to ensue among the board of trustees for the final hiring of a coach, but the trustees followed the athletic board's recommendation and offered the job to Hayes.

Things worked out for the best. Hayes held the OSU post until 1978, becoming one of the winningest coaches in college football history. Brown won six more conference titles and two league crowns over the next 12 seasons.

Brown came up with two more innovations in his first few years of coaching in the NFL. Although he had used a messenger guard for bringing in plays back in the AAFC days, he began to go to it far more often in 1951 and beyond. Otto Graham was not always happy about it, and frequently failed to use Brown's messengered plays because he believed the players on the field knew best what to do. Still, it was merely a case of agreeing to disagree between coach and quarterback, and not any raging controversy.

The other innovation was to put a thin plastic bar across the helmet to protect a player's mouth, a forerunner of the face mask now worn

by all NFL players. The idea came courtesy of 49ers rookie middle guard Art Michalik, who severely cut Graham's mouth on a hit out of bounds during a 1953 game in Cleveland, won by the Browns, 23-21.

Everything else remained the same. Brown still worked his players hard in training camp, but kept practices light between regular-season games. There was still plenty of classroom work, and rookies who couldn't follow Brown's system were not kept around no matter how highly touted they were coming out of college.

The Browns lost to the 49ers in the 1951 season opener, then rolled over 11 straight foes en route to an 11-1 record, and another American Conference championship. Cleveland's defense was outstanding, with linebacker Tony Adamle, middle guard Bill Willis and end Len Ford getting Pro Bowl nods. The secondary featured future Pro Bowlers Warren Lahr and Tommy James at cornerback and veteran Cliff Lewis alternating with a rookie named Don Shula at safety.

The opponent for the NFL championship game was again the Rams, a team the Browns whipped 38-23 in Game 2 of the regular season. Things wouldn't go so well the second time

SIGNS OF THE TIMES: *Cigarette and beer ads are the Polo Grounds backdrop for Dub Jones on a 20-yard gain versus the Giants in November 1951. He accounted for Cleveland's only TD on a 68-yard run in the 10-0 win, then scored six more the following week against the Bears, tying an NFL single-game record. He led the Browns in rushing that season with 492 yards.*

around. Norm Van Brocklin, who hardly played in the 1950 title game, connected with Tom Fears on a 73-yard touchdown reception to break a 17-17 tie and give the Rams a 24-17 win in Los Angeles Coliseum.

Although the Van Brocklin-to-Fears pass embarrassed the defense, a pair of rookies — Andy Robustelli and Norb Hecker — did the same to the Browns' offense. Robustelli, an end who would go on to a Hall-of-Fame career, beat Marion Motley on a rush and scooped up a fumble caused when Larry Brink sacked Graham. Robustelli fumbled himself, but the ball somehow fell back in his arms as he was going down at the Browns' two-yard line.

Hecker, a Cleveland native and an alumnus of Baldwin-Wallace College (in Berea, Ohio, where the Browns now have their headquarters) put the nail in the Browns' coffin by sniffing out a screen pass intended for Dub Jones on

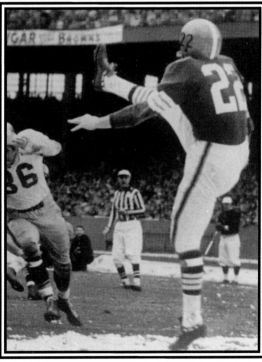

NEW FACES OF THE FIFTIES: *Rebuilding an aging roster, Paul Brown found fiercely-competitive new talent as shown here. Top: Chick Jagade saw time at fullback as Marion Motley's knees gave out. Left: Half-back-receiver Ray Renfro succeeded Dub Jones. Right: Ken Konz joined as a defensive back and punter.*

Cleveland's final drive and smacking Jones two yards behind the line of scrimmage.

It was Paul Brown's first loss in a championship game. It was the first year since 1944 that the city of Cleveland could not boast of a pro football champion.

Cleveland won another American Conference championship in 1952, but without the same smooth-running engine. Graham had his poorest year and several players (Jones, Speedie, Motley) were suffering injuries. On defense, tackle Chubby Grigg moved on to the Dallas Texans and safety Cliff Lewis retired. They were replaced by rookies Bob Gain and Bert Rechichar respectively.

The Browns were 8-3 and one game ahead of the Eagles going into the last game of the season, against the Giants. New York won, but the Browns caught a break when the Washington Redskins upset the Eagles to give Cleveland another conference title.

But the Browns did not redeem themselves for a lackluster season in the 1952 title game. The newest NFL powerhouse, the Detroit Lions, had just beaten the Rams in a playoff for the National Conference crown.

Detroit was led by quarterback Bobby Layne, who was definitely not Paul Brown's kind of guy. Layne was known as a braggart and as one who enjoyed the nightlife. He demanded his teammates' respect as much as he earned it. He bullied anyone he thought was not putting out 100 percent to the point where many considered him to be more of a coach than the real head coach, Buddy Parker.

Two critical fumbles led to two Detroit touchdowns. The Browns were on the Lions' two-yard line with a first down and a chance to tie the score at 14-14, but a five-yard loss, a 12-yard sack and a one-yard gain killed the drive. The final score in Cleveland Stadium was Lions 17, Browns 7.

It was clear by the end of the 1952 campaign that Mickey McBride was tiring of owning a pro football team. He sold the club to a

syndicate headed by longtime steel magnate David Jones, former Cleveland Indians president Ellis Ryan, Randall Park Raceway owner Saul Silberman and Homer Marshman, who had founded the Cleveland Rams in 1937. The selling price was a record $600,000.

"I never made anything (from owning the Browns)," McBride said, "but I didn't lose anything either, except maybe a few thousand dollars. I've simply had my fling at pro football and convinced myself Cleveland will always buy the best. Now I'm getting out. I have a few other things to keep me busy."

McBride wasn't the only man to walk away from the Browns after the 1952 season. Mac Speedie, the club's all-time leading receiver at the time and the man who led the AAFC in receptions three times and the NFL once,

OTTO'S INJURY: *Otto Graham rolls right before being knocked out of bounds versus the 49ers in November 1953. A late elbow hit in the mouth by middle guard Art Michalik forced Graham from the game. He returned in the second half with 15 stitches and a Paul Brown-invented plastic face bar on his helmet, a forerunner of today's high-tech face masks.*

LAST ORIGINALS: *Paul Brown poses in 1953 training camp with seven of the eight players remaining on the Browns' roster from his first team in 1946. From left to right are Dante Lavelli, Bill Willis, Marion Motley, Frank Gatski, Otto Graham, Lou Groza and George Young. (Not pictured: Lin Houston.)*

signed with a Canadian Football League team. Defensive tackle John Kissell also went to the CFL, but rejoined the Browns in 1954. None of these changes seemed to have any effect on the club. Rumors the Browns were slipping in 1953 were quashed as the team won its first 11 games and was set to become the first in the NFL since the 1942 Chicago Bears to sail through a regular season unbeaten and first ever to win every game of the year.

It didn't happen. On the last weekend of the season a Browns defense that hadn't allowed more than 21 points in a game suddenly caved in to the Philadelphia Eagles in a 42-27 loss. The championship battle, again versus Detroit, was closer, but no better. Jim Doran caught a 33-yard touchdown pass from a scrambling Bobby Layne with two minutes to go to give the Lions a 17-16 victory in Detroit.

It was Doran's only touchdown of the year. Doran, a starting defensive end, came in to play offense because star receiver Leon Hart suffered a twisted knee in the first period. It was Paul Brown's third straight championship loss. Although Brown was bitter after the defeat, the

'53 season was perhaps a vindication of his system. Many of the original Browns — Speedie, Cliff Lewis, George Young, Lin Houston, Lou Rymkus — were either gone or relegated to backup roles. But Brown knew talent and was able to rebuild while still contending. In place of the originals came Walter Michaels, Bob Gain, Don Colo, Doug Atkins, Ken Gorgal, Ken Konz, John Sandusky, Ray Renfro and others.

Even Marion Motley, slowed by injuries and age, finally had to share fullback duties with Harry "Chick" Jagade. Motley played his last game for the Browns in '53. He sat out 1954 and came back with the Steelers as a linebacker for the 1955 season.

Also retiring after the 1953 season were Dub Jones, Bill Willis, Lin Houston, linebacker Tommy Thompson and defensive tackle Derrell Palmer. Jones would later un-retire.

Prior to the 1953 season, Brown had made the biggest trade in NFL history, a 15-player deal with the Baltimore Colts. The Browns sent 10 men to the Colts, including starting defensive backs Bert Rechichar and Don Shula, in exchange for five players, three of whom were serving in the military. Defensive tackle Don Colo and middle guard Mike McCormack were the key pickups for the Browns. After one season as the successor to Bill Willis, McCormack moved to right offensive tackle in 1955 where he remained through 1962.

The Browns were back in the NFL championship game in 1954 with a 9-3 record, despite having given up 55 points in a loss to the otherwise mediocre Steelers. For the third year in a row they would meet the Lions, who had defeated Cleveland 14-10 on the last weekend of the season, on another Layne-to-Doran pass.

This time was much different. The Browns slaughtered the Detroiters 56-10 before 43,827 in Cleveland Stadium. Graham, who had completed only two of 15 passes in the '53 title game, was 9-of-12 with three touchdown passes and three TD runs in the avalanche.

A 9-2-1 record in 1955 got the Browns to the championship game an unprecedented sixth straight season. They had little trouble beating the Rams, 38-14, in the Los Angeles Coliseum for their third NFL crown.

Graham, who had tried to retire after the '54 campaign only to be coaxed back by Brown, called it quits for good after the '55 title game. The retirement of Graham signaled the end of

OVER AND OUT: *Otto Graham scores the final touchdown of his 10-year career on a one-yard run in the third quarter of Cleveland's 38-14 victory over the Rams in the 1955 NFL title game. Graham retired again, but this time it was permanent.*

an era that may never be equaled. With a 30-team league now it would be nearly impossible for any team to win 10 straight conference titles and seven league championships.

Unquestionably, the Browns were the team of the 1950s just as the Packers, Steelers and 49ers were the teams of the latter decades. And like Bart Starr with Green Bay of the '60s, Terry Bradshaw with Pittsburgh of the '70s and Joe Montana with San Francisco of the '80s, Graham was the on-field symbol of a dynasty.

Paul Brown, of course, with his snap-brim fedora, was as familiar a sight on the sidelines as the Packers' Vince Lombardi with his dark-rimmed glasses, the Steelers' Chuck Noll with his square jaw and the 49ers' Bill Walsh with his white hair and various sweaters.

A Team & Times in Transition

The retirement of Otto Graham was the symbolic end of the "dynasty" years of the Cleveland Browns franchise. For the next seven seasons, the Browns would bear little resemblance to their predecessors. Perennial contenders, yes, but no longer were they the dominant team of the NFL, or even the Eastern Conference — the New York Giants had assumed that role. Everything changed. Instead of Graham, there was Ratterman, then O'Connell, then Plum, then Ninowski, then Ryan. By 1956, the familiar names of the '40s and early '50s were retired or nearly so. Although Paul Brown did a skillful job of rebuilding, the new talent did not respond as well to his old ways. That, combined with the lack of championships, helped lead to Brown's dismissal. By 1963, the changes included a new coach, a new owner and a new symbol of greatness: Jim Brown.

Bob Gain

By Steve Byrne

The arrival of Brown in 1957 coincided with the emergence of professional football as a television sport. After baseball's Giants and Dodgers left New York for the West Coast after the '57 season, the New York media focused attention on the football Giants, NFL champs in '56 and loaded with quality talent. The major exposure given the Giants, their famed overtime battle with the Colts in the '58 title game and their revitalized rivalry with the Browns, helped spark new interest in the NFL with television viewers nationwide.

Brown provided a perfect show for television. His moves, his style, his wide sweeps around end, his long runs, his tackle-breaking power — they exemplified NFL football at its entertaining and professional best.

While Brown was the one constant in the 1956-62 era, the rest of the roster was in transition. By Brown's first season, the Browns were in the second year of an ongoing search for Otto Graham's successor. The process had begun in 1954 when Paul Brown traded Bob Garrett, a quarterback from Stanford and the Browns' bonus selection in the draft, to Green Bay for

veteran quarterback Vito "Babe" Parilli, whom he expected would be the Browns' No. 1 quarterback for the 1956 season. Parilli had two years of solid NFL experience, having split time with Tobin Rote with the Packers in 1952-53. George Ratterman had scant experience as Graham's backup. But Parilli had real trouble learning Brown's system and Ratterman, who had four years of bench time to pick it up, was ahead of Parilli and became the starter.

Brown, ever the innovator, brought to the game a new technological device — a citizen's band radio, set in Ratterman's helmet, with an

NEW DIRECTION: *Jim Brown's arrival in 1957 gave purpose to the Cleveland offense following the end of the Otto Graham era. Paul Brown could now rebuild around his new star. Brown hit full stride in Game 9 (above) with 237 yards rushing against the Rams, a career high, tied once in 1961 versus the Eagles.*

FCC-assigned frequency between Brown and his quarterback for the purpose of feeding Ratterman the plays. The system, developed by Cleveland resident George Sarles in his basement, worked OK, but the Browns lost 31-14 to the Lions on its maiden voyage. The whole thing finally blew up. The Cardinals, who beat

A QUARTERBACK CARROUSEL: *George Ratterman (far right) began the 1956 season as Otto Graham's successor, but his career ended on a knee injury in Game 4. It left Paul Brown (above) to work with Tommy O'Connell (left) and Babe Parilli.*

the Browns in the season opener, claimed to have had their own electronic play-calling system via a wire buried just below the ground surrounding the sidelines, whose signal was picked up by hearing aids worn by the team captains.

The Giants claimed they were intercepting the Browns' signals with a receiver on their bench and knew what the Browns would do on every play (a violation of FCC signal-stealing law). The Giants later admitted they planted the story about signal stealing just to ridicule the whole idea of electronic communication between coach and quarterback.

Whatever, the Browns abandoned that system and Commissioner Bert Bell declared all electronic devices in helmets illegal. But the '56 season was just as disastrous. Brown had only his second losing campaign in 27 years of

coaching as the Browns finished 5-7. A victory over the eventual NFL-champion Giants was the lone bright spot.

Ratterman suffered a career-ending knee injury in the fourth game. Brown was down to one quarterback. He found another in a man cast off by the Bears, Tommy O'Connell, who eventually became the starter in 1957.

Like the quarterback position, the entire offense was in transition. The line was solid, but aging with veterans Frank Gatski, Abe Gibron, Mike McCormack and Lou Groza still in position. Pete Brewster and Ray Renfro were quality receivers, but Dante Lavelli was at the end of his Hall-of-Fame career.

Rookie Preston Carpenter led the team in rushing as part of a backfield that featured a wide variety of performers: Maurice Bassett, Ed Modzelewski and Curly Morrison. The club that had scored 349 points in 1955 scored half that many in '56. The Browns needed help.

Enter Jim Brown.

If a case could be made for a greatest athlete of all time, Jim Brown would be an excellent

candidate. In his senior year at Manhassett, N.Y., High School, Brown averaged 14.9 yards per carry on the football team and 38 points a game on the basketball squad.

At Syracuse University, he was a member of the varsity football, basketball, lacrosse and track teams. In that latter sport he finished 10th in a national AAU meet, despite not having the time to train due to his other athletic endeavors. It's highly likely that had he been able to dedicate himself to the decathlon, Brown would have posed a serious challenge to Olympian Rafer Johnson at that meet.

On the recreational side, Brown consistently shot in the low 80s on the golf course, bowled games of 200 or better and earned the rank of marksman on the rifle range. He was once offered a chance to become a professional boxer and also was invited to a tryout with the Cleveland Indians.

But Paul Brown wasn't looking for a new fullback when the draft rolled around. Quarterback was the Browns' No. 1 concern after the 1956 season, and there were a bunch of good

TRANSITION TALENT: *Entering the mid 1950s, Lou Groza (76) was one of the solid, but aging, veterans remaining on the offensive line. Maurice Bassett (30) was one of a variety of backfield performers in the post-Motley, pre-Brown time period.*

ones coming out of college. Unfortunately, other teams were shopping for them too.

The Packers chose Paul Hornung, the Heisman Trophy winner from Notre Dame. San Francisco took a local star, Stanford's John Brodie. The Browns figured they'd take Len Dawson of Purdue, a local kid of their own from Alliance, Ohio. But a flip of the coin to determine if the Browns or the Steelers would get the fifth draft choice didn't go Cleveland's way, and Pittsburgh selected Dawson. The Browns had to "settle" for Jim Brown.

Brown gained 942 yards (78.5 per game) on 202 carries (16.8 per game) with nine touchdowns as a rookie in 1957. He gained 89 yards in his NFL debut against the Giants and had a league-record 237 against the Rams in Game 9.

More importantly, the Browns won the Eastern Conference at 9-2-1 and beat the previ-

SWARMED: *Tommy O'Connell's injured ankle and Milt Plum's pulled hamstring put the Browns in a quarterback crisis for the 1957 title game. Detroit overpowered the Browns, 59-14. Plum (16), played in the second half of what would be Paul Brown's final championship game as a pro football coach.*

ous year's champions, the Giants, twice. It may have been Paul Brown's best coaching job. He did it without Otto Graham. Only offensive tackle Lou Groza remained from the 1946 original Browns. Only Groza, defensive end Len Ford and defensive back Warren Lahr were starters from the 1950 NFL champions.

The title game was another matter. The Lions, who rallied from a 27-7 halftime deficit

to beat the 49ers in a playoff for the Western Conference crown, were peaking. The Browns, on the other hand, had lost Tommy O'Connell to a broken ankle in Game 10 and saw his back-up, rookie Milt Plum, pull a hamstring in practice during game week. Although both played against the Lions, neither was effective and Detroit rolled to a 59-14 victory.

The Lions were without Bobby Layne, but had an adequate backup in former Packers starter Tobin Rote. They also had Frank Gatski, one of the original Browns, starting at center on an outstanding offensive line.

That game would be the last NFL title contest in which Paul Brown would coach. The

1958 team finished 9-3 and tied with the Giants for first place. The Browns had lost to New York in the final regular-season contest on a last-minute field goal by Pat Summerall, then fell again to the Giants, 10-0, in the playoff game.

Paul Brown would never lead the Browns to first place again. He did two more times, with the Cincinnati Bengals in the '70s, but the

Costello, cornerback Bernie Parrish, defensive end Paul Wiggin, outside linebacker Jim Houston, wide receiver Gary Collins, offensive tackle Dick Schafrath, guards Gene Hickerson and John Wooten and defensive back Ross Fichtner were all Paul Brown's draft selections.

But it was Jim Brown in those years who made the Browns a glamour team. In fact, it

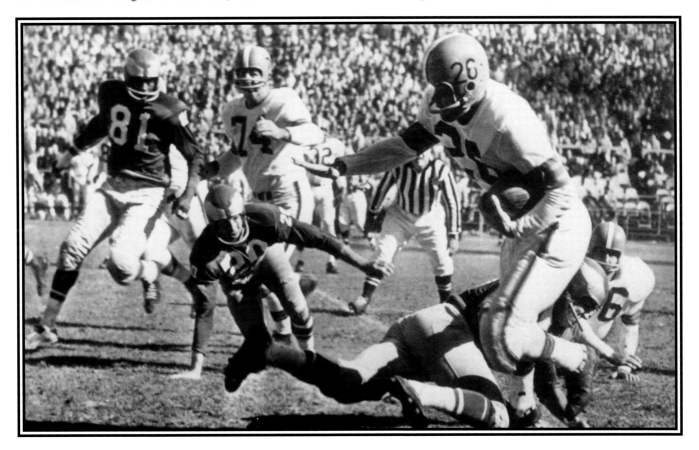

RELIABLE: *Ray Renfro (26) provided veteran stability during the influx of new players from 1956-62. He gained most of his 5,508 career receiving yards during those years, retiring after the '63 season. His total is second only to Ozzie Newsome's 7,980.*

Browns finished second in 1959 and '60 and third in 1961 and '62.

The Browns certainly were not without top talent in the years 1956-62. Jim Brown made the Pro Bowl every year in his nine-year career. Offensive tackle Mike McCormack, defensive tackle Bob Gain and guard Jim Ray Smith made it five times each. Walter Michaels was a four-time Pro Bowler. Cornerback Don Paul made it three times. Milt Plum, linebacker Galen Fiss and receiver Ray Renfro were chosen twice.

The transition years also saw the drafting of the players who would lead the Browns back to glory in the mid '60s. Middle linebacker Vince

was Brown and the 1958 Giants-Colts championship contest (alias "The Greatest Game Ever Played") that did more to make the league so attractive to television. Brown led the league in rushing in all but one of his nine seasons. He retired as the all-time touchdown leader with 126, a record that stood for 29 years until Jerry Rice of the 49ers broke it in 1994.

The Browns' principal rival in the years 1956-62 was the New York Giants, and the bat-

CLASSIC CONFRONTATION: *The Jim Brown-Sam Huff battles provided visual imagery made for pro football's rise to popularity on television. Huff is the winner on this play from a 1959 Giants victory in Yankee Stadium. Jim Ray Smith (64), Milt Plum (16), Bobby Mitchell (49) and Mike McCormack (74), plus New York's Rosey Grier (76) get a close-up view.*

tles between Jim Brown and Sam Huff, the Giants' outspoken middle linebacker, were media events within the games.

Huff was a folksy West Virginian who joined the Giants in 1956 and started at middle linebacker that season. In 1960, a TV documentary entitled "The Violent World of Sam Huff," a brutal, profanity-laced program in which Huff was wired for sound, helped glamorize the game by showing it at its most unglamorous. There were no gallant open-field

touchdown runs, no cheerleaders mobbing a quarterback — just guys with dirt and grass stains all over themselves slugging each other for all they were worth. Naturally, the Huff-Brown wars were the highlight of the program.

In truth, Brown won the majority of those battles. The subsequent years have shown Huff to be a good linebacker, but not in the class with the top men at that position such as the Lions' Joe Schmidt or the Bears' Bill George.

But the games often went to the Giants. New York possessed a team of stars led by two Pro Bowl quarterbacks, Charlie Conerly and Y.A. Tittle. They threw to Del Shofner, Kyle Rote and Bob Schnelker; and handed off to Frank Gifford, Mel Triplett and Alex Webster. Blocking for them were Rosey Brown, Jack Stroud, Ray Wietecha and Darrell Dess.

A defense that included linemen Andy Robustelli, Dick Modzelewski, Rosey Grier and Jim Katcavage, linebacker Cliff Livingston and defensive backs Emlen Tunnell, Jim Patton, Erich Barnes and Dick Lynch was tough on all offensive stars, not just Jim Brown. The series went 9-5-1 in favor of the Giants in Paul Brown's last seven seasons (1956-62).

The biggest change in the Browns occurred on March 21, 1961, when a young advertising executive named Art Modell headed a syndicate that paid almost $4 million for the franchise. Modell, only 35 years old, envisioned pro football and television as a marriage made in heaven. He had hit it big in realizing how to use daytime television to market products to housewives, and dreamed of using TV to market the NFL to fans nationwide.

Football was Modell's passion. It was his only diversion from the go-go world of Madison Avenue. He followed the NFL religiously. One of the men he most admired was Paul Brown. Modell got word the Browns were for sale on a tip from ex-Brown Curly Morrison, communicated by a mutual acquaintance, theatrical agent Vince Andrews, in October of 1960. Modell wasted no time trying to acquire the club.

It was ironic that Modell, who was a big fan of Paul Brown, would be the man to relieve Brown of his head coaching duties. Unlike Mickey McBride or David Jones and their partners, Modell would not be a spectator in the daily operations of his team.

The 1962 season wasn't a happy one. Paul Brown coveted Heisman Trophy winner Ernie Davis of Syracuse University, which would give the Browns a 1-2 punch in the backfield much like the league-champion Packers enjoyed with

Paul Hornung and Jim Taylor. Brown traded halfback Bobby Mitchell and the Browns' second first-round pick in the '62 draft, running back Leroy Jackson, to the Redskins for the rights to Davis. It was an excellent deal for the Redskins, who were under increasing pressure from the other teams, civil rights groups and the federal government to integrate. Mitchell became the first black to play in a Redskins uniform.

The deal resulted in second-guessing in Cleveland. Mitchell had averaged 32 receptions and 106 carries in his four years with the Browns. He had scored 38 touchdowns. He was dealt for someone who had never been in a National Football League game.

Worst of all, Brown didn't tell Modell what he was doing. The owner wasn't pleased. He did tell the boss about trading quarterback Milt Plum, who had publicly criticized Brown for not allowing audibles. (All plays were being brought in from the coaching staff.) Modell

GIANT LEAP: *Milt Plum fires over Dick Modzelewski's charging pass rush in 1960, typical of the hard-fought Browns-Giants rivalry. "Mo" later became a key member of the Browns' 1964 title team.*

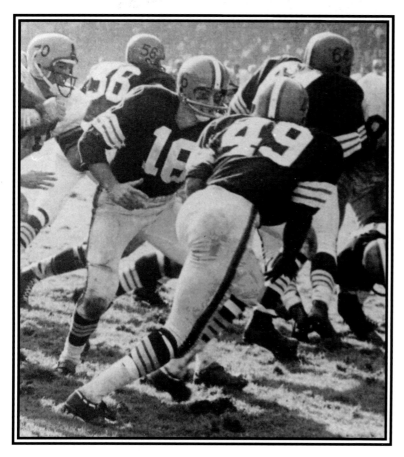

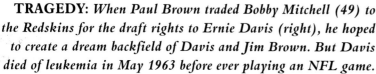

TRAGEDY: *When Paul Brown traded Bobby Mitchell (49) to the Redskins for the draft rights to Ernie Davis (right), he hoped to create a dream backfield of Davis and Jim Brown. But Davis died of leukemia in May 1963 before ever playing an NFL game.*

OK'd the deal, which sent Plum to the Detroit Lions for quarterback Jim Ninowski, whom Brown promised would be the starter. A later trade brought Frank Ryan, a Phi Beta Kappa (Rice), from the Rams to back up Ninowski.

Ninowski had served as Plum's backup in 1958-59 before being dealt to the Lions prior to the 1960 season. Presumably, life would be better the second time around for the former Michigan State star, but it was not to be.

Ninowski was flattened on a pass attempt in the second quarter of the seventh game by Pittsburgh's Gene "Big Daddy" Lipscomb, suffering a dislocated shoulder and broken collarbone. He was replaced by Ryan who directed the Browns to a 41-14 victory that day and three more wins that season. "Dr. Frank" never looked back, leading the Browns to five straight

winning seasons (1963-67) and the National Football League title in 1964. Ninowski, meanwhile, became Ryan's backup through 1966, taking over when the score was out of reach and often adding a TD or two.

Davis never played for the Browns. He was diagnosed with leukemia and missed all of the 1962 season. He died on May 18, 1963. Ernie Green, acquired from the Green Bay Packers during the 1962 training camp, eventually became Jim Brown's – and later Leroy Kelly's – backfield mate.

As for Paul Brown, the dissatisfaction was growing. Several players went to Modell and complained about the way Brown was handling personnel. Losing was not the problem, they said, but Brown's attitude was. The coach who had been football's greatest innovator, unfortunately, had failed to remain one step ahead of the competition. Every coach was imitating Paul Brown, but some were doing it with better players and/or building on what Brown had started 17 years earlier.

RYAN'S ROLE: *Opening the 1962 season as the starting quarterback, Jim Ninowski (above) passes to Ray Renfro versus Baltimore in Game 5. Two weeks later, Ninowski suffered a broken collarbone and separated shoulder against Pittsburgh. It took Frank Ryan off the sidelines (left) and into the starter's role.*

After playing in title games in 11 of their first 12 seasons, the Browns had failed to reach a championship contest for five straight years. The well-established Giants and the emerging Green Bay Packers were the new symbols of NFL domination.

Modell announced on Jan. 9, 1963, that Paul Brown had been relieved of his coaching and general manager duties. He would be paid for the remaining six years on his contract and given "other duties." Blanton Collier, offensive backfield coach, replaced Brown. All other assistant coaches were rehired.

The Paul Brown era was over, the Art Modell era had begun and the Cleveland Browns were about to enter a new period of consistent title contention.

KELLY'S IMPACT: *Leroy Kelly became the Browns' most visible symbol of success in the late 1960s. Succeeding Jim Brown, Kelly quickly became a premier running back. In 1966 (above), his first season as a starter, Kelly gained 1,141 yards and tied for the NFL touchdown crown with 16 (15 on the ground).*

New Success in the Sixties

After 17 seasons, the Cleveland Browns entered 1963 for the first time without Paul Brown in charge. But if anyone could take the sting out of Brown's dismissal, it was Blanton Collier. He had been a Paul Brown assistant for the team's first eight seasons and the head coach at the University of Kentucky before rejoining the Browns as a backfield coach in 1962. He was 56 years old when he became an NFL head coach for the first time. But it was not just experience that made Collier what he was. He was ready to follow Paul Brown's legend because he knew Brown's coaching system inside out, although almost a complete opposite of his mentor personality-wise. "We're going to be watched by the entire football world in the coming season," Collier told his players at the start of training camp, "and we will be judged on only one basis: if we win or lose.

"The world doesn't want the nice guy," he continued. "I think the world would sort of like a winner to be a nice guy, but first he's got to be a winner. Each year you have to produce or get out. That's not Collier's law or Modell's law. It's the law of professional sports.

"I won't be mild mannered or easygoing. I do not know how I acquired that reputation. I'm not a tough person, and I don't try to be. But I get fired up about things, especially lack of effort and lack of attention. What you do and how soon you do it will determine how dedicated you are."

Collier professed to being as tough as his predecessor, but everyone saw a coach dedicated to winning without being dedicated to a style that many believed had become passe. Perhaps no player noticed it more than Frank Ryan, the cerebral quarterback who had taken over the starting job in 1962 after an injury to Jim Ninowski.

Under Collier, Ryan was now allowed to call his own plays, and was given the freedom to change a play at the line of scrimmage if he saw the defense was stacked against it. Without

Frank Ryan

By Steve Byrne

the messenger system, Ryan was able to use his intelligence as effectively as he was able to use his physical talent.

The Browns also had to deal with three players' deaths in preseason. Ernie Davis' death in May followed that of Tom Bloom, a cornerback from Purdue drafted in Round 6. Bloom was killed in an automobile accident Jan. 18. Don Fleming, a starting safety and a Browns player since 1960, died when he was electrocuted on June 4 while working at a construction site in Florida. The turbulence and

COMMUNICATION: *Coach Blanton Collier confers with Jim Brown during the 1963 training camp. There was an excellent rapport between the two men and Brown responded with 1,863 yards rushing that season, the best of his career.*

tragedy of the off-season was put on hold as Collier and the assistant coaches set about to tinker with their talented club, while adding a new measure of youth to the mix as well.

On the offense, second-year wide receiver Gary Collins (22) replaced Ray Renfro (32), in the final season of Renfro's 12-year career. Ernie Green (24) and Ken Webb (27), pickups from the Packers and Lions, respectively, shared duties as Jim Brown's backfield mate.

John Wooten (26), a fifth-year vet, moved from right to left guard, replacing Jim Ray Smith (30), who had been traded to Dallas for Monte Clark (26). (Clark became a starting right tackle in 1965.) The move allowed Gene

Hickerson to take over the right guard spot that he held through 1971. Second-year right tackle John Brown (24) succeeded the retired Mike McCormack.

On defense, Jim Houston (25), a No. 1 draft choice in 1960, was inserted in the lineup at left linebacker after having played defensive end his first three years. Left linebacker Galen Fiss was switched to the right while Vince Costello remained in the middle.

Collier and staff also worked a 21-year-old rookie, Jim Kanicki, into the defensive line for Bob Gain (34) who suffered an injury-plagued year. In the secondary, veterans Bernie Parrish and Jim Shofner remained at the corners. Ross Fichtner moved from left to right safety, allowing rookie Larry Benz (22) to take over the left.

Collier appeared to have made all the right moves in the years ahead as the Browns now had most of the personnel in place for their run of five playoff appearances over the next six seasons.

The 1963 season saw no Browns player respond more positively to the change of coaches than Jim Brown, who in 1962 had failed to gain 1,000 yards for the first time since his rookie season and for the first time in a six-year career had failed to lead the league in rushing. (Jim Taylor, the fullback of the league-champion Packers, did it.) Jim Brown had been running primarily between the tackles in Paul Brown's last few years as head coach. Under Collier, the star had the whole field with which to work.

"In Paul's latter years ... we were just so conservative, it was as if we were afraid," Jim Brown said. "Then Blanton came, and it wasn't a dictatorship anymore. Any play that would give me an easy opportunity to move the ball, Blanton was all for it, and he came up with those plays."

"I have never seen anyone [have] a relationship with a superstar like Blanton had with Jim," John Wooten said. "From the time Blanton returned to Cleveland he and Jim had liked

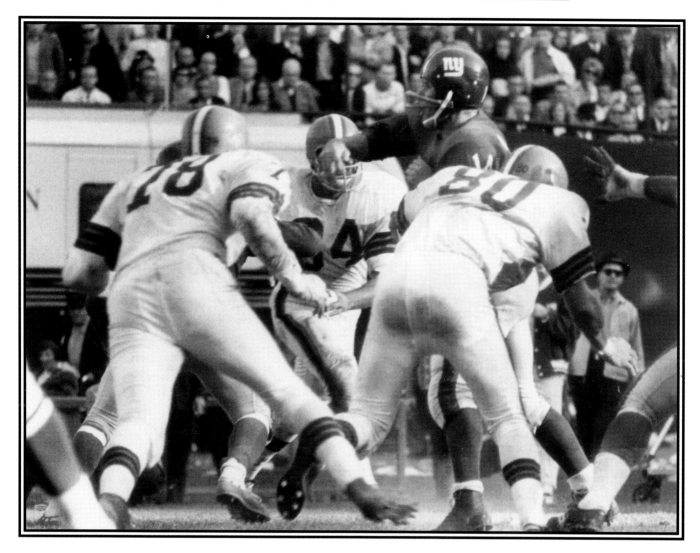

CLOSING IN: *Frank Parker (78), Paul Wiggin (84) and Bill Glass (80) surround New York's Y.A. Tittle in a 1963 Browns victory. The Browns nearly won the Eastern Conference that season, finishing at 10-4, a game behind the Giants, whose dynasty would end when the Browns finally won the crown in 1964.*

and respected each other. Blanton could motivate anyone, from a superstar such as Jim Brown, to the most insecure man, to all of us in between."

Brown improved his rushing yards from 996 in 1962 to 1,863 in '63, with a staggering 6.4 yards-per-carry average. The team itself went from 7-6-1 to 10-4, but still finished a game behind New York in the Eastern Conference race. The Browns, Giants and Cardinals were tied at 8-3 with three games to go.

Cleveland beat the Cards in Week 12, but were annihilated by Detroit on the next-to-last weekend to fall from a first-place tie with New York. The Giants won their last three games, clinching it via a victory over Pittsburgh, a team that routed them 31-0 in the second week of the season.

Y.A. Tittle had been brilliant in 1963. He completed 60 percent of his attempts and threw 36 touchdown passes to only 14 interceptions. Only John Unitas of the Baltimore Colts had a year equal to Tittle's. But 1963 was a last hurrah for an old team that had created a minidynasty in its conference. Tittle was 37 years old. The club was loaded with players with 10 or more years of service.

It all unraveled in a hurry for the Giants. The team plunged to 2-10-2 in 1964 and weren't a force again in the league until 1970. By that

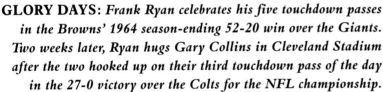

GLORY DAYS: *Frank Ryan celebrates his five touchdown passes in the Browns' 1964 season-ending 52-20 win over the Giants. Two weeks later, Ryan hugs Gary Collins in Cleveland Stadium after the two hooked up on their third touchdown pass of the day in the 27-0 victory over the Colts for the NFL championship.*

time the National Football League and American Football League had merged, and the Browns found themselves as one of the three teams switched from the older league to the AFL. The merger destroyed the once-fierce Browns-Giants rivalry for good.

The Browns won the Eastern Conference in 1964, but had trouble earning respect for doing it despite the fact the club was in a hot race with the St. Louis Cardinals all season. It was thought the Browns simply won the conference through attrition, rather than on merit. The Giants had fallen, so who else BUT Cleveland should win the East? Not only that, but the Baltimore Colts began tearing up the Western

Conference. An opening-day loss was followed by 10 straight victories. They smashed the Chicago Bears, the NFL champions in the previous year, 52-0 in the third game of the season. They defeated Vince Lombardi's Packers twice, and racked up 428 points to just 225 for their opponents. John Unitas threw 19 touchdown passes and a mere six interceptions.

Baltimore was coached by Don Shula, 34, one of the youngest heads in NFL history. He had grown up in Painesville, Ohio, just outside of Cleveland, played college football at John Carroll University in Cleveland Heights, Ohio, and started his NFL career with the Browns in 1951. Shula had also been an assistant under Collier at Kentucky and replaced another former Browns assistant coach, Weeb Ewbank, with the Colts.

The Baltimore defense, led by veteran Gino Marchetti, led the league in fewest points allowed and fewest touchdowns allowed (28).

The linebacking was solid, with 12-year veteran Bill Pellington in the middle and young veterans Jackie Burkett and Don Shinnick on the outside. Cornerback Bobby Boyd was the leader of a revamped secondary.

Blockers for Unitas included future Hall of Famer Jim Parker, a first-round draft choice from Ohio State in that banner year of 1957. Parker had moved to guard in 1963 because young Bob Vogel was a budding star at left tackle. Dick Szymanski was the All-Pro center, and on the right side of the line were two men who had been starters when Baltimore won back-to-back NFL crowns in 1958-59 — Alex Sandusky and George Preas.

Unitas' arsenal of pass receivers included Raymond Berry, double-threat halfback Lenny Moore, tall flanker Jimmy Orr, and John Mackey, considered by many the first superstar tight end in history. Unitas, Berry, Moore and Mackey all became Hall of Famers.

Moore led the Colts in rushing and in touchdowns with 16 by run and three by reception. Jerry Hill, Tony Lorick and converted quarterback Tom Matte, another Ohio Stater, shared the fullback duties.

Oddly enough, it was the Giants who might have given the Browns a shot at the title. One of New York's two victories and one of its two ties were against St. Louis, despite the latter's superior record. The Browns beat the Giants twice, including the last game of the season, to edge the Cards by a half game for the conference crown. The Browns had a tie and a loss in their two games against St. Louis. The Colts probably helped, too, by punishing the Cardinals, 47-27, in their regular-season meeting.

Everyone expected the Colts to do the same to Cleveland in the championship game. The offenses were considered equally explosive, but

BOOTING BALTIMORE: *Lou Groza kicks a 43-yard third-quarter field goal to open the scoring in the 1964 title game against the Colts. Bobby Franklin is Groza's holder.*

the Colts' vaunted defense was supposed to provide the difference. Almost all experts had a high-scoring game in sight.

It was a high-scoring game: for the Browns in the last two quarters, because that is when they scored all their points in a 27-0 triumph. Frank Ryan fired three touchdown passes to Gary Collins and Lou Groza kicked two field goals as the Browns dominated the second half before almost 80,000 in Cleveland Stadium. Collins gained 130 yards receiving. Jim Brown had 114 yards rushing on 28 carries. But it was the defense that got itself some respect that Dec. 27 day by limiting Unitas to 96 yards passing and intercepting him twice.

The Browns ruled the Eastern Conference again in 1965 with an 11-3 record, their best mark ever in a 14-game season. They were four games ahead of the Dallas Cowboys and the

IN FRONT OF THE PACK: *After his three-TD effort in the 1964 title game, Gary Collins tunes up in this 1965 preseason contest against the Packers. Collins led the Browns in receiving four times in his career, including the '65 season. Green Bay would later beat the Browns for the 1965 NFL championship.*

New York Giants, who finished tied for second place. They did this without Paul Warfield, the wide receiver who had had such a great rookie year in '64, for 10 games because of a broken shoulder suffered in the annual preseason game between the defending NFL champion and the College All-Stars.

Frank Ryan wasn't the healthiest man in 1965, either. Gino Marchetti of the Colts separated Ryan's shoulder in the Pro Bowl, and Ryan was in a cast for most of the off-season. He was injured again in Game 2 of the regular season, a 49-13 loss to St. Louis. Jim Ninowski came in to lead the Browns to a victory over Philadelphia the next week, and Ryan returned the following Saturday to fire a 44-yard TD pass to Collins in a 24-19 win over the Steelers.

The championship game was against the Packers in Green Bay. Nature wasn't kind to the Browns that day, as a morning snowfall started to melt during the game. The field had been hard and dry the day before as the Browns went through their final tune-up, but it was a mud bath in the second half. Jim Brown's running was rendered a non-factor by such a dreadful surface and the Browns fell, 23-12, after trailing by just one point, 13-12, at halftime.

The title was the third of five Coach Vince Lombardi would win with the Packers in the 1960s, as Green Bay became the team of that decade just as the Browns had been the team of the '50s. As for the Browns, they would be the underdog in two more NFL championship contests before the decade would end. They would do it without Jim Brown.

On July 14, 1966, Brown became the second football legend with that name to leave the Cleveland Browns in 3 1/2 years. He was in England, shooting a film called "The Dirty Dozen" at the time. He had assured the Browns he would be back, and it was Owner Art Modell's Hollywood connections that had helped Brown land a role in that film in the first place. So the best-paid football player of 1965 (Brown was earning $80,000) walked away from the game at the age of 30, informing Collier he was "no longer mentally prepared to play."

But the Browns kept winning. With little time to ready itself for the Post-Jim Brown Era, the Browns finished 9-5 and tied for second in the division. Leroy Kelly, a three-year veteran who had mainly been a punt returner over his first two seasons, gained 1,141 yards rushing and led the league in yards-per-carry average at 5.5, and touchdowns rushing with 15. Only Gale Sayers of Chicago had more yards rushing than Kelly.

"I don't expect to replace [Jim Brown]," Collier said. "Runners such as Jim come along once in a lifetime. But I do expect someone from this squad to make a name for himself."

Ernie Green, who had been better known as the guy who blocked for Jim Brown, made a bit of a name for himself in 1966 as well. Green gained 750 yards that season, 224 more than he'd had in his previous best year (1963) and caught 45 passes, 17 more than his career high (also 1963).

The Browns ended 9-5 again in '67 and won their division, the Century in the new NFL alignment that had four four-team divisions. They were crushed, however, 52-14, by the ris-

ing star of the Eastern Conference, Capitol Division champion Dallas.

Cleveland's next two seasons were more successful as the Browns ruled the Century Division again with records of 10-4 and 10-3-1. They reached the championship games in 1968 and '69, but were blown out both times by the Western Conference champions, the Colts, 34-0, in 1968, and the Vikings, 27-7, in 1969.

While the Browns were maintaining their winning tradition through the 1960s, their old

ONCOMING COWBOYS: *By the mid '60s, the Dallas Cowboys had replaced the New York Giants as the Browns' principal rival in the Eastern Conference. Frank Ryan hands off to Leroy Kelly in this 1966 Browns victory, 30-21, in Cleveland Stadium. George Andrie (66) and Bob Lilly (74) approach on the left.*

division rivals, the Giants, Eagles and Cardinals, were experiencing periods of inconsistency. New York never finished better than 7-7 in the last six years of the decade. Philadelphia had only one winning season in the years 1962-77. The Cardinals rallied in 1968 to finish 9-4-1 and one-half game behind the Browns, after new head coach Charley Winner's housecleaning following ugly racial confrontations, but fell back to 4-9-1 the next year.

The new power was the Dallas Cowboys, coached by Tom Landry since the team's birth

UNBREAKABLE: *Galen Fiss was a key member the Browns' Rubber Band Defense of the '60s, dubiously dubbed because it "stretched, but didn't break." Fiss, Vince Costello and Jim Houston formed a solid corps of linebackers, joined at various times by Dale Lindsey, Johnny Brewer and Sidney Williams.*

in 1960. Landry was a Browns nemesis for many years, first as a defensive back in the AAFC with the Brooklyn-New York Yankees, then as a member of Coach Steve Owen's New York Giants Umbrella Defense of the early '50s, then as an assistant coach on the Giants teams that knocked the Browns from Eastern Conference dominance in the late '50s, and finally as coach of Dallas.

The Cowboys made it to the championship game in 1966 and '67, only to lose close ones to the Packers. Landry himself presented an interesting contrast to the intimidating Vince Lombardi of Green Bay. Both men were assistants with the Giants in the glory days of the

'50s, but Landry was more in the Paul Brown mold. He was a quiet, gentlemanly figure who had an uncanny eye for talent. His methods were the antithesis of Lombardi and his Sturm and Drang.

In truth, there were no reasons the Browns should have fallen off the radar screen. They put eight players in the Pro Bowl every season from 1966-69. It was the same number who went after the 1965 season and one more than made it after their NFL championship year. Right guard Gene Hickerson was All-Pro five consecutive years from 1966-70. Leroy Kelly made All-Pro each year from 1966-69. Paul Warfield and Gary Collins were All-Pro twice.

Collier was never afraid to tinker with success. When longtime right linebacker Galen Fiss neared the end of his brilliant 11-year career in 1966, Collier replaced him with tight end Johnny Brewer, a rugged blocker and just as sure a tackler. Brewer responded to the move and made the Pro Bowl after the 1966 season.

The switch paved the way for the team to put Milt Morin in Brewer's tight end position. After dividing his time with Ralph "Catfish" Smith in 1966-67, Morin held the job through 1975 and became the first pass-catching tight end in Browns history.

Defensive players were moved from one side of the line to the other with great frequency. Defensive ends Paul Wiggin and Bill Glass were flip-flopped with regularity. So were tackles Jim Kanicki and Walter Johnson.

The linebackers were even more interchangeable. It was usually Jim Houston at left linebacker, except when it was John Garlington or Bob Matheson. Houston would then be in the middle, because middle linebackers Matheson and Dale Lindsey would be somewhere else. If Houston was in the middle, Lindsey

LEAGUE LEADER: *In 1968 (above), Leroy Kelly led the NFL in rushing for the second straight year with a career-high 1,239 yards, his third straight 1,000-yard season. His 20 TDs (16 on the ground) also led the league. Kelly was a Pro Bowl pick in '68, the third of six times he would be selected for the honor.*

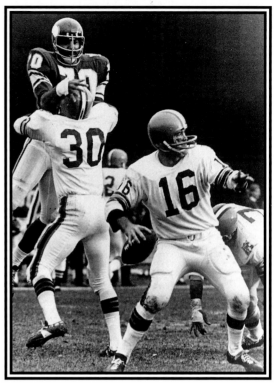

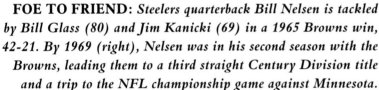

FOE TO FRIEND: *Steelers quarterback Bill Nelsen is tackled by Bill Glass (80) and Jim Kanicki (69) in a 1965 Browns win, 42-21. By 1969 (right), Nelsen was in his second season with the Browns, leading them to a third straight Century Division title and a trip to the NFL championship game against Minnesota.*

would be at right linebacker, unless it was Garlington there. Only the right linebacker, Billy Andrews, wasn't constantly on the move.

Also on the move was Leroy Kelly. The man who had carried the ball just 43 times in the two years he and Jim Brown were members of the team, led the league in rushing in 1967 and '68, scoring 27 touchdowns in those seasons.

Not all Browns stars in the '60s were homegrown. Defensive end Bill Glass came over in the Milt Plum trade in 1962 and was selected for the Pro Bowl four times with his new club. Erich Barnes, who'd worn out his welcome first with the Bears and then with the Giants, found a home in the Browns' secondary and made the Pro Bowl after the 1968 season.

Frank Ryan left the Browns just before the start of the 1969 season. It was not a real sur-

prise, as Ryan had earned a doctorate in mathematics and had been teaching the subject at Case Western Reserve University. The Browns acquired Bill Nelsen from the Steelers in anticipation Ryan would call it quits. Nelsen was Pittsburgh's No. 1 quarterback in 1965, but injuries plagued his career there and he was dealt for Cleveland's backup quarterback, Dick Shiner. Ryan made his way to the Washington Redskins, where he played two seasons.

Nelsen performed far above expectations in both 1968 and '69, leading the Browns to two straight upsets of the Cowboys in divisional playoff games. In the '68 game, interceptions by Mike Howell, Ben Davis, Dale Lindsey and Erich Barnes helped Nelsen's cause considerably in a 31-20 victory. In the '69 game, Nelsen completed 18 of 28 passes, with six third-down completions resulting in first downs, as the Browns won, 38-14.

But Nelsen had a history of knee problems and was never considered the club's long-term answer. The team was in the market for a topflight quarterback for the 1970 season.

At 10-3-1, however, the Browns were far down in the draft order. There was no way

Cleveland could get the two quarterbacks who had been considered "can't miss" future NFL stars — Louisiana Tech's Terry Bradshaw or Purdue's Mike Phipps — without trading with a weaker team.

Pittsburgh had the first selection and said it would take Bradshaw. Green Bay, which was in dire need of defensive linemen, announced it would select Mike McCoy of Notre Dame. Miami was next and no one was certain what Dolphins General Manager Joe Thomas would do.

What he did was tell the Browns the price for his club's No. 1 draft choice was either Leroy Kelly or Paul Warfield. How badly DID the Browns, Art Modell and Blanton Collier want that quarterback? Badly enough, apparently. Warfield went to the Dolphins and the Browns drafted Phipps. Warfield was the one Miami had wanted all along. The running back stable already included Larry Csonka, Eugene "Mercury" Morris and Jim Kiick. Kelly was not needed, but a deep threat like Warfield, to make the trio of running backs all the more potent, was.

Warfield had enjoyed his best year two seasons before with career highs in receptions with 50, yards with 1,067 and touchdowns with 12. His 1969 figures included 42 catches, 886 yards and 10 TDs.

The reaction to the trade, of course, was one of shock. Warfield had been one of the most popular Browns ever. He was a native of Warren, Ohio, and an Ohio State alumnus. Nelsen said the news made him feel as if *he* had been traded. The Browns' community reacted as if a family member had left home.

Business was business, however, and Paul Warfield was a Dolphin as the 1970 season, the first in which the NFL and AFL would operate

DEALT TO DOLPHINS: *Paul Warfield continued his Hall-of-Fame career after being traded in 1970 for Miami's No. 1 draft choice, which the Browns used to select quarterback Mike Phipps. Warfield was a member of three Dolphins Super Bowl teams and played in the WFL before returning to the Browns in 1976-77.*

as one league, rolled around. The Browns tried to fill the Warfield void with Giants speedster Homer Jones, who had caught 184 passes for 4,019 yards and 34 touchdowns over the past four years. Cleveland sent two starters, fullback Ron Johnson and defensive tackle Jim Kanicki, to the Giants to get him. But Jones lasted just one season and the job eventually went to Fair Hooker, who held the position through 1974.

The trade of Paul Warfield, who was one of the symbols of the successful '60s, marked the end of an era in Browns history as much as the passing of a decade and the entrance to a new alignment of the league had for many other teams. Soon, losing a coach would be added to that list. The Browns and the National Football League were about to begin a period in which almost nothing would be the same.

Realignment & Rivalries

By Steve Byrne

Greg Pruitt

Following the 1970 NFL season, the Browns' first in the American Football Conference of the realigned NFL, team owner Art Modell had this to say: "We were not prepared for the American Football League. That was my fault. We were just not prepared for their style of play, and had a so-so year." The Browns finished 7-7 that season and lost the Central Division title to Paul Brown's third-year Cincinnati Bengals.

It was the only non-winning record in Blanton Collier's eight-years as the Browns' head coach. But maybe no one, even the big winners, was prepared for 1970. The National Football League, working the same stand in its two-division format since 1933, and the American Football League, the six-year-old challenger, had formally merged in 1966, but television contracts did not allow permanent inter-league play until their 1970 expiration.

With it came football as we know it — two conferences of three divisions each, a two-week playoff schedule (since expanded to three) culminating in a world-championship game, played at a neutral site. That's the way it has been for more than 25 years, the longest stretch through which the NFL has gone without a major upheaval.

The break-even record the Browns managed in the first season might have been the only thing that could have made Art Modell ashamed in 1970. The former ad man from Brooklyn became a major player in the NFL in almost no time. Granted, Modell was a man who knew television and who came into the league at a time when TV was helping all sports become a lucrative venture, but he brought more than just knowledge to the table. Modell was a shrewd negotiator who, as chairman of the NFL's television committee, made both TV and professional football extremely wealthy.

But it was a decision of Modell's made in the spring of 1969 that had the most impact, both on the league and on the Browns. Negotiations over the makeup of the new NFL were at an impasse. The AFL owners wanted the conferences to have equal numbers of clubs and have AFL and NFL franchises mixing within the divisions. Leading this group was Paul Brown, now the vice president, general manager and head coach of the Cincinnati Bengals, who joined the AFL in 1968.

The NFL owners wanted to maintain the old alignments, which meant the 16 teams of the senior league would make up one conference and the 10 clubs of the AFL would form another, with the latter catching up through expansion.

Modell proposed a compromise in which the Browns, Steelers and Cardinals would join the conference composed of AFL teams and stay in the same division. The Bengals, with whom the Browns would have a ready-made rivalry, would be the fourth team in the circuit. The Cleveland Browns, Modell said, wouldn't move unless Art Rooney, owner of the archrival Steelers, would agree to it.

Rooney agreed, but Bill and Stormy Bidwell, owners of the St. Louis Cardinals, would not. The whole ordeal took a toll on Modell, and the Browns' owner was hospitalized for a bleeding ulcer by the time the other owners eventually reached an agreement (only because NFL Commissioner Pete Rozelle locked them in their New York hotel meeting room until they did). Modell's plan finally was approved, although it was the Colts who became the third NFL club to switch to the AFL, now called the American Football Conference. Baltimore was put in the AFC East, while the Houston Oilers became the fourth team in the AFC Central with Cleveland, Pittsburgh and Cincinnati.

Once again the Browns had a major role in how the NFL would look for years to come. Just as Paul Brown's revolutionary coaching methods and the Browns' unparalleled success of the early- and mid-1950s made pro football more attractive to millions of fans, so too would Art Modell's foresight help make football the greatest professional sports spectacle.

The Browns were rewarded by being named one of the teams to play in the first regular

PROMISING: *1970 rookie quarterback Mike Phipps was the Browns' hope for the future in the AFC Central Division.*

Monday night football game in league history. The Cardinals had been playing one game per season on Monday nights for several years, and now the idea was adopted as a weekly game in which all teams could participate. Again, Modell was instrumental in hammering out the details for the game. The Columbia Broadcasting System had the rights to the NFC, stemming from its having broadcast the NFL for years, and the National Broadcasting Co., which televised the AFL since 1965, was given domain over AFC

NEW CHALLENGES: *Fierce Central Division rivalries with the Bengals and Steelers were established in 1970. Gary Collins (86) blocks for Leroy Kelly on a short gain in a 14-10 loss in Cincinnati on Nov. 15. Jim Houston sends Pittsburgh's Preston Pearson airborne in a 15-7 win in Cleveland Stadium on Oct. 3.*

contests. The Monday night games, however, went to the American Broadcasting Co., which at first had the AFL (1960-64) but was better known for its telecasts of college football. The Browns' opponent in that first "Monday Night Football" game was the New York Jets. The matchup, played on Sept. 21, 1970, was a natural. One of the winningest teams of the NFL would play an old-line member of the AFL, as both teams were now cousins in the new AFC.

Not only that, but the Jets had stunned the pro football world by upsetting the 19-point favorite Baltimore Colts in the third Super Bowl two seasons earlier to give the young league the respectability it had sought for nine years. Joe Namath, the Jets' brash and talented quarterback who had "guaranteed" the Super Bowl victory, was the big drawing card for the game, to be played in Cleveland Stadium.

Namath was brilliant, completing 19 of 32 passes for 299 yards. But it was the Browns' defense, which intercepted Namath three times and recovered a Jets fumble, that was responsible for Cleveland's 31-21 victory despite a 445-221 disadvantage in total yardage. Browns right linebacker Billy Andrews picked off a Namath pass and returned it 25 yards for a touchdown to ice it for Cleveland. Gary Collins put his name in the trivia books when he caught a 55-yard pass from Bill Nelsen to score the first touchdown in a "Monday Night" game.

Perhaps a more important and significant game was actually played in the 1970 preseason when the Browns met their intrastate rivals, the Cincinnati Bengals, for the first time. The Bengals won that game, 31-24.

The first-ever regular-season Browns-Bengals game took place on Oct. 11 in Cleveland, site of Paul Brown's greatest success as coach of the Browns for 17 years. The game will likely be remembered for the deafening boos that greeted Brown on his first visit to Cleveland Stadium as a coach in eight years. Brown did not shake hands with Blanton Collier after the preseason game in Cincinnati and declined to do so after the first regular-season meeting as well, won by the Browns, 30-27.

A rivalry was born. The Bengals won the second regular-season contest, 14-10. The game was the second victory in a seven-game winning streak the Bengals put together en route to an 8-6 record and the AFC Central Division championship. Two weeks after the season ended, Blanton Collier announced he would retire.

The announcement came after the Steelers game, which the Browns lost 28-9. Cleveland's record was 5-6 at the time, one game behind Cincinnati in the Central Division standings. But Collier said it was not a ploy to motivate his club. The fact was the coach's hearing, which had always been impaired, was getting worse. He could barely hear on the sideline and feared the affliction would affect his ability to coach.

The Browns did finish the season with a bang, although not enough of one to allow Collier to leave as a champion. They sandwiched road-game victories over the Houston Oilers and the Denver Broncos around their most heartbreaking loss of the season, 6-2 to the Cowboys at home. Dallas got two field goals in the second half to win it, but it was the Browns' mistakes — three interceptions, a blocked punt to set up one field goal, a fumble by Gary Collins inside the Cowboys' 10-yard line, two offensive interference calls on Collins — that sunk the Browns.

Offensive coordinator Nick Skorich was named to replace Collier. Skorich had previously been head coach of the Philadelphia Eagles from 1961-63 and remains in 1995 the only man the Browns ever hired for the head coaching job who had previous NFL head coaching experience.

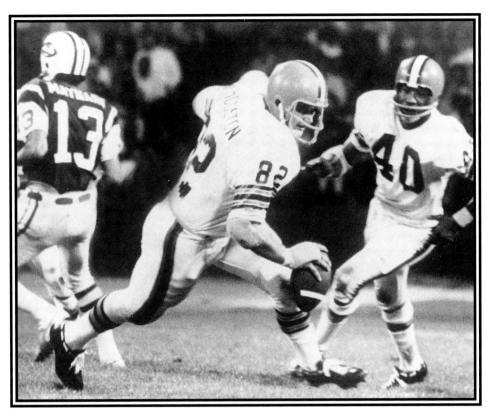

MONDAY NIGHT INAUGURAL: *The Browns opened the 1970 season in the first-ever ABC Monday Night Football game, beating the Jets, 31-21, in Cleveland Stadium. Jim Houston (82) runs back a second-quarter interception past the Jets' Don Maynard (13) while Erich Barnes (40) trails the play on the right.*

The Browns rebounded in 1971 to win the Central Division with a 9-5 record, then lost to the Colts, 20-3, in the playoffs. However, the Browns would not win another division championship for nine seasons (1980). They actually improved to 10-4 in 1972 and entered the playoffs as a wild-card team, but lost to the Miami Dolphins, 20-14.

The rise of the Pittsburgh Steelers, which had begun in 1969 with the hiring of former Browns linebacker-guard Chuck Noll, would be realized in 1972 and completed two years later with a Super Bowl victory. The rivalry, which the Browns had until then dominated (33 victories to the Steelers' 11) was suddenly one of the hottest in the league.

The Browns beat the Steelers, 26-24, in Week 10 of 1972 on a 26-yard field goal by Don Cockroft with 13 seconds to play, to leave each

FAMILIAR STANCES: *Many longtime Browns veterans departed in the 1970s, paving the way for new talent to emerge in the Kardiac Kids era. Included were cornerback-safety Erich Barnes (40) and receiver Gary Collins (86) in '71, guard Gene Hickerson (66) in '73 and defensive tackle Walter Johnson (71) in '76.*

team at 7-3. But the Steelers slapped a 30-0 loss on the Browns two weeks later in Pittsburgh. Both teams won their last two games easily, as Pittsburgh won the Central championship, its first title of any kind in 40 years of National Football League membership.

The Steelers dominated the Browns in the standings, but not always on the field. Though the Browns would lose 16 straight in Three Rivers Stadium from 1970-85, they would win five games in Cleveland Stadium from 1970-77.

The Browns fell to 7-5-2 in 1973 and 4-10 in '74. Skorich was fired and replaced by offensive line coach Forrest Gregg on Jan. 22, 1975. Gregg had been an All-Pro offensive tackle for the Green Bay Packers from 1956-70 and was only 42 years old when Art Modell picked him to be the fourth head coach in Browns history. Gregg brought Blanton Collier, 69, out of retirement to coach the quarterbacks.

Gregg, known as a stern, gruff man and a true taskmaster, didn't produce results immediately. The Browns were 3-11 in 1975, their poorest season in history until 1990, but bounced back to go 9-5 in '76. Cleveland even had a shot at the Central Division title on the last week of the season.

The Browns, Bengals and Steelers were 9-4 entering the final game, but Cleveland was stunned by the Kansas City Chiefs, 4-9 at that point, by a score of 39-14. Pittsburgh and Cincinnati, meanwhile, were burying weak opponents, the Oilers and Jets, by a combined score of 63-3. The Steelers won the division because they had swept the season series with the Bengals.

The years 1970-77 saw the departure of most of the team's stars of the '60s. Leaving were receiver Gary Collins and halfback Leroy Kelly, who each played briefly in the World Football League. Retiring were guard Gene Hickerson, offensive tackle Dick Schafrath, defensive tackle Walter Johnson, linebacker Jim Houston, defensive back Erich Barnes and tight end Milt Morin.

Also retiring would be wide receiver Paul Warfield, who had left the Dolphins for the WFL, then returned to the Browns for two seasons (1976-77) after the WFL went out of business in 1975.

In their spots came many of the players who would form the Kardiac Kids outfit that won the AFC Central in 1980. Defensive tackle Jerry Sherk arrived with the 1970 draft. The 1971 draft produced defensive back Clarence Scott, linebacker Charlie Hall and, in the sixth round, offensive tackle Doug Dieken. Defensive back Thom Darden was the first-round draft pick of 1972 and running back Greg Pruitt was No. 2 in '73. Linebacker Dick Ambrose arrived in 1975. Fullback Mike Pruitt and wide receiver Dave Logan were drafted in 1976. Outside linebacker Robert L. Jackson was the Browns' top choice in '77.

Coming to the Browns via trades or free agency were wide receiver Reggie Rucker, center Tom DeLeone, guard-center Robert E. Jackson and cornerback Ron Bolton.

Perhaps the biggest disappointment of the years 1970-77 was that Mike Phipps never became the quarterback almost everyone said he would be. Bill Nelsen remained the starter in Phipps' first two seasons. By 1976 Phipps was no longer a starter. He'd had only one year in which he completed more than 50 percent of his passes and threw 81 interceptions to 37 touchdown passes. He was traded to the Bears in 1977 for Chicago's fourth-round draft selection that year and its first-round pick in '78.

It wasn't Phipps who benefited most by the return of Blanton Collier as quarterback coach in 1975. The old master was more help to a man few predicted would be a star when the Browns nabbed him in the 13th round of the 1972 draft.

ARRIVAL: *Safety Thom Darden, a No. 1 pick in 1972, was one of a long line of successful high-round draft choices in the 1970s that formed the nucleus of the Kardiac Kids of 1979-80.*

IN COMMAND: *Brian Sipe was a passing champion in college. But with the Browns, he directed a more balanced offense featuring strong runners, quality receivers and rock-solid linemen. Sipe helped lead the Browns to a steady climb in the AFC Central and some of the most memorable victories in team history.*

Rutigliano & the Kardiac Kids

There might never be two men in the same profession more different than Forrest Gregg, the tough disciplinarian who coached the Browns from 1975-77, and his successor, the kinder, gentler Sam Rutigliano, who took over in 1978. Gregg was known as a stern taskmaster who got the most out of young players with a no-nonsense, demanding approach. He was a Hall-of-Fame offensive tackle for Vince Lombardi in the glory days of the Green Bay Packers when they were dominating professional football in the 1960s. But while Lombardi, the ultimate tough-guy coach, could still motivate veteran players, Gregg had his problems with the guys who had been there and done that. He was dismissed by Art Modell and replaced by Dick Modzelewski with one game to go in the 1977 regular season, which ended with a 6-8 record after a 5-2 start.

Ozzie Newsome

By Steve Byrne

"Forrest was a Hall of Famer," wide receiver Reggie Rucker said. "You have to look at his background. You have to take into consideration that the apple doesn't fall far from the tree. He played for Vince Lombardi.

"I think in the '70s you had a different kind of athlete. You couldn't just tell a player what to do. The player wanted to know why he was doing it, and that just wasn't Forrest's way."

In his place came Rutigliano. Unlike Gregg, Nick Skorich and Blanton Collier, Rutigliano had not served as an assistant coach with the Browns when Modell hired him on Dec. 28, 1977. Like Gregg, Collier and Paul Brown, however, Rutigliano had no head coaching experience in the NFL.

Cleveland, in fact, was one of the few places Rutigliano had never lived. A son of an Italian immigrant from the Sheepshead Bay section of Brooklyn, Rutigliano had gone to junior college in Decatur, Miss., and to four-year college at the universities of Tennessee and Tulsa. He was an end on the 1951 NCAA championship team at UT as a junior before moving to Tulsa for his senior season. He was back in New York for his

OVER THE TOP: *Although short by NFL quarterback standards at 6-1, Brian Sipe took Cleveland's passing statistics to new heights. In 1995, he was the team's all-time leader in NFL passing attempts (3,439), completions (1,944), yardage (23,713) and TD passes (154).*

first coaching job, Lafayette High School, while he attended Columbia University at night. After several years in the preps, he accepted college assistant coach's jobs at the universities of Connecticut and Maryland, the latter position working under the former Browns linebacker Lou Saban.

When Saban was named head coach and general manager of the Denver Broncos, Rutigliano joined his staff. The Patriots, Jets and Saints were his next employers. He was with four teams in a stretch of 11 seasons. "He bounced around pretty good," Modell said of Rutigliano, but added that he believed he had the next Blanton Collier as his new head coach.

"He's a teacher by background," the Cleveland owner said, "just like Collier was. Beyond

that, he relates with today's attitudes. He's contemporary in his relationship with players. I could have gotten a name coach, but that's not what I wanted."

What Modell really wanted was to start from scratch. The old order was no longer. Everything would be different.

Different it certainly was. Where Forrest Gregg had been intensity and boiling blood, Rutigliano was a coach who wanted to make sure that the players avoided emotional peaks and valleys. Rutigliano was fond of saying you can't have players swinging from the rafters one day and expect to have them calm down the next.

"You were dealing with a team that was frazzled and unsure of its direction," Rucker explained. "I remember I asked Peter Hadhazy [Browns executive vice president], 'Why don't you get Sam?' The team couldn't use another dictator. It needed someone to bring a new flavor. I knew Sam from when I was a player and he was coach for the Patriots, and when Sam came in, I knew the guys would love him. He could be firm, but he wasn't into telling adults how to conduct their lives."

One thing that did not change was the Browns' commitment to Brian Sipe at quarterback. Sipe was a 13th-round draft choice in 1972 from San Diego State, where he was NCAA passing champion. He did not even make the Browns' roster until 1974 and was never expected to oust Mike Phipps, the club's No. 1 draft choice in 1970 and the man for whom the Browns traded future Hall of Fame inductee Paul Warfield to acquire.

Phipps never became the star the experts said he would be, and when he broke a shoulder in the first regular season game of 1976, Sipe went in and never went out. The slender Californian who guided the Browns to a 9-5 record played well enough to spur the club to trade Phipps to the Bears on May 3, 1977.

It was a long road for Brian Sipe. Sure, he had set all those records at San Diego State, but that was when he was playing for the pass-happy head coach Don Coryell in the pro-set offense. Sipe was considered small by quarterback standards (6-1, 195 pounds) and didn't possess a strong arm.

But Coryell would later take another quarterback considered lacking in physical skills, Dan Fouts, and see him make a mockery of many old NFL passing records with the San Diego Chargers.

Rutigliano liked Sipe. Watching films of the quarterback in Modell's basement, the Browns' head-coach candidate said he was impressed by the fact that Sipe never missed open receivers, never turned his shoulders when he set up to pass and would move in the pocket only to find his receivers and not out of panic.

A broken shoulder blade knocked Sipe out for the second half of the 1977 season, but he came back in 1978, Rutigliano's first year as head coach, to become the most prolific passer in Browns history. He set team records for attempts and completions in '78 and broke them both for two years running.

There was plenty of talent around Sipe. The offensive line of Doug Dieken and Barry Darrow at tackles, Henry Sheppard and Robert E. Jackson at guards and Tom DeLeone at center had played together for two seasons. Reggie Rucker was a quality veteran wide receiver and young, athletic Dave Logan was ready to move into the other wide receiver spot being vacated by the aging Paul Warfield (who had rejoined the Browns in 1976 after five years with the Dolphins and one year in the World Football League). Greg Pruitt was an All-Pro in the Cleveland backfield.

The holes to fill were at tight end and fullback. Milt Morin's last season with the Browns was 1975 and his replacements at tight end, Oscar Roan and Gary Parris, had only 20 catches combined in 1977. Cleo Miller, a free agent pickup from the Kansas City Chiefs, who also got him as a free agent, was starting at fullback while No. 1 draft choice Mike Pruitt was mostly sitting. Pruitt carried only 99 times over his first two seasons, as he was not a favorite of Forrest Gregg.

CALM COMMUNICATOR: *Head Coach Sam Rutigliano's ability to relate to modern-day players helped the talented Browns to mature into a cohesive unit in the late 1970s, culminating in the Kardiac Kids' dramatic seasons of 1979-80.*

To solve the tight end problem Rutigliano drafted a wide receiver, Ozzie Newsome of Alabama, in the first round of 1978. Crimson Tide coach Paul "Bear" Bryant had called Newsome the best receiver he'd ever coached, and Rutigliano was convinced his draftee would be a tight end with the moves of a wide receiver. He wasn't wrong. Newsome caught 38 passes as a rookie for a 15.5-yard average per catch. He increased that to 55 receptions and nine touchdowns in 1979.

The fullback situation was solved by making Mike Pruitt the starter over Cleo Miller. Pruitt greatly increased his number of carries from 47 in 1977 to 135 the next season. Miller's dropped from 163 to 89 in the same period. Pruitt would have his breakout season in '79

with 264 carries for 1,294 yards (4.9 yards per carry), 41 receptions and 11 TDs.

There was talent on defense, too. Defensive tackle Jerry Sherk and free safety Thom Darden were All-Pro. Cornerback Clarence Scott had been a starter since 1971 and outside linebacker Charlie Hall had been one since '72. Dick Ambrose was solid at middle linebacker and Ron Bolton had started at cornerback since 1973, first with the Patriots and since 1976 with the Browns.

But with two first-round draft choices in 1978, Rutigliano had the luxury of drafting a defensive player as well as a tight end. Clay Matthews of the University of Southern California was the Browns' No. 1 pick. He started two games in 1978 and all 16 the following year.

PRUITTS DO IT: *Under Sam Rutigliano, Greg Pruitt (left) was joined by Mike Pruitt (above) in the Browns' backfield with immediate success. In 1979, Mike Pruitt's 1,294 yards rushing was the best Browns total since Jim Brown's 1,544 in 1965.*

The Browns improved to an 8-8 record in 1978. Sipe threw for 2,906 yards and 21 touchdowns. Greg Pruitt was working less, but enjoying it more. He had 60 fewer carries, but improved his rushing average from 4.6 yards a carry to 5.5.

Sipe was even more awesome in 1979. He had coolly led the Browns to come-from-behind victories in the first three regular-season games with fourth-quarter rallies, then watched the defense put it all together in a 26-7 victory over the Dallas Cowboys, the defending NFC cham-

TRIO OF TARGETS: *The 1980 Kardiac Kids featured three clutch pass receivers who caught the majority of quarterback Brian Sipe's team-record 337 completions. From left to right are Reggie Rucker, Ozzie Newsome and Dave Logan.*

pion, in a Monday night game in Cleveland Stadium. Then reality set in. Three straight losses made the Browns 4-3. They were still 9-5, with a shot at a wild-card playoff berth, but no late heroics were in order in a 19-14 loss to the Oakland Raiders in Week 15 and a 16-12 setback to the Cincinnati Bengals in the finale.

Still, 12 of the 16 games were decided by a touchdown or less. The thrilling finishes to so many games that season earned the Browns the nickname "Kardiac Kids" for their ability to induce heart failure among the team's followers.

They did it without Greg Pruitt for the most part. He suffered a sprained knee in the victory over the Cowboys and re-injured it in Week 9, finishing him for the year. Pruitt was limited to 62 rushing attempts and 14 receptions. Calvin Hill, an 11-year veteran who had been a star with the Dallas Cowboys from 1969-74, played mostly in Pruitt's place.

Even more serious was the health of Jerry Sherk. A staph infection in his left leg, diag-

nosed after the 10th game of the season, put the defensive tackle in the Cleveland Clinic for five weeks. His condition was listed as critical and it wasn't known whether he'd even survive. He did, but spent the off-season rehabilitating the leg and trying to regain the strength he lost from a 35-pound drop in his weight.

Consequently, 1980 hardly looked like a year that was going to live in the memories of Browns fans for eternity. The defense was considered porous, having yielded 22 points a game. To resolve that situation, Rutigliano appointed Marty Schottenheimer defensive coordinator. Schottenheimer, a former linebacker with the Bills and Patriots who had been linebackers coach at Detroit the previous two seasons, set about to create a 3-4 alignment. The four-linebacker setup was intended to stop the run, but would not provide much of a pass rush.

It would have to be done without Jerry Sherk, who left after two quarters of the first regular-season game and never played again in 1980. Sherk had 10 1/2 sacks in 1979, further reducing the Browns' ability to rush the opposing quarterback.

Lyle Alzado, an All-Pro with the Denver Broncos who was acquired for the start of the

FIRED UP: *Ex-Broncos defensive end Lyle Alzado brought his emotional brand of leadership to the Browns' line in the 1980 playoff season. He was joined by end Marshall Harris and nose tackle Henry Bradley.*

1979 season, also had 10 1/2 sacks that year. He was the only starting defensive lineman in '79 who would keep his job in '80. Henry Bradley, who was cut in training camp of '79 and was driving a truck in Cleveland when he was called back to the club to replace Sherk after the 10th game, became the nose tackle in the 3-4 defense. Marshall Harris, a second-year veteran acquired from the Jets, was the other defensive end. Harris took over for Jack Gregory, the 1979 starter who retired after a 13-year career.

Robert L. Jackson, the Browns' No. 1 draft selection in 1977, moved into the starting line-up as the fourth linebacker. Charlie Hall and Clay Matthews played outside while Jackson and Dick Ambrose were the inside linebackers.

But the biggest deal the Browns pulled was to get an offensive star, Buffalo Bills guard Joe

DeLamielleure, to join an already strong line that included veterans Doug Dieken, Tom DeLeone, Robert E. Jackson, Henry Sheppard, Cody Risien and Gerry Sullivan.

DeLamielleure was unhappy with the Bills and boycotted their training camp. Although the general consensus was that defensive players should be the top priority, the team said it couldn't pass up a player with DeLamielleure's credentials, which included never missing a start since his rookie season of 1973, five straight Pro Bowl selections and blocking for record-setting rusher O.J. Simpson.

What Rutigliano had assembled was a team without a big name, even though Sipe would become the living symbol of the Kardiac Kids. The Browns were a collection of talented, low-profile players who never let individual success cloud the purpose of the season-long mission, or let the occasional failures knock them off their even keel. It was Sam's way, and he insisted it was working.

The 1980 preseason, however, was a disaster. The Browns won just one of four games and gave up a combined 111 points in three of them. The offense was no great shakes either, averaging 13 points a game. The regular season started just as badly. Cleveland was beaten by the Patriots, 34-17, in the opener and lost the home debut the next week, 16-7, to the Oilers.

Then came the turnaround. Sipe marched the Browns 66 yards in four plays to shatter a 13-13 tie in the third quarter of a 20-13 win over Kansas City. A touchdown pass to No. 1 draft choice Charles White was the winner.

Next, Sipe completed 13 straight passes, a club record, in a victory over Tampa Bay, 34-27. Calvin Hill's 43-yard TD catch in the fourth quarter gave the Browns a 31-27 lead.

A loss to the Broncos was followed by five straight victories, with a 27-26 conquest of the defending Super Bowl champion Pittsburgh Steelers being the highlight as the Browns erased a 26-14 deficit in less than four minutes.

On Nov. 30, the Browns moved into first place by themselves at 9-4 with a 17-14 victory over the Oilers. They fell back into a tie with

LINE MATES: *Right tackle Cody Risien (above) joined left tackle Doug Dieken (above left) and left guard Henry Sheppard (below left) on the 1980 offensive line that also included center Tom DeLeone and right guard and ex-Bill Joe DeLamielleure.*

Houston two weeks later, but won the AFC Central title with a 27-24 triumph over the Bengals in Cincinnati on the last week of the campaign. Don Cockroft's 22-yard field goal with 1:25 to play broke a 24-24 tie.

The Browns and Oilers both finished 11-5, but the Browns were the division champions on the strength of an 8-4 record among AFC foes to Houston's 7-5 mark.

Sipe was later named NFL Most Valuable Player. He had passed for 4,132 yards, second in league history at the time to San Diego's Dan Fouts. He became only the third quarterback to ever eclipse the 4,000-yards passing plateau (Joe Namath did it with the Jets in 1967). Sipe broke his own team records for pass

SEASONED VETS: *Running back Calvin Hill (top), defensive tackle Jerry Sherk (right) and safety Clarence Scott (above) added 10, nine and eight years of NFL experience, respectively, to Sam Rutigliano's first "Kardiac Kids" team of 1979.*

BEHIND THE LINE: *Robert L. Jackson (56), Dick Ambrose (52) and Clay Matthews (57) formed three-fourths of Cleveland's 1980 linebacking corps. They were joined by Charlie Hall.*

attempts (554) and completions (337), and threw for 30 touchdowns and just 14 interceptions. Mike Pruitt had the second of his four 1,000-yard rushing seasons and also led the team with 63 receptions.

Once again, 12 of the 16 games were decided by a touchdown or less. This time, however, the Kardiac Kids won nine of those close ones. And the fans were ecstatic. There were 15,000 of them at Hopkins Airport when the team arrived from Cincinnati. Cleveland mayor George Voinovich was one of them, as he called the Browns' AFC Central championship the most important thing to happen to the community since he'd been in office. The eight-year playoff drought was over. All was now good in Brownsland.

The Kardiac Kids would play one more close game, although it would not result in heart failure, but rather heartbreak. The Oakland Raiders had crushed Houston, 27-7, in a wild-card playoff game for the right to visit Cleveland and take on the Browns. Had the Oilers won, the Browns would have hosted the AFC East champion Buffalo Bills, as the league attempted not to match teams from the same division in the playoffs until the conference championship.

The Cleveland area was going through two weeks of Browns madness. The 20,000 tickets available for the playoff battle were sold in two hours. Fans camped all night in front of ticket outlets, waiting for the 10 a.m. window opening. Christmas shoppers were buying up Browns merchandise as fast as the shopkeepers could put it out for them.

The area needed this. Like many other northern cities that had been manufacturing giants in the late 19th and early 20th centuries, and a magnet for European immigrants, Cleveland's future was precarious. Jobs in the smokestack industries were vanishing and the population was dwindling. Clevelanders were leaving the city in droves, both to the ever-sprawling suburbs and to the ballooning "Sun Belt" states. "Cleveland jokes" were becoming popular, as the city became the nationwide symbol of the declining Northeast-Midwest industrial corridor.

In Oakland, the Raiders had been consistent winners for more than a decade. Jim Plunkett, the 1970 Heisman Trophy winner, had

RED RIGHT 88: *In the nightmare ending to a dream season, Oakland's Mike Davis intercepts Brian Sipe's end-zone pass to Ozzie Newsome (82) in Cleveland Stadium. The play halted the Kardiac Kids' hopes to advance in the 1980 AFC playoffs.*

resurrected his career with the Raiders. So had vicious defensive end John Matuszak, the first overall draft choice of 1973 whose unruliness almost swept him out of the league until he joined the Raiders in '76.

The defense was extremely tough. Cornerback Lester Hayes, who led the NFL with 13 interceptions, and veteran linebacker Ted Hendricks were All-Pro. On offense, Plunkett had two excellent wide receivers in Cliff Branch and Raymond Chester and a budding young star at tight end, Todd Christensen. Plunkett could hand off to running backs Mark van Eeghen and Kenny King, behind an outstanding offensive line with veterans like Gene Upshaw, Art Shell and Dave Dalby.

Game day was bitterly cold in Cleveland, with temperatures around zero. Still, 77,000 fans decided not to watch the game on television and come to the Stadium. Nothing could dampen, or chill, this party.

The Browns scored first when Ron Bolton intercepted Plunkett's pass and returned it 42 yards for a touchdown. Hendricks blocked Don Cockroft's extra-point try and Cleveland led 6-0. Van Eeghen scored on a one-yard run just before halftime and the Raiders were up 7-6 at the intermission.

Cockroft kicked two field goals in the third quarter to make it 12-7 Browns, but van Eeghen scored again, with 9:22 remaining, to put the Raiders ahead 14-12.

The Browns stopped Oakland at the Cleveland 15-yard line with 2:22 to play. Sipe then drove them 72 yards to the Raiders' 13, at the open end of the Stadium. But on second down Sipe's pass intended for Ozzie Newsome was

intercepted by defensive back Mike Davis in the end zone. The season was over and the play, known in the playbook as "Red Right 88," would forever live in Cleveland Browns infamy.

Plunkett defended the Browns' decision to try to get a touchdown, even though it seemed as if they were well within field goal range. He said all the points, with the exception of Bolton's interception return, were scored in the closed end of the Stadium. He added that a field goal kicked in the open end would never have been a sure thing from any distance.

It was some consolation that the Browns gave the Raiders their toughest playoff game. Oakland went on to defeat the Philadelphia Eagles, 27-10, in Super Bowl XV.

The 1980 season was the last hurrah for the Kardiac Kids. They fell to 5-11 in '81 and watched the Bengals win the AFC Central and go to the Super Bowl. Forrest Gregg was the Cincinnati coach, proving his military style

FRUSTRATION: *Sam Rutigliano paces the Astrodome sideline during a 34-27 loss to Houston in 1983. Although the Browns finished at 9-7 that season, the close-win Kardiac Kids era would completely reverse itself in 1984 as the team lost seven of its first eight, six by 10 points or less, leading to Rutigliano's dismissal.*

was effective with a team with a lot of younger talent on the roster.

The Browns went 4-5 in the strike-shortened 1982 campaign and made the playoffs under the NFL's makeshift post-season schedule that year. They were 9-7 in 1983, which became the last for Brian Sipe in the NFL as he was lured away by the new United States Football League. In 1984, after the Browns lost seven of their first eight, Rutigliano was dismissed and replaced by Marty Schottenheimer.

The Kardiac Kids days unofficially ended with Sipe's jumping leagues. It was time for a new era in Browns history as hearts were soon replaced by bones.

Kosar, Canines & Contenders

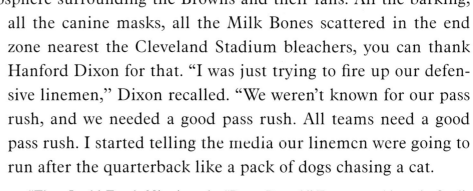

Hanford Dixon would probably be remembered anyway. The Browns' No. 1 draft choice of 1981 was a three-time All-Pro and, with Frank Minnifield, formed what was regarded as the best cornerback tandem in the late 1980s NFL. But Dixon's on-field accomplishments in his nine-year career may be overshadowed by what he brought to the atmosphere surrounding the Browns and their fans. All the barking, all the canine masks, all the Milk Bones scattered in the end zone nearest the Cleveland Stadium bleachers, you can thank Hanford Dixon for that. "I was just trying to fire up our defensive linemen," Dixon recalled. "We weren't known for our pass rush, and we needed a good pass rush. All teams need a good pass rush. I started telling the media our linemen were going to run after the quarterback like a pack of dogs chasing a cat.

Kevin Mack

By Steve Byrne

"Then I told Frank Minnifield we should start barking at the linemen, you know, to get them fired up. Pretty soon the fans started barking, and you know the rest."

The rest is that the Cleveland Browns' fans adopted Dixon's persona faster than Walter Payton could hit a hole off left tackle. For every game in the latter half of the 1980s otherwise rational folks would behave like dogs (or, as it came to be spelled, "Dawgs," in imitation of Dixon's Alabama drawl). The bleachers, where the most dedicated barkers held seats, became

the "Dawg Pound." Fans poured into the Stadium wearing masks that made them look like bulldogs, bloodhounds, golden retrievers, et al. They carried bones, both real ones and replicas, and wore clothing adorned with dog references as the apparel manufacturers moved quickly to take advantage of the situation.

It was infectious. The image of the good-timing, slightly rowdy football fan sitting in a 55-year-old stadium with a grass field, barking like a maniac, caught on across the nation. Fans who had never been within an all-day drive of Cleveland suddenly found a team with which

FOUNDER & POUNDERS: *When Hanford Dixon (left) and Frank Minnifield began barking at Browns linemen to inspire a pass rush "like a pack of dogs chasing a cat," a tradition was born for the team and the fans. By the mid '80s (above), the Dawg Pound had a permanent home in Cleveland Stadium.*

they could identify. The emotional outlet of the Dawg phenomenon was unprecedented.

The Oakland Raiders had cultivated an image for themselves in the 1970s. They were the nasty boys of pro football who looked like Paul Brown's worst nightmare — unshaven, unshorn and dressed like motorcycle gang members. Characters like Ken Stabler, Jack "Assassin" Tatum, John Matuszak, Ted Hendricks, Otis Sistrunk and George Atkinson glamorized the "silver and black" for people who followed the NFL on television.

Their opposite number was the Dallas Cowboys, who were clean-cut and businesslike and never approached games as if they were street rumbles. While Oakland was coached by super-animated John Madden, Dallas had taciturn Tom Landry and quarterback Roger Staubach, an Annapolis graduate who made the Cowboys "America's Team."

The Chicago Bears became an image team about the same time the Browns were beginning the Dawg shtick. Chicago had recogniz-

able figures such as the tough-guy coach (Mike Ditka), the iconoclastic quarterback (Jim McMahon) and the endomorphic rookie (defensive tackle William "The Refrigerator" Perry).

But in all those cases it was the players who upheld the image. With the Browns, their fans were the show, and the media were quick to play it up. John Thompson, alias "Big Dawg," had as familiar a face to football fans nationwide as Art Modell, even if it was hidden by a bloodhound mask. Standing in the front row of the bleachers, the Big Dawg's exhorting the team to victory was constantly being captured by the TV cameras and shown on highlight films on Sunday nights.

It was harmless, for the most part. But the Browns occasionally had to curb their Dawgs. The throwing of real marrow bones on the field was halted for the safety of the players, and the team attempted to better police the Pound after reports of unruliness increased. Oddly enough, however, Dixon and Minnifield weren't the best

MARTY'S MAGIC: *After replacing Sam Rutigliano in 1984, Marty Schottenheimer guided the Browns to their best run of success since the '60s. From 1985-88, the Browns won three Central Division titles, appeared in the AFC title game twice and in 1986 enjoyed their highest regular-season win total (12) since the 14-0 undefeated AAFC season of 1948.*

known, or even the best loved, of the Browns in the late 1980s. That honor went to quarterback Bernie Kosar, the Northeast Ohio native who led the Miami Hurricanes to an NCAA title in 1983, then said in 1985 that he would skip his last two years of college eligibility if he could fulfill his lifelong dream of playing for Cleveland.

The Browns were happy to oblige. Brian Sipe had jumped to the USFL after the 1983 season. His replacement, Paul McDonald, had a dismal year in 1984 despite having four seasons as Sipe's backup. McDonald threw 23 interceptions to just 14 touchdown passes.

He wasn't helped by Mike Pruitt's knee problems, which sidelined the All-Pro rusher for four games after undergoing arthroscopic

surgery. Pruitt had his worst season with 506 yards and a 3.1 per-carry rate, and was released before the start of the 1985 campaign.

Age and injury caught up to the offensive line. Doug Dieken played in his 14th (and final) season in 1984. Right tackle Cody Risien missed all of the regular season after suffering a preseason knee injury. Joe DeLamielleure was released after 12 seasons in the league.

Head Coach Sam Rutigliano was fired eight games into the season, as the Browns were 1-7. It was the first time that Art Modell had ever replaced a head coach in mid season. Defensive coordinator Marty Schottenheimer took over. The team won four more games to finish 5-11.

The club spared no expense to get Kosar. They gave the Buffalo Bills their first draft choices in 1985 and '86, a third choice in '85 and a sixth pick in '86 for the Bills' first choice in the supplemental draft of 1985. The Browns picked up another quarterback in 1985, Gary Danielson of the Detroit Lions, for a third-round draft pick in 1986. Danielson had been in professional football since 1974, first with the World Football League and two years later with the Lions.

Danielson started the first five games of '85 before injuring his right shoulder. Kosar got the nod and led the Browns to an 8-8 record and the first of three consecutive AFC Central championships. Kosar completed half of his passes (124 of 248) with eight touchdowns to seven interceptions.

While the quarterbacking was in transition, the Browns were mainly a running team. Fullback Kevin Mack gained 1,104 yards and Earnest Byner added 1,002. Mack and Byner became the third pair of running backs on the same team to each gain 1,000 yards in the same season (Miami's Larry Csonka and Eugene "Mercury" Morris in '72, and Franco Harris and Rocky Bleier of Pittsburgh in '76). Their combined yardage was second in team history to Jim Brown and Ernie Green in 1963.

Byner had a great game in the 1985 divisional playoff game versus Miami: 161 yards to break the club's record for yards rushing (114

BORN TO BE A BROWN: *Bernie Kosar was a lifelong Browns fan from Boardman, Ohio, who gave up his last two years of college eligibility to be selected by Cleveland in the 1985 supplemental draft. By 1989 (above), he was leading the team to its fifth straight trip to the playoffs and third AFC title game.*

IMMEDIATE IMPACT: *With rookie Bernie Kosar taking control, the Browns returned to the playoffs in 1985. In Game 13 (above), Kosar and the Browns beat the Giants, 35-33, on their way to an 8-8 record and the AFC Central Division title.*

by Jim Brown in 1964) in a playoff game. His 66-yard run was also a Browns playoff record for longest gain rushing. But Cleveland lost, 24-21, after leading 21-3 at one time. After the game Kosar criticized the coaching staff for using an offensive plan he considered too conservative, and said something had to be done.

What was done was the hiring of Lindy Infante as offensive coordinator. Infante most recently had been head coach of the Jacksonville Bulls in the USFL and was considered one of the greatest offensive minds in football. He was better known to Browns fans as designer of the 1981 Super Bowl-bound Cincinnati Bengals' offense, led by the passing of Ken Anderson to receivers Cris Collinsworth, Isaac Curtis and Dan Ross.

Infante installed an offense that would highlight Kosar's assets (reading defenses, accuracy) and disguise his weaknesses (a basic lack of mobility, average offensive line).

The Browns also set about to find a wide receiver, though they didn't have a first-round draft choice. Paul Warfield was assigned to scout the nation to find one with speed and good hands the Browns could draft in Round 2. Warfield recommended San Diego State's Webster Slaughter.

The team obviously did something right. The Browns compiled a 12-4 record in 1986, best in the AFC, and improved their scoring by 104 points over 1985. After an opening-day loss to the defending Super Bowl champion Chicago Bears, and a Week 3 pounding by the Bengals, the Browns started soaring. They won their last five games, eight of their final nine and 11 of the last 13.

Kosar had career highs in pass attempts (531), completions (310) and yards (3,854). Suddenly there was a new contingent of quality receivers. Third-year veteran Brian Brennan led the club with 55 catches and six touchdowns. Slaughter had a great rookie year with 40 catches and four TDs. Tight end Ozzie Newsome and second-year man Reggie Langhorne had 39 receptions each.

The running backs got into the act, too. Herman Fontenot grabbed 47 passes, Earnest

HIGH FIVE: *Under defensive specialist Marty Schottenheimer's direction, this was a common scene of celebration in the mid '80s. In 1985 (above), starters included defensive end Reggie Camp (96), linebackers Eddie Johnson (51) and Tom Cousineau (50), and defensive backs Frank Minnifield (31) and Don Rogers (20).*

Byner had 37 catches and fullback Kevin Mack had 28 receptions.

After Mack and Byner both broke 1,000 yards rushing in 1985, the running game took a back seat in '86 to Infante's pass offense. Mack led the team in rushing with 665 yards.

The offensive line provided good protection for Kosar and quality blocking for Mack and Byner. Starters were Rickey Bolden or Paul Farren at left tackle, Farren or Larry Williams at left guard, Mike Baab at center, Dan Fike at right guard and Cody Risien at right tackle.

The Dawg Defense, meanwhile, solidified around four Pro Bowlers: nose tackle Bob Golic, outside linebacker Chip Banks and cornerbacks Dixon and Minnifield. Outside linebacker Clay Matthews was reaching his prime, while defensive ends Reggie Camp and Carl Hairston provided solid play along with inside linebackers Anthony Griggs and Eddie Johnson, and safeties Ray Ellis and Chris Rockins.

The 1986 season was the Kardiac Kids all over again. Brownsmania was everywhere. The record, coupled with the Dawg persona, had the area delirious with Super Bowl dreaming. Songs by professional and amateur recording artists started popping up on radio stations with ever greater regularity. Nowhere could a Northeast Ohio resident get away from the Browns in the last months of 1986.

But, as with every other year, the Super Bowl would have to wait for the Browns. The

REVAMPED RECEIVING: *Three new wide receivers joined tight end Ozzie Newsome as Bernie Kosar's targets in the '80s. Brian Brennan (above), Reggie Langhorne (left) and Webster Slaughter (top) became Browns in 1984, '85 and '86, respectively.*

BACKFIELD BRILLIANCE: *Kevin Mack (left) and Earnest Byner (right) provided a power rushing attack not seen since the '60s. In 1985, the pair each gained more than 1,000 yards as the Browns' offense featured a new emphasis on the running game.*

road almost took a detour in the divisional playoffs, as the Browns had to rally from 10 points behind late in the fourth quarter to pull out a 23-20 double-overtime victory over the Jets in one of the most dramatic games in the history of the NFL.

But if the Browns had won one they should have lost that week, they lost one they should have won the following week in the AFC championship contest in Cleveland Stadium. The Denver Broncos came to town fresh off a divisional playoff victory over the defending AFC champion Patriots. The Broncos were led by quarterback John Elway, one of the best all-around athletes in the National Football League, and a stubborn defense led by Pro Bowlers Rulon Jones, Karl Mecklenburg and Dennis Smith.

A field goal by the Browns' Mark Moseley with 20 seconds left in the first half tied the game at 10-10. It was 13-13 with 5:43 remaining in the fourth quarter when Kosar found Brian Brennan behind the Denver defense and threw a 48-yard touchdown pass to him to put the Browns ahead, 20-13. Celebrating was prema-

ROLLING OUT: *Bernie Kosar avoids pursuit in the 1986 AFC title game against Denver in Cleveland Stadium. Kosar directed the Browns to a fourth-quarter 20-13 lead, only to be tied on "The Drive" and beaten in overtime on a Rich Karlis field goal.*

ture. Marty Schottenheimer's prevent defense couldn't prevent Elway and the Broncos from embarking on a 98-yard, 15-play drive that managed the clock to perfection. "The Drive," ended on a five-yard pass to Mark Jackson with 37 seconds remaining to tie the score and force the Browns into overtime for the second playoff game in a row.

Cleveland won the coin toss to begin the overtime and elected to receive. The Denver defense stopped them and Jeff Gossett punted to the 24-yard line. The Broncos then marched 60 yards to set up Rich Karlis' 33-yard game-winning field goal with 5:48 to go. The final: 23-20 Denver, the same score by which the Browns beat the Jets a week earlier.

In 1987, the Browns won the AFC Central again despite a strike by the players' union that cancelled one game and had the teams using replacement players for three others. The regular Browns had an 8-4 record and the replacements won two of three games. Kosar enjoyed another banner year, leading the league in completion rate (62 percent) and topping the AFC in quarterback rating (95.4).

The Browns and the Broncos met for the AFC championship again in 1987, but this time it was in Denver. The Broncos jumped to a 21-3 halftime lead and were up 28-10 at one point in the third period. But two touchdowns by Earnest Byner, one on a pass and the other via rushing, cut the margin to 28-24. Rich Karlis nailed a 38-yard field goal with 10 seconds left in the third quarter to make it 31-24.

Cleveland tied it with 4:12 gone in the final period on a four-yard pass from Kosar to Webster Slaughter. Denver untied it with 4:01 left on a 20-yarder from Elway to Sammy Winder.

The Browns were driving for another tying score when disaster hit. They were at the Broncos' eight-yard line when Kosar handed to

Byner, who pushed ahead to the three, but was stripped of the ball by Jeremiah Castille, who recovered with 1:12 to play. A safety when Broncos punter Mike Horan ran out of the back of the end zone was meaningless.

The Broncos had won again, 38-33. "The Drive" of the '86 season had been followed by "The Fumble" of '87. Added to "Red Right 88" of the 1980 season and the Browns' most painful playoff memories of the 1980s forever had memorable monikers.

The '88 season might be forever remembered by Browns fans as the Year of the Injured Quarterback. Bernie Kosar was hit on the elbow of his throwing arm in a 6-3 victory over the Chiefs in Game 1. The next week Gary Danielson was lost when he broke his left ankle in a 23-3 loss to the Jets. Mike Pagel went down in the sixth game, a 16-10 loss to Seattle.

Thirty-eight-year-old Don Strock, who was brought out of retirement and signed after Danielson's injury, became the quarterback. He responded by leading the Browns to an upset of Philadelphia in Week 7 and by playing an outstanding second half as the Browns defeated the Oilers 28-23 in Week 16.

The latter contest got the Browns a wild-card playoff berth. They had been trailing the entire game and were behind 23-7 when Houston's Warren Moon fired a seven-yard TD pass to Haywood Jeffires at the six-minute mark of the third quarter.

But Strock led the Browns back. A two-yard touchdown pass to Earnest Byner at 6:06 left in the third period was followed by two-yard TD run by Byner two minutes into the fourth stanza. The game-winner was a 22-yard pass from Strock to Slaughter at the 8:37 mark. The drive featured three catches by Reggie Langhorne for 47 yards. The final second-half figures for Strock showed 16-for-23 passing for 215 yards, two touchdowns and no interceptions.

There was no such miracle rally the following week when the two teams met again in Cleveland Stadium for their wild-card playoff game. Strock suffered a hand injury trying to recover his own fumble in the first quarter and

THE FUMBLE: *Denver's Jeremiah Castille prepares to strip Earnest Byner of the ball on the Broncos' three-yard line in the fourth quarter of the 1987 AFC title game in Mile High Stadium. The Browns were driving for a tying touchdown, but instead were again denied a trip to the Super Bowl.*

Mike Pagel, just activated off the injured reserve list (shoulder separation) was called to duty. Pagel did well, completing 17 of 25 passes for 179 yards and two touchdowns, but the Oilers went home after two straight weekends in Cleveland with a 24-23 victory.

Pagel's 14-yard TD pass to Webster Slaughter in the third frame put the Browns ahead 16-14, but Houston came back on a touchdown run by Lorenzo White and a 49-yard field goal by Tony Zendejas with 1:54 remaining to take a 24-16 edge.

Slaughter caught another touchdown pass from Pagel with 31 seconds remaining, but the Browns' onside kick was recovered by the Oilers as time expired.

The game would be the last one Marty Schottenheimer would coach with the Browns. A growing philosophical gap between Schottenheimer and owner Art Modell led to an agreement that the head coach would step down. Schottenheimer was soon after hired to coach the Kansas City Chiefs. In his place came Bud Carson, a longtime defensive coach who was being given his first shot at a head coaching position at the age of 58.

Carson was the architect of the Pittsburgh Steelers' "Steel Curtain" defense of the 1970s, which helped them win Super Bowl titles in 1974 and '75. He was defensive coordinator for

> *But Strock led the Browns back. A two-yard TD pass to Earnest Byner at 6:06 left in the third period was followed by a two-yard touchdown run by Byner two minutes into the fourth stanza.*

WRIST TAKER: *Don Strock (12) became the Browns' fourth starting quarterback in 1988 following injuries to Bernie Kosar, Gary Danielson and Mike Pagel. Strock took plays into the huddle strapped to his wrist, then took the Browns to the playoffs.*

the Rams in 1978-79 and helped them to an NFC championship. Along the way, Carson's Rams defense held the Seattle Seahawks to minus-seven yards in a game, an all-time low in NFL history. He also was defensive coordinator of the Jets in 1985-88, where he improved that club's defense from No. 23 overall in 1984 to eighth the following season.

Carson's first season as coach in 1989 was an odd one. In the regular-season opener versus the Steelers, the Browns set club records for the most lopsided shutout score and the fewest yards of total offense allowed (53) in a 51-0 rout. The Browns forced eight turnovers and had seven sacks.

The Browns were 7-3 at one point. They had beaten their archrivals, the Broncos, but lost an overtime battle to Miami and dropped their rematch with the Steelers. Things started to look really bleak when they could only reach a 10-10 tie in a home game against the Chiefs and former coach Marty Schottenheimer, who was rebuilding the fortunes of Kansas City. That was followed by three consecutive losses and the Browns were 7-6-1.

But the Browns next beat the Minnesota Vikings in overtime with a bit of trickery. Matt

BIG DADDY & FAMILY: *Browns defenders demonstrate the intensity typical of the Browns-Bengals battles of the late '80s. End Carl "Big Daddy" Hairston (left) wraps up quarterback Boomer Esiason. Nose tackle Bob Golic (below) does likewise. Above, linebackers Clay Matthews (57) and Mike Johnson (59), and safety Felix Wright (22) tackle running back Ickey Woods.*

Bahr set up for what looked to be a 31-yard field goal try in overtime, but holder Mike Pagel took the ball, stood up and hit linebacker Van Waiters with a 23-yard pass in the end zone to win a game by that means for the first time in 12 years.

Bahr had sent the game into overtime with a 32-yard field goal with 24 seconds to play. The triumph set up a showdown for the divisional title with the Oilers in Houston.

The Browns built a 17-3 advantage by halftime, but Warren Moon and the Oilers dominated the second half. A field goal by Tony Zendejas was sandwiched by touchdown passes to Drew Hill to give the Oilers a 20-17 lead. The second TD pass to Hill happened one play after one of the most bizarre events in Browns history. Moon, operating from a shotgun formation, had the snap go over his head. Clay Matthews recovered, but tried to lateral to a teammate. The ball was loose and recovered by Hill at the Browns' 27-yard line.

Kevin Mack finally gave the Browns the victory on a four-yard run with 39 seconds to go.

TOP DAWG'S EXIT: *Hanford Dixon's nine-year career ended after the 1989 season. He retired as a three-time leader in Browns interceptions, a three-time Pro Bowl selection and the one-time creator of the famed symbol of "rabid" Browns fans: the Dawg.*

Mack, who played only four games in 1989, did the bulk of the running on the winning drive and finished with 62 yards on 12 carries.

The divisional playoff game was another wild affair as the Buffalo Bills visited Cleveland. The Browns led for good when Bernie Kosar tossed a three-yard touchdown pass to Ron Middleton with 1:06 to go in the first half to make the score 17-14. The Browns were ahead 34-24 when Thurman Thomas grabbed a

TD pass from Jim Kelly with four minutes to play. The extra-point try was no good, which forced the Bills to have to go for a touchdown if they were in the position to win. They got in the position, but couldn't convert.

Ronnie Harmon dropped Kelly's 14-yard pass in the end zone and Clay Matthews intercepted a Kelly pass on the one-yard line with nine seconds left. Matthews didn't attempt a lateral that time and the Browns survived with a 34-30 victory.

Survived is the word. The defense allowed Kelly 405 yards passing, a Cleveland playoff record. The 656 yards passing by both clubs was also a record for a regulation-length playoff game, as were the seven TD passes the two teams threw.

But for the third time in four seasons the Browns were defeated by the Broncos in the AFC title game. This time it wasn't close. Denver outscored Cleveland 13-0 in the fourth quarter to register a 37-21 conquest. John Elway threw four touchdown passes, including a 70-yarder to Mike Young and two to running back Sammy Winder. Brian Brennan had two touchdown catches for the Browns as Cleveland scored all its points in the third period.

The loss made the Browns 0-5 in games that could have sent them to the Super Bowl: NFL championship games in 1968 and '69, and AFC title games in 1986, '87 and '89.

It would be another five years before the team reached a playoff game. They would do it without Bernie Kosar. The young man who wanted to lead his boyhood favorite team to Super Bowl glory was released in 1993. The loyalty and devotion Browns fans had for Kosar made the end of the line much more difficult to face.

Hanford Dixon retired after the 1989 season, but the Dawgs did not retire with him. The image he and fellow cornerback Frank Minnifield created for the club is around today, although not as feverish as was when the "Corner Brothers," as Minnifield and Dixon called themselves, were patrolling the secondary.

The Browns have never had a helmet logo. The only mascot the franchise had known prior

DEFENSIVE DIRECTION: *Head Coach Bud Carson guided the Browns to a 9-6-1 mark in 1989 and a playoff win over Buffalo before losing to Denver in the AFC title game. The architect of Pittsburgh's Steel Curtain defense of the '70s, Carson watched his Browns defense shut out the Steelers in the '89 opener, 51-0.*

to the mid-'80s was the frowning elf, or "Brownie," with the football tucked under his arm, a symbol that was more or less retired when the NFL and AFL merged in 1970.

Since then, the Browns have officially adopted a dog as the club's mascot. Fans can now see a human wearing a bulldog suit walking the sidelines at Cleveland Stadium. His name? Rover Cleveland.

Rebuilding in the New NFL

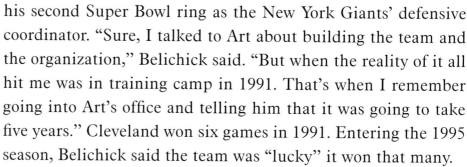

Bill Belichick knew the Cleveland Browns were a team in trouble long before he was named their head coach on Feb. 5, 1991. He figured as much based on conversations with Browns front office personnel such as Ozzie Newsome, Mike Lombardi, Ernie Accorsi, Jim Shofner and team owner Art Modell. But seeing it on the field was a whole different experience for the 38-year-old who 10 days earlier had won his second Super Bowl ring as the New York Giants' defensive coordinator. "Sure, I talked to Art about building the team and the organization," Belichick said. "But when the reality of it all hit me was in training camp in 1991. That's when I remember going into Art's office and telling him that it was going to take five years." Cleveland won six games in 1991. Entering the 1995 season, Belichick said the team was "lucky" it won that many.

Vinny Testaverde

By Mark Craig

Of the 3-13 team from 1990 that Belichick inherited, he said: "It was just a mess. Just look at the players who were here at the time." Belichick got up, walked around his desk and picked up a board with the names of every player the Browns have had on their roster since 1991.

"Paul Farren, Mike Baab, Ralph Tamm, Ben Jefferson," Belichick said, tapping his desk with each player's name. "Tim Manoa, Bob Buczkowski, who we traded, John Talley, Ken Reeves, Van Waiters."

Belichick pointed out that few players from that 1991 Browns team were still active in the league as early as three years later. Even Bernie Kosar, the popular quarterback who was released in Belichick's most highly controversial decision on Nov. 8, 1993, had become no more than a backup in Dallas and Miami.

"Of the ones who were still in football in 1994, very few were still playing," Belichick said. "Kosar, Scott Galbraith, Ralph Tamm, guys like that are still hanging on in the league. Now a guy like Webster Slaughter, that's different. It's unfortunate that we lost him, but he just got turned loose (as a free agent) by the courts in 1992. We didn't really have a chance to keep him."

When the Browns were preparing for the 1995 season, only four players were left from when Belichick took control of the team: running back Leroy Hoard, left tackle Tony Jones and defensive ends Anthony Pleasant and Rob Burnett.

"When you're as bad as we were in 1991, it's going to take more than one or two moves to make it happen," Belichick said. "It's going to take some time. Unfortunately, I don't know how you can speed up the process."

Modell accepted Belichick's reasoning. He gave Belichick a five-year contract in 1991 and extended it by two years in 1993. "We were in a tailspin before Bill Belichick arrived," Modell said. "We were going nowhere very, very fast. We had to change our whole approach."

When Belichick started, he had four basic methods to acquire players: the draft, trades, the waiver wire and Plan B free agency, which was the earliest form of free agency that made every team's fringe players free to switch teams. Two years later, the league's new seven-year collective bargaining agreement drastically changed the rules of the National Football League.

"In the old days, you drafted a guy and he played for you for 12 years," Belichick said. "As long as he was good enough to make the team, you kept paying him and he kept playing."

Unrestricted free agency for players after their fourth season and an unyielding salary cap that kicked in for the 1994 season ended that sort of stability. "The way the game is in this era, you have to be flexible," Belichick explained. "It's a little bit like being a college coach because you know no matter what you do, you just can't keep a team together."

The new system was far from perfect when it went into effect, but Belichick said at least everybody began playing by the same rules. "The playing field is level now," Belichick said.

MEETING THE CHALLENGE: *Bill Belichick accepted a major rebuilding task when he became the Browns' head coach in 1991. In 1994, the team finished at 11-5, its best record since 1986, and made the AFC playoffs for the first time in five years.*

"Whoever is the best is a reflection of the best organization, from management to ownership to coaching to scouting.

"If you compare that to the 1993 season, you'll see what I mean. That was the year before the salary cap, but the year everyone was keeping cap figures. You had teams like Miami and New Orleans with $50 million payrolls,

PLAN B PICKUP: *Ex-Giant Matt Stover signed as a Plan B free agent in 1991. In 1994, he became the most accurate field goal kicker in Browns history, closing out the season with a team-record 20 straight.*

and ours was at $32 million. That's a big difference."

In 1994, the year the cap and free agency came together, the Browns reached the playoffs for the first time since 1989. Their 11-5 record was the best since 1988, good for second in the AFC Central Division. The Browns then beat New England in the opening round of the playoffs before losing to Pittsburgh in the second round.

In the new era of pro football, the Browns, like all teams, had to make tough decisions. Long gone were the days when talent was the only thing a coach looked for. "A player's worth is just as important as whether he can make your team or not," Belichick said. "It's like you have to appraise real estate. If you appraise it wrong, then that's going to hurt your football team competitively."

Modell believes the collective bargaining agreement signed in 1993 raised the NFL to a level of competition unmatched to that point.

And with players moving around, a salary cap to deal with and off-season activity being scrutinized as closely as the regular-season games, Modell also said the pressure to win became higher than ever before.

"It's more demanding now in the Belichick era than it was in the Paul Brown era," Modell explained. "The pressure is public pressure, peer pressure, self-imposed pressure and, most importantly, media pressure. This was not the case when I first bought the team in 1961. It's overwhelming."

Modell was happy with the way Belichick stood up to the pressure of finding players in the most difficult era of player acquisition.

"Belichick's greatest strength is his ability to judge talent," Modell said. "Say what you want about his X's and O's, and his motivational abilities and player relations. Putting all that aside, I haven't had anybody in a long, long time who has the ability to judge talent as he has.

"Look at his No. 1 draft picks from 1991-95. The proof is in the pudding. There it is. History has shown the job he's done."

Heading into 1995, Belichick said he was most proud of his first-round draft picks. He picked Eric Turner second overall in 1991, Tommy Vardell ninth in 1992, Steve Everitt 14th in 1993, Antonio Langham and Derrick Alexander ninth and 29th, respectively, in 1994, and Craig Powell 30th in 1995.

"Nobody really had us taking Turner as the second player in 1991," Belichick said. "We took some criticism for taking him, but I never had any doubts he would be an outstanding player in this league, and I think he became clearly one of the top defensive players in the league.

"It may have seemed easy, what with him being the second pick. But there were a lot of misses in that draft. Pittsburgh took Huey Richardson [15th], Tampa Bay got Charles McRae [seventh], and Atlanta used the third pick on Bruce Pickens. Meanwhile, I think we

FINAL HOLDOVERS: *After four years of rebuilding the Browns' roster, only four players remained in 1995 from Bill Belichick's first season in 1991: defensive ends Rob Burnett (90) and Anthony Pleasant (98), running back Leroy Hoard (33) and offensive tackle Tony Jones (66).*

BUILDING BLOCKS: *Entering the 1995 season, first-round draft choices were the pride of Bill Belichick. Safety Eric Turner (opposite page) was the top pick in 1991 followed by running back Tommy Vardell (above) in '92, center Steve Everitt (above right) in '93, cornerback Antonio Langham (right) and receiver Derrick Alexander in '94, and linebacker Craig Powell in '95.*

got a good player in that draft out of a guy people thought was a reach, a guy that a number of people wouldn't have taken in the spot we were sitting."

Turner tied for the league lead in interceptions with nine in 1994. He had 17 in his first four seasons.

The draft wasn't the only tool the Browns used to improve themselves in the 1990s. Plan B free agents, unrestricted free agents, waiver wire castoffs and players picked up through trades all have contributed to the Browns' overall turnaround in the mid-'90s.

The Browns took care of their place-kicking needs when they signed Matt Stover as a Plan B free agent from the New York Giants in 1991. Stover had not kicked in a regular-season game, but by 1994 he had moved ahead of Matt Bahr as the most accurate field goal kicker in

Browns history, including a team-record 20 straight to close out the season.

In 1992, safety Stevon Moore was signed as a Plan B free agent. Basically thrown away by Don Shula's Miami Dolphins, Moore joined Turner and gave the Browns one of the strongest safety tandems in the league in 1994.

When the unrestricted free agent market opened in 1993, the Browns signed, among oth-

UNWAIVERING CONSISTENCY: *Guard Bob Dahl squares off against Cincinnati's Tim Krumrie. Dahl was waived by both the Bengals and Steelers before the Browns signed him in 1992. Entering 1995, he had started 41 straight games for the Browns.*

ers, receiver Mark Carrier and quarterback Vinny Testaverde in 1993, linebacker Carl Banks and cornerback Don Griffin in 1994, and receiver Andre Rison and running back Lorenzo White in 1995.

Belichick also plucked running back Randy Baldwin from Minnesota's practice squad in 1991, and by 1993, he was one of the league's most dangerous kick returners, not to mention one of the best downfield tacklers on the Browns' special teams.

In 1992, the Browns found offensive lineman Bob Dahl on the waiver wire after both Cincinnati and Pittsburgh had given up on him. Dahl, a defensive lineman at the University of Notre Dame, was drafted in the third round of the 1991 draft by Cincinnati. He landed on the Bengals' practice squad and was released that season. The Steelers picked him up and put him on their practice squad as they tried to convert him to offense. They gave up too early and released Dahl.

The Browns then picked him up before the 1992 season and put him on their practice squad until activating him on Halloween that year. Ironically, he made his first start the following week against Cincinnati. Heading into the 1995 season, Dahl had started 41 straight games for the Browns.

Belichick also agreed to take in linebacker Pepper Johnson when the Giants were rebuilding their linebacking corps in 1993. A year later, Johnson moved into the starting middle linebacker position in Cleveland. He registered more than 200 tackles and was a team leader.

The Browns also found a mammoth offensive tackle that everyone overlooked in the 1993 draft. Orlando Brown, a 6-foot-7, 325-pounder from South Carolina State, was signed as a free agent in 1993. By mid-season a year later, he had developed into a solid player at right tackle.

In the way of trades, the Browns picked up a couple starters for mid-to-low draft picks in 1992 and 1993. In '92, they gave the Rams an eighth-round pick for linebacker Frank Stams. In 1993, they acquired Miami offensive lineman Gene Williams for a fourth-round pick.

Not all of the Browns' moves of the 1990s have worked. Belichick admits that. "There are a lot of things you'd like to do over again," Belichick said. "Obviously, the Jerry Ball trade in 1993 didn't go particularly well for us. I'd say that's the biggest mistake, only because we gave up something for him. We gave up a third-round pick."

GIANT ACQUISITIONS: *Bill Belichick's rebuilding efforts included former New York Giants familiar to him when he was defensive coordinator for the Giants' Super Bowl champs of the 1986 and '90 seasons. Linebackers Carl Banks (left) and Pepper Johnson (right) joined the Browns in 1994 and '93, respectively.*

Other personnel decisions haven't worked out, but Belichick isn't as upset about them because the price the team paid was low.

"A guy like [offensive tackle] Freddie Childress obviously didn't work out, but all we gave up for Childress was an eighth-round pick. So what," Belichick said. "Those are the kinds of moves you've got to make when you're not very good. Freddie Childress didn't work out, but Randy Baldwin did, Frank Stams did, Matt Stover did, and so did a lot of others."

Player development in the 1990s was another key to the Browns' success in 1994. For example, defensive ends Rob Burnett and Anthony Pleasant went from not being very

MOVING ON: *Eric Metcalf provided spectacular thrills as a Browns kick returner and running back from 1989-94. But as part of what would become a trend in the mid '90s, he was traded to Atlanta in '95 as the Browns cleared room under the salary cap to sign perennial All-Pro receiver Andre Rison.*

good as rookies in 1990 to being solid starters in 1994.

Punter Tom Tupa is another classic case. He came to the Browns as an NFL quarterback who also was Ohio State's all-time leading punter. He lasted five seasons (1988-92) with the Phoenix Cardinals and Indianapolis Colts, playing in 45 games with 13 starts at quarterback. He punted the ball only six times, averaging 46.7 yards.

Tupa signed with the Browns for two games in 1993, but didn't see any action and was released. They brought him back in the spring of '94, made him their full-time punter and were not disappointed in the fall.

"To win in the NFL, you have to find good players," Belichick said. "You can't think you're going to out-trick or out-coach everybody at this level. It doesn't work."

Belichick said it's getting harder to find players as the NFL unfolds into the 21st century. "You have the new rules, and you have eight rounds in the draft as compared to 12," Belichick said. "There are fewer four-year college players and a lot more junior college guys. You have more ground to cover, but it's just something you work your way through."

The Browns, he added, have been much more thorough in that department since player personnel director Mike Lombardi took over the department in 1992. "The 1991 and 1992 drafts weren't very good drafts for us," Belichick said. "I think we did OK early in the draft when we really knew what we were doing, but we blew some picks in the later rounds."

In 1992, the Browns drafted a man by the name of Marcus Lowe, a defensive tackle from Baylor, in the 10th round. Guys like Lowe are long shots to begin with, but Lowe was a man who spent only one day in Cleveland.

He rode the stationary bike for a day and was told to go home and come back when he wasn't the size of the Goodyear blimp. Marcus never returned, and was cut because he was simply too large.

A guy like Lowe taught Belichick a lesson he will never forget. "There were a couple cases in the later rounds in 1991 and 1992 where I didn't have a chance to see the guy we took," Belichick said. "I found out then that if I see a player and we miss on him, I won't be nearly as ticked off as if I don't see the guy, we take him and he doesn't make it."

By the 1993 draft, Belichick said the organization had been pretty well-schooled in what he wanted in a football player. "We're definitely going in the same direction," Belichick said. "The information from the scouting department is a lot better. The quality of the scouts is a lot better. The scouts adhering to the philoso-

"In four years, we took a team that was second-worst in the league to the fourth-best record in the league. It was slow and it was steady, and maybe it wasn't spectacular. But we built a team."

phy of the football team is a lot better. And the players are a lot better."

Of course, all this work has left Belichick and his staff with basically two weeks off a year. They take a two-week vacation before the start of training camp. But Belichick believes it has been worth the effort.

"I think we basically rebuilt the whole team," Belichick said. "Four years later, in 1995, I don't look at any area and think we're deficient. Obviously, we could always be better. But provided we can stay healthy, and the younger players can continue to improve as the ones who have been here before have, I think we're going to have a good football team for quite a few years."

Belichick looked back on his training-camp meeting with Modell in 1991 and shook his

SUCCESSFUL SIGNINGS: *The Browns used free agency to best advantage in rebuilding all aspects of the roster. Ex-Colt and Cardinal Tom Tupa (left) became the Browns' punter, kick holder and backup quarterback in 1994. Ex-Buccaneer Vinny Testaverde (right) succeeded Bernie Kosar as the starting quarterback in '93.*

head. "The biggest thing this organization has to be proud of is coming off a 3-13 season, going 6-10 when we probably were lucky to be 6-10 and ending up 12-6, including the play-offs, in 1994," Belichick said.

"In four years, we took a team that was second-worst in the league to the fourth-best record in the league. It was slow and it was steady, and maybe it wasn't spectacular. But we built a team. And it's a team that I think will last. I don't think it's going to be a team that goes 11-5 one year and 4-12 the next."

The Greatest Victories

For the Cleveland Browns, a 50-year winning tradition not only translates into great historic eras, but it also means important victories that symbolize and define those eras.

It all began in the AAFC when the powerful Browns won four straight titles, highlighted by a 29-game unbeaten streak that included three victories in eight days during the 1948 season.

Then there was the first game in the NFL in 1950 against the champion and heavily-favored Eagles. Next there were the great championship wins during the dynasty years of the 1950s when the Browns gave pro football new credibility and respectability in the eyes of the American sporting public.

In 1964 came the most memorable and most recent title, 27-0 over Unitas and the Colts. When the Browns moved to the AFC in 1970, the Browns faced Paul Brown as an opponent for the first time and a rivalry with his Bengals was born. Ten years later, it was the Bengals again as the Kardiac Kids palpitated the hearts of fans one more time by beating Cincinnati to make the playoffs.

In 1987, the Browns took two overtimes to beat the Jets en route to the AFC title game. Then in 1994, the improving Browns showed their playoff-bound spirit by beating the champion Cowboys.

The 1948 Browns were the first major professional football team to go through a season undefeated. The 1972 Miami Dolphins have been the only one since. The Chicago Bears twice had been unbeaten in regular seasons, only to lose the NFL championship game each time.

Although the Dolphins are well remembered for their 17-0 mark in '72, they never had to face a schedule such as the Browns saw in late November of 1948. Their last four games were on the road, and three of them were played over an eight-day stretch.

Cleveland beat the New York Yankees, 34-21, on a Sunday, then flew to Los Angeles for a Thanksgiving Day game. They whipped the Dons, 31-14, but Otto Graham injured a knee and was considered doubtful for the Browns' next game, which was only three days away in San Francisco.

The Browns were in trouble. Not only were they carrying a 12-0 record that season, but had a 21-game unbeaten streak put in jeopardy by Graham's injured knee, which stiffened in the days following the Dons game. And the 49ers were 11-1 themselves, as only a 14-7 loss to the Browns on Nov. 14 had marred their season.

For the first time in their history, the Browns were underdogs. There was even talk that they wanted to finish tied for the division championship to force a playoff, and another big gate, in Cleveland.

With his knee heavily taped, Graham put on his uniform on Sunday, but told Coach Paul Brown he couldn't play. But when 49ers return man Forrest Hall fumbled the kickoff and the Browns recovered, Graham and his head coach both seemed to forget about what the quarterback had said. Graham went out with the offensive unit and, on the first play, threw a 28-yard touchdown pass to Dante Lavelli.

Although Graham played the whole game, his customary mobility was not there. After a field goal by Lou Groza gave the Browns a 10-0 lead, San Francisco answered with a TD run by Joe Perry and a scoring pass from Frankie Albert to Alyn Beals to give the 49ers a 14-10 halftime lead.

Graham attempted a quarterback sneak on fourth down in the third period, but with his knee immobilized it failed. The Niners tacked on another Albert-to-Beals touchdown and it was 21-10. Graham then led one of the finest comebacks in Browns history. He completed a 24-yard pass to Edgar "Special Delivery" Jones that set up a one-yard touchdown run by Marion Motley on the succeeding drive.

On the Browns' next possession, Graham threw a 20-yard touchdown pass to Dub Jones to put Cleveland in front, 24-21. San Francisco tried a halfback option pass on the next drive, but

Keeping the Streak Alive

Browns 31
49ers 28

Otto Graham plays with an injured knee, but the Browns are winners for the third time in eight days.

Game Stories by Steve Byrne

defensive back Tom Colella intercepted.

Graham then threw 33 yards to Edgar Jones for a TD that gave Cleveland a 10-point lead, 31-21. Perry scored again to decrease the Browns' advantage to three points with seven minutes to play. Cleveland proceeded to hold possession for the next six minutes.

The 49ers finally got the ball back at their own 12-yard line with a mere 50 seconds remaining. Albert was sacked by Tony Adamle and the Western Division title of the All-America Football Conference was Cleveland's for the third straight year. The Browns had won three games and scored 96 points in eight days. Their unbeaten streak was 22 games. They would keep it for seven more before finally experiencing defeat, a 56-28 loss to the 49ers on Oct. 9, 1949.

Considering the Browns' four-year run of success in the All-America Football Conference, it is difficult to believe that anyone could look at their first game in the National Football League objectively and predict a blowout in favor of their opponent: the Philadelphia Eagles.

Sure, but who would have thought the game would end the way it did, with the Browns routing the two-time defending NFL champions by a 35-10 score?

Probably no one, not even the Browns themselves, thought the latter would come true. But most fans, and almost everyone not connected to the old AAFC in some way, expected the former.

Philadelphia, the NFL champions of 1948 and '49, was installed as the seven-point favorite, but many believed that was much too conservative. Some were talking seriously of 50-0. This against a team that had not only made a mockery of its league, going unbeaten only two years before, but one that had strengthened itself considerably in the off-season through a separate transaction with a member of the defunct league and through a common draft of players from the former AAFC teams.

Halfback Rex Bumgardner, defensive tackle John Kissell and guard Abe Gibron came from Buffalo when Bills owner Jim Breuil became part owner of the Browns, then brought the trio with him as part of the

deal. The Browns added defensive end Len Ford (Los Angeles) and linebacker Hal Herring (Buffalo) through the draft.

After the game, Frank "Bucko" Kilroy, the Eagles' All-Pro tackle, called attention to Cleveland's revised roster. Noting the influx of new talent, Kilroy said the Browns had become a team of AAFC all-stars and that Philadelphia wasn't up to beating an all-star team.

But the Browns were up to beating the NFL champions, because Head Coach Paul Brown prepared for the game down to the last detail. When the Eagles played the Rams for the 1949 title, Browns assistant coaches Blanton Collier and Fritz Heisler were in the L.A. Coliseum stands. Their notes would provide the foundation of Paul Brown's pre-game preparation.

It was only natural the Browns' maiden flight in their new league should be against the other champion. It was like a Super Bowl, with nine months and a training camp in between.

That's where the Eagles might have lost it. Fullback Steve Van Buren, the leading rusher in the NFL four of the previous five seasons, injured a toe on his right foot in Philadelphia's 17-7 loss to the College All-Stars and missed all of the Eagles' other pre-season games.

All-Pro tackle Alvin Wistert suffered a knee injury and halfback Bosh Pritchard injured a shoulder. Still, there was no indication that Van Buren wouldn't play, and the sorry showing the Eagles made in the preseason didn't seem to give a hint of what was to come.

The Browns, meanwhile, had beaten four old-line NFL teams during their exhibition-game schedule. The victory over the Detroit Lions was most critical because it essentially served as a dress rehearsal for the game with the Eagles.

The Lions employed the famed "Eagle Defense," Neale's innovative formation designed to slow opposition passing attacks while still providing plenty of pressure on quarterbacks and the running game.

The Eagle Defense featured a five-man line, two linebackers to jam the receivers as

In a League of Their Own

Browns 35
Eagles 10

The Browns are already the class of the NFL, beating the confident champs in the season opener.

they started their routes, and four defensive backs to enable double coverage on the receivers. Against the Lions, Brown first experimented with a double-wing formation that sent halfback Bumgardner in motion on each play. The additional receiver forced single coverage by the Lions' secondary on Dub Jones.

Secondly, Brown took advantage of the lack of a middle linebacker in the Eagle Defense. By spreading the Cleveland tackles further apart on each play, the defensive tackles followed suit, thus isolating their middle guard and opening up the middle for the Browns' running game, particularly the trap plays to Marion Motley.

There were 71,237 spectators in Philadelphia's Municipal Stadium (site of the Army-Navy game) on Sept. 16, 1950, for the opening of the NFL season and what Commissioner Bert Bell said was "the most talked about game in the history of the NFL."

The Browns lost offensive left tackle Lou Groza, also pro football's best field goal kicker, when he hurt a shoulder on the first series. The Browns looked to be in trouble. Kicking was one area in which even the staunchest defenders of NFL superiority believed the Browns had an edge.

That edge was lost, and the Browns proved it on their second series. Eagles second-year punt returner Clyde "Smackover" Scott fumbled Horace Gillom's punt at the Philadelphia 39. Rookie Jim Martin recovered the ball for Cleveland and the Browns moved to the Eagles' 16-yard line. Stalled there, defensive tackle and backup kicker Chubby Grigg, who had not kicked a field goal since high school, was called to give the Browns the lead. His 25-yard attempt was tipped at the line of scrimmage.

The Eagles got to the Cleveland eight-yard line and made it 3-0 on Cliff Patton's field goal. Each team stopped the other on the next two series, but the brilliant but one-dimensional Eagles defense suffered a lapse. As Paul Brown had planned, Cleveland halfback Rex Bumgardner had been going in motion to draw linebacker Joe

Muha to the sidelines, thus forcing single coverage on Dub Jones.

Jones, who had been running sideline patterns all evening, caught defensive back Russ Craft cheating up on him. When Craft inched his way up, Jones suddenly turned and headed downfield. He was 10 yards in front when Craft realized his mistake, and Otto Graham got him the ball on the Eagles'

Linebacker Hal Herring (20), one of several ex-AAFC players to join the 1950 Browns, tackles the Eagles' Frank Ziegler.

25. Jones scored easily and the score was 7-3 in favor of the inferior league's champion with 1:37 remaining in the first quarter.

Things got worse for the Eagles. Scott suffered a broken shoulder as Philadelphia was driving on the Browns. That meant the three Eagles ball carriers were gone. Their running game, with which they thought

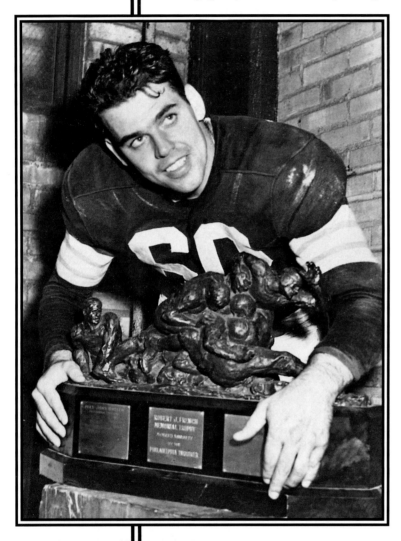

Otto Graham, who threw three touchdown passes and ran for another, displays the trophy he received as the game's best player.

they could dominate the Browns even without Van Buren and Pritchard, was finished. Four plays from the Cleveland 14-yard line netted only three yards.

Swift Browns right end Dante Lavelli was in a mismatch versus linebacker Alex Wojciechowicz, a 13-year veteran. On the following series Lavelli outran Wojciechowicz and got to the end zone where Graham found him

for a 26-yard touchdown pass. It was 14-3 in the Browns' favor at halftime.

Mac Speedie made it 21-3 six plays into the second half. The big left end was far too tall for Philadelphia's diminutive defensive backs while possessing just as much speed. Speedie caught a 12-yard touchdown pass after a leaping grab at the two.

The Eagles then started double-covering Lavelli and Speedie, so Cleveland started throwing to its running backs. Graham and Bumgardner found each other three straight times before Philly gave up double coverage to pick up the backs.

The Eagles got their only touchdown when All-Pro Pete Pihos beat Cliff Lewis and Hal Herring on a pass from Bill Mackrides, who replaced starter Tommy Thompson, from 17 yards away with 14:17 to play.

Any hopes Eagles fans had of watching their favorites come back were dashed when the Browns used a bruising running game to waste time. The famous trap to Marion Motley, which Cleveland had disdained at first in favor of a passing attack, began to churn away yards and time precious to the Eagles. Graham ended the drive with one-yard TD run to make it Browns 28, Eagles 10.

Warren Lahr intercepted a pass on Philadelphia's next series. Jones then swept 57 yards to the Eagles' seven before defensive back Frankie Reagan stopped him. Bumgardner took it the rest of the way to the end zone on the next play. Final score: Browns 35, Eagles 10.

The game not only proved that the Browns were a team with which the older league had to reckon, but also proved Paul Brown's system was the wave of the future. Brown and his staff had Philadelphia scouted to a fare-thee-well, while the Eagles simply remained with what had worked so effectively in the past.

Likewise, the Eagles' run of success was now in the past as they would not win another conference crown for 10 years. The new standards of excellence in coaching, innovations, and on-field play would now be set by Paul Brown and his Browns.

Were there still any disbelievers three months and eight days following the Browns' whipping of the Philadelphia Eagles, the defending NFL champions, in their first game in a "real" professional league?

Oh sure there were. The Browns, after all, were 10-0 in 1950 against teams with losing records. They played only one team with a winning mark, the New York Giants, and were 1-2 against them. That revolutionary passing game Paul Brown had used to make a shambles of the All-America Football Conference had been grounded by the Giants' "Umbrella Defense." New York yielded only 19 points and one touchdown to the Browns' offense over three games.

However, the Giants had scored only 26 points themselves and had lost their playoff game to the Clevelanders, 8-3, on Dec. 17 in Cleveland Stadium. The Browns *had* won only against teams with losing or breakeven records, but they also hadn't lost to any of those clubs, either.

Now Cleveland would take on a powerhouse, the Los Angeles Rams, who had survived a playoff of their own against the Chicago Bears on the same day the Browns were dispatching the Giants. Just like New York, Chicago had beaten the Rams twice in the regular season.

There could hardly have been a better matchup for the crown. From a local angle, the game featured Cleveland's current team against the team it had replaced. Five years earlier, the "Cleveland" Rams defeated the Washington Redskins in Cleveland Stadium for the NFL crown, then packed up and moved to Los Angeles.

From a national angle, had the Browns not made such a splash in their first season in the league, it would have been the Rams the NFL would have canonized in 1950. Regardless, this was to be a battle of wide-open, innovative passing offenses featuring future Hall of Famers from both sides.

Los Angeles, under new head coach Joe Stydahar, set 22 league records and scored a whopping 490 points. No team could hold them to fewer than 14 points in any one

game. Three times they topped 50 points in a game. They scorched Baltimore for 70 points and Detroit for 65. Their two quarterbacks, Bob Waterfield and Norm Van Brocklin, both made the Pro Bowl.

Van Brocklin had been first in passing efficiency that year, with Otto Graham rated No. 2. But the battle within the battle never took place because Van Brocklin had broken a rib in the playoff victory over the Bears. Stydahar had to go with Waterfield, a dilemma any head coach would gladly face.

Waterfield was, however, also the Rams' punter and place-kicker, and an injury to him would have

put Los Angeles at a disadvantage at three positions.

The Rams had lost to Philadelphia in the 1949 championship game on a rain-drenched Los Angeles Coliseum field that inhibited their highly-sophisticated passing attack of Van Brocklin and Waterfield throwing to their outstanding receivers such as Tom Fears and Elroy Hirsch.

With the '50 game in the American Conference champion's city (the NFL used National/American Conference names from 1950-52), no doubt Stydahar had the field conditions on his mind. He started with a big backfield of Paul "Tank" Younger and rookie "Deacon" Dan Towler at halfbacks, rather than the usual smaller, quicker halfback duo of Glenn Davis and V.T. Smith. The coach believed that Younger, also a star linebacker, and Towler, really a fullback,

Taking control after the Rams scored on the game's first play, Otto Graham picks up 12 yards on this first-quarter run. Dante Lavelli delivers a brutal block behind Graham.

wouldn't need a hard, dry field to do well against the Browns' defense.

And that defense was almost without one of its most vital cogs. End Len Ford had been on the sidelines since Oct. 15 after a collision with fullback Pat Harder of the Chicago Cardinals. Ford was given clearance to play, but was 15 pounds underweight at game time.

The condition of the playing field was not unlike that of the championship game the previous year. A warming trend hit Cleveland and thawed the frozen ground at the Stadium. A light rain fell in the morning and made the footing softer than it should have been.

So was the Browns' defense, on the game's first play. Perhaps overly conscious of Tom Fears, the Los Angeles end who had a record 84 receptions that year, Glenn

Davis slipped out of the backfield unnoticed and caught an 82-yard TD pass.

But it took the Browns only six plays to get an equalizer. Graham gained 21 yards rushing and completed three passes on the drive, the final one to Dub Jones for a 31-yard touchdown.

The Rams needed eight plays to get the game's third touchdown on an afternoon when offense was king. Dick Hoerner, the Rams' top rusher and a man once drafted by the Browns, finished the march with a three-yard run. Fears had a 44-yard reception on the drive.

Back came the Browns. A pass interference call against Rams rookie Woodley Lewis and a 17-yard pass to left end Mac Speedie got the Browns from their own 35-yard line to the Los Angeles 26.

Graham then hooked up with Dante Lavelli for Cleveland's second touchdown early in the second quarter. The score, however, stayed 14-13 as the PAT failed when the snap to holder Tommy James was high.

James attempted a pass to Tony Adamle in the end zone, but Adamle dropped it.

It was now time for the Browns' defense to stiffen. The Rams used their running game to march to the Cleveland seven, but V.T. Smith was charged with holding and Ken Gorgal intercepted Waterfield to end the drive.

The Browns offense stalled again and punter Horace Gillom uncharacteristically shanked one for only nine yards to the Browns' 46. The Rams got to the Cleveland 12, but could gain only four more yards on the next three plays. Waterfield then missed a 15-yard field goal attempt.

After entering the game in place of rookie Jim Martin, Len Ford was particularly effective in shutting down the Rams. On one series Ford threw V.T. Smith for a 14-yard loss, sacked Waterfield for an 11-yard setback and tackled Glenn Davis 13 yards behind the line of scrimmage.

In the third quarter, Graham and Lavelli connected on another TD pass, a 39-

yarder, to give the Browns their first lead of the game, 20-14. But the Rams then responded with two of their own, just 25 seconds apart. Hoerner hit the end zone from a yard away and Larry Brink picked up Marion Motley's fumble and ran it six yards for a score.

Motley was not a strong factor in carrying the ball. The Browns had decided to go with a passing game and Motley was used mainly as a blocker. Plus, the Rams' defense was heavily geared to stop him and he was getting hammered at the line of scrimmage on almost every play.

Warren Lahr intercepted a pass at the end of the third quarter, giving Graham the opportunity to begin one of the most pressure-filled drives in the history of the Browns. Twice Cleveland converted on

Cleveland's ground game was minimized in favor of a passing attack, but fullback Marion Motley picked up 12 yards on this fourth-quarter play before being tackled by Tank Younger. Dub Jones (86) scored the Browns' first TD on a 31-yard pass from Graham in the opening quarter.

Warren Lahr, Weeb Ewbank, Paul Brown and Tony Adamle (l-r) watch from the sideline as Lou Groza prepares to kick the winning field goal.

back was hit on his blind side and fumbled. Linebacker Mike Lazetich recovered and it looked as if the Rams had the game in the bag. A first down would allow them to run out the clock.

They did not get it. Cliff Lewis took Waterfield's 51-yard punt at the Browns' 19 and ran out of bounds 13 yards later, with 1:50 left to play. Graham gained 14 yards on a scramble, completed passes of 15 to Bumgardner, 16 to Jones and 12 to Bumgardner. Then Graham ran it to the 10, making sure he was in the middle of the field to set up Groza's field goal attempt.

With a strong 30-mile-per-hour wind at his back, Groza made his most memorable kick, a 16-yarder with 28 seconds left.

After the kickoff, the Rams gained possession on their own 46. Although Waterfield had completed 18 of 22 passes, Stydahar inserted the broken-ribbed Van Brocklin for the final possession. On the first play, Van Brocklin's pass was picked off by Lahr, Cleveland's fourth of the day. The Browns had a 30-28 victory and a championship in their first season in the NFL.

More important than the Browns proving their capabilities was the fact the game was played between two teams with offenses far ahead of their time. The Browns and the Rams emphasized the pass. No longer were the run-oriented offenses the only keys to success. Paul Brown later said it was "the greatest game I ever saw, not because of the game itself, but because of the tremendous exhibition of passing by both teams."

The sparks generated on that cold Cleveland day by two high-profile, pass-oriented teams helped to heat up fan interest in pro football nationwide. The NFL had entered a decade of increasing prominence and credibility within the American public.

fourth down, on a seven-yard pass from Graham to Lavelli on fourth-and-four and later on a quarterback sneak. Graham found Rex Bumgardner on a 14-yard pass play to the back of the end zone for the score. The last play was the only one in the drive in which Graham did not either run himself or throw underneath the Los Angeles defense.

Graham and the Browns were driving for a touchdown again when the quarter-

Players look skyward to see Lou Groza's 16-yard winning field goal sail over the uprights with 28 seconds remaining in the game. The Browns were NFL champions in their first season in the league.

There was a brand new look to the Browns for 1954. Only 10 starters remained from the team that won the NFL title in 1950. One-third of the 1954 roster was new as Paul Brown rebuilt the team while keeping the Browns in contention. Two things didn't change, however. The Browns were still champions of the Eastern Conference and they were still having trouble beating the Detroit Lions.

Detroit had beaten Cleveland in the last two NFL championship games. The Lions would win again on the final weekend of the '54 regular season, Dec. 19, in Cleveland. A week later, the teams were to meet in Cleveland Stadium for another title match.

The Lions' 14-10 victory a week before had Browns fans hoping for the best, but preparing for the worst. Including the pre-season, Detroit had an eight-game unbeaten

streak against the Browns and were confident their devil-may-care approach was superior to Brown's reliance on a system.

Lions quarterback Bobby Layne had thrown 37 passes in the victory on Dec. 19 while the Browns' Otto Graham had passed only six times. Graham had not thrown a TD pass in the four previous meetings between the two NFL powers.

After beating the Browns 17-7 in '52 and 17-16 in '53, the Lions were ready to become the first club in NFL history to win three consecutive league titles.

Head Coach Buddy Parker had installed a pass-oriented offense similar to the Browns and the Los Angeles Rams. Layne threw to players like Leon Hart, Doak Walker, Dorne Dibble, Cloyce Box, Jug Girard and Jim Doran. Lew Carpenter, formerly of the Browns, and ex-AAFC star Bob Hoernschemeyer were dependable ball carriers for the Lions.

Several Browns veterans reportedly met in private during the week between the games to discuss how to overrule the coaches and use the plays they knew were needed to beat the Lions. They would, in effect, be staging a mini-rebellion against Paul Brown's system of sending in plays through a messenger guard rotation.

Brown, too, sensed the old ways would never beat Detroit. So instead of flanking the halfbacks on the outside, which showed a defense just what the Browns were planning to do, Brown decided to run out of a T formation that was the standard in the NFL in the 1950s. He would also turn Graham loose and open up the offense, attacking the Lions before being attacked.

It looked like more of the same in the first quarter, however, when Lions linebacker Joe Schmidt intercepted Graham's pass and Doak Walker was good on a 36-yard field goal to open the scoring.

But it was all Browns from there. Gil Mains was called for roughing punter Horace Gillom on the Browns' first possession and Graham made the Lions pay by tossing a pass through the Detroit secondary to Ray Renfro for an easy touchdown.

Then came the deluge. Don Paul intercepted Layne's pass and returned it 33 yards to the eight. Graham passed to Pete Brewster in the end zone for a 14-3 lead.

In the second quarter, the Lions had to punt and Billy Reynolds returned it to Detroit's 12. Soon after, Graham scored from the one, his first of three TDs on the ground. Rookie running back Bill Bowman then scored Detroit's final TD on a five-yard run to make it 21-10.

But before the half ended, the Browns would score twice more for a 25-point half-time lead. To make it 28-10, middle guard Mike McCormack ripped the ball from Layne's cocked arm, setting up Graham's second TD run, a five-yarder.

Next, linebacker Walt Michaels intercepted Layne at the Lions' 31 and Graham immediately went to Renfro, who beat All-Pro and future Hall-of-Fame defensive back Jack Christiansen at the three and plunged into the end zone. At halftime, the score was Browns 35, Lions 10.

In the third quarter, Graham scored his third touchdown, a one-yard run, following a 43-yard completion to Brewster. Next, Ken Konz intercepted a pass and returned it to Detroit's 13-yard line to set up a TD run by Fred "Curly" Morrison that made it 49-10. Finally, in the fourth quarter, a second Konz interception led to a 19-yard touchdown run by Chet "the Jet" Hanulak.

The final score was 56-10. The Browns forced seven Lions turnovers. Cleveland had its receivers running amok through the Detroit secondary as the Lions had to abandon their seven-man rush that once had shackled Graham.

Taming Layne and the Lions

Browns 56
Lions 10

After back-to-back title-game losses, Graham and the Browns finally dominate their nemesis.

Graham had one of his greatest games ever, running for three TDs and passing for three more. After completing nine of 12 passes for 163 yards, he exited the field in the fourth quarter to a standing ovation. Following the game, the 33-year-old Graham confirmed what had been rumored all season: that he was retiring. He would "go out on top." He returned, of course, in 1955 to lead the Browns to another championship.

The game was a watershed for the Browns. Talk of the team getting too old to win another NFL championship was put to rest. In fact, the game, and the 1954 season, signalled what appeared to be a successful transition to new talent. On offense, third-year man Ray Renfro became a full-time receiver. Pete Brewster finished his second

Billy Reynolds runs back a kick with the help of a block by Chet "the Jet" Hanulak (44). Future Hall of Famer Joe Schmidt (56) pursues on the right.

season as Mac Speedie's very capable successor. And rookie Maurice Bassett, in Paul Brown's opinion, had become a better inside runner than Marion Motley, whose aging knees led to retirement in the '54 preseason (though he later finished his career in Pittsburgh).

On defense, middle guard Mike McCormack, who was acquired in the 1953 10-forfive deal with Baltimore, provided a powerful pass rush to offset the retirement of veteran Bill Willis. Tackle Don Colo and linebacker Tom Catlin, also acquired from the Colts, had become "bruising defensive players" according to Brown.

Rookie Carlton Massey played so well at defensive end that opposing offenses could no longer simply plan to avoid the other end, Len Ford, as the safest running route. And finally, second-year safety Ken Konz played like a savvy veteran, intercepting seven passes in '54, including two for touchdowns.

Furthermore, the new aggressiveness exhibited by the Browns in the title game made Buddy Parker eat his words of Dec. 19, when he said "I only wish it was next Sunday."

In contrast, his post-game comments after the 56-10 thrashing included this statement: "I hope I never have to go through another one like this. If I do, I'll probably be out picking cotton."

Entering 1995, neither Parker, nor any other NFL head coach, has had to "go through another one like this" since that day in '54. Although the 45-point spreads in the Browns' loss to Detroit in 1957 (59-14) and the 49ers' victory over the Broncos in Super Bowl XXIV (55-10) were nearly as great, no team since the 1954 Lions has lost an NFL championship game by a margin that wide. In fact, in the history of the NFL, only the 1940 Bears' 73-0 win over the Redskins was more lopsided.

Everything went right for the Browns. When Pete Brewster attempted this catch inside the Lions' five yard line, the ball was knocked into the air, but was caught by Ray Renfro.

Baltimore's overtime victory over the New York Giants in the 1958 NFL championship contest in which quarterback John Unitas led the Colts on two rallies, one to tie the score in regulation play and one to win, is generally credited as the consummation of the marriage between the NFL and network television.

So how could either have asked for anything more less than a year later when Unitas' Colts hosted the Cleveland Browns and the best running back in the league — Jim Brown?

The Browns and the Colts hadn't played each

November 1, 1959

Jim Brown Jolts the Colts

Browns 38
Colts 31

Big Daddy, Gino and Fatso are no match for the Cleveland fullback's five-touchdown performance.

other since 1956. Unitas was a rookie, and a good one, although his young team would be only 5-7 that year. Brown was a senior at Syracuse University in the fall of 1956, as his future club was also 5-7 and learning how to live without quarterback Otto Graham, who retired the year before.

But Unitas and Brown were NFL superstars three years later, and they proved it on Nov. 1, 1959. Brown scored five touchdowns, a career high, while rushing for 178 yards on 32 carries. Unitas tossed four touchdown passes.

There were 57,557 on hand at Baltimore's Memorial Stadium to see the greatest offensive players in the NFL match brilliance in an inter-conference battle. The final score was 38-31, as defense wasn't the order of the day. It was much more like a

tennis match, as heads turned from side to side while the teams marched up and down the field at will.

But it was a defensive play that "broke the serve." Cleveland safety Junior Wren intercepted a Unitas pass early in the third quarter with the Browns ahead, 17-10. That set up a short touchdown by Brown to give Cleveland a 24-10 lead. The teams alternated touchdowns from that time, just as they had done in the first half.

The Browns kicked a field goal on their first possession. The Colts answered with a three-pointer from Steve Myhra. Brown then gave Cleveland a 10-3 lead with his most impressive run of the day. Taking a pitch from quarterback Milt Plum, Brown escaped several potential tacklers, bowled over defensive back Ray Brown and took off on what became a 70-yard touchdown run. Milt Davis, the Colts' right cornerback, had a chance to catch up to Brown, but Bobby Mitchell threw a block to keep Davis at bay.

All of Unitas' touchdown passes were from short yardage. The Colts came back with a touchdown pass to Lenny Moore from three yards away to tie it at 10-10. Brown gave Cleveland its halftime lead with a 17-yard run.

After Wren's interception and Brown's third TD run, Unitas returned with an eight-yard scoring pass to Jerry Richardson. Brown scored from a yard away and Unitas hit Raymond Berry from 11 yards out to make it 31-24.

Then came the only punt of the afternoon, by Wren, early in the fourth quarter. The Colts marched to the Cleveland seven-yard line, but Unitas' pass intended for Richardson in the end zone was picked off, again by Wren, to keep the Browns ahead.

The fifth Jim Brown TD was on a one-yard plunge. Baltimore scored its final touchdown as Unitas fired a five-yarder to Jim Mutscheller.

Unitas completed 23 of 41 passes for 397 yards, an excellent effort by any measurement. Because the Colts were always behind, pressure mounted on Unitas to keep his team within striking distance. Unitas called just 19 runs for the game, and Bal-

timore's own standout fullback, Alan "the Horse" Ameche, gained only 18 yards on nine attempts.

Milt Plum had an excellent day likewise, going 14-for-23 for 200 yards. Bernie Parrish, a rookie cornerback, intercepted a Unitas pass on the Browns' four-yard line in the second frame. Mitchell caught five passes for 66 yards for the Browns, while Berry made 11 grabs for 156 yards and Moore caught five for 115 yards for Baltimore.

All of that was overshadowed by Brown and his quintet of touchdown runs. It was made more impressive by the fact it was done versus the defending NFL champion, which possessed an awesome front four that included future Pro Football Hall of Famers Gino Marchetti and Art "Fatso" Donovan, plus Eugene "Big Daddy" Lipscomb and Don Joyce.

"He's everything everybody's said, and more," said Weeb Ewbank, the head coach of the Colts and a former Browns assistant. "We did not tackle as well as usual, but maybe that's because we were trying to bring down Jim Brown."

The offensive line had something to do with it. Willie Davis, later to become a star defensive end and Hall of Famer with the Packers, replaced Lou Groza in the first quarter after Groza hurt his back. The rest of the offensive line had another future Hall of Famer, Mike McCormack, at right tackle, Gene Hickerson and Jim Ray Smith at guards, and Art Hunter at center.

"I guess this is my most satisfying day," said Jim Brown, who would win the 1959 league rushing title with 1,329 yards. "There's nothing like beating the champs. I just might have been hitting with a little something extra today."

Losing to the powerful Baltimore Colts would not have been a disgrace in 1964. Only twice in that autumn did Colts fans not see their favorites win. Baltimore finished 12-2, the third-highest scoring team in NFL history at the time. Only the Vikings and the Lions had beaten the Colts.

Few expected anything special from the Cleveland Browns, champions of the Eastern Conference. The Browns finished 10-3-1 in 1964, only a half-game better than the year before. Some said the '64 Browns didn't look much different from the team that finished second the previous season, and maybe they had only won the title because the New York Giants, who had captured the East five times in the last six years, had completely collapsed.

Besides, the Western Conference was thought to be superior. It had won the NFL championship six times in the last seven years. The Colts, Green Bay Packers and Chicago Bears were considered the league's dominating teams.

But on this day in 1964, the word "domination" would belong to the Cleveland Browns. Their defense, adequate, but not nearly in a class with the Colts, Packers or Bears, shut down a strong Baltimore offense loaded with future Hall of Famers: Johnny Unitas, Lenny Moore, Raymond Berry, John Mackey and Jim Parker.

On offense, quarterback Frank Ryan and receiver Gary Collins had their greatest days as Browns, hooking up on three second-half touchdown passes that, along with Lou Groza's two field goals, gave the Browns their first NFL title since Otto Graham's final year, 1955, and their most recent heading into the 1995 season.

Collins, in only his second full season as a starter, was the Browns' most visibly confident player going into the game. During the week preceding the contest, he boasted to a Cleveland television interviewer that the Browns would "win big." And the night before the game, he told teammate Paul Wiggin that he would catch three touchdown passes and win MVP honors.

The game was supposed to be interesting only because Jim Brown, the league's premier running back, would play. Brown had almost singlehandedly demolished the defending champion Colts in a regular-season tilt in 1959 with 178 yards rushing and five touchdowns, but was shackled in a 1962 game, with only 11 yards on 14 carries.

Whether or not Brown had a good game was not supposed to matter. It was on defense where the difference would lay. The Colts had the finest defense in the NFL, giving up a league-low 215 points. Cleveland, on the other hand, gave up more yardage to its opponents than any other club in the circuit. The Browns had yielded 293 points.

There wasn't much the defense was supposed to be able to do against John Unitas, the best quarterback of his day. Unitas was also battle-tested. He had paced the Colts to an overtime victory in the 1958 NFL championship game, also known as "The Greatest Game Ever Played," and led them to victory again in the 1959 title contest. Frank Ryan, meanwhile, had never been in a championship game. Nor had most of his teammates.

But some had. Brown, linebackers Galen Fiss and Vince Costello and defensive end Paul Wiggin were around when the Browns lost to the Detroit Lions in the 1957 title game. Kicker Lou Groza had been with the club since the first day in 1946, while defensive tackle Bob Gain was a starter on the Browns' 1955 champions.

However, it was a player for whom the Browns traded, defensive tackle Dick Modzelewski, who owned the most recent stretch of title-game experience: six over the previous eight seasons with his former team, the Giants, including the NFL cham-

pionship in 1956. Modzelewski had become available after Giants Head Coach Allie Sherman embarked on a housecleaning mission on his aging defense. Already he had swapped tackle Rosey Grier to the Los Angeles Rams and linebacker Sam Huff to the Washington Redskins.

When Modzelewski became available, Blanton Collier and Art Modell were more than willing to give up split end Bobby Crespino for the veteran lineman. Along with his experience, Modzelewski brought enthusiasm and a winning attitude to the Browns.

In addition to the acquisition of Modzelews-

The Ultimate Championship

ki, it was clear that in spite of a solid 10-4 record in 1963 and three defenders – Bill Glass, Galen Fiss and Bernie Parrish – making the Pro Bowl team, defensive improvements were needed for the Browns to overcome the Giants in the standings.

Bob Gain, a five-time Pro Bowl selection, was winding down his fine career. Collier already had begun working second-year man Jim Kanicki into that position. And shortage of speed in the defensive secondary led Collier to insert another two-year player, Walter Beach, at cornerback in place of veteran Jim Shofner. It also led to a great amount of zone defense because the Browns couldn't depend on man-to-man coverage.

Going into the 1964 championship game, Baltimore was installed as a seven-

Browns 27
Colts 0

The underrated Browns overpower and shut down the favored Colts in all phases of the game.

The defense continued to play the game of its life. Baltimore punted again, this time to Cleveland's 34. Jim Brown swept around left end for 46 yards and Frank Ryan found Gary Collins for an 18-yard TD pass.

The Browns sacked John Unitas six times. Dick Modzelewski (74), Bill Glass (80), and Jim Kanicki (69) corral the Colts' QB in the first quarter.

The weather in Cleveland Stadium on Dec. 27, 1964, was cold, windy and overcast. Passing into the wind was a chore. Neither team could get its offense in gear in the first two quarters, but that was to the Browns' advantage. The Colts were supposed to score points in bunches against this so-so defense, and failure to do so was frustrating the visitors.

Baltimore elected to receive the second-half kickoff and the Browns chose to defend the open end of the Stadium, to have the wind behind them in the third quarter. The gamble paid off when Tom Gilburg's punt traveled only to the Browns' 48-yard line. Cleveland could make only 14 yards from there, but with the wind at his back Groza kicked a 43-yard field goal. The scoreless deadlock had been broken, and the momentum was clearly with the Browns.

The defense continued to play the game of its life. Baltimore punted again, this time to Cleveland's 34. Jim Brown swept around left end for 46 yards and Frank Ryan found Gary Collins for an 18-yard pass and the game's first touchdown.

On the next series, the defense held the Colts without a first down. Gilburg again had trouble punting, and a 28-yarder into the wind put the ball at the Baltimore 40. From the 42 Ryan and Collins connected again and the Browns had a 17-0 lead.

Lenny Moore fumbled near midfield and Paul Wiggin recovered. Ryan tossed passes to tight end Johnny Brewer and receiver Paul Warfield. Brown added a 23-yard run to get the Browns to the Baltimore two. Groza's second field goal, in the early moments of the fourth quarter made it 20-0.

Next, Ryan and Collins did it a third time, from 51 yards away, to give the Browns a 27-0 lead. That's how the game

point favorite. And why not? Hadn't Charley Johnson, the St. Louis Cardinals' fourth-year quarterback, scored 61 points on the Browns' defense in two games that year? Johnson was considered a fine passer, but hardly the equal of Unitas. The Cardinals became the Browns' primary rivals in the Eastern Conference in 1964, finishing at 9-3-2. The Giants, meanwhile, dropped to last at 2-10-2.

ended, making it one of the most stunning upsets in championship-game history and proving that the Browns' defense was not to be taken lightly.

The Browns sacked Unitas six times. Jim Kanicki led the charge with consistent penetration despite going against a future Hall of Famer, guard Jim Parker, most of the afternoon.

The offensive line was great, too. Right tackle Monte Clark, who was acquired in a trade with Dallas in '63 for Jim Ray Smith, played the best game of his life against left defensive end Gino Marchetti. Clark was only playing because regular right tackle John Brown injured his left knee at midseason. The Colts had 57 sacks in 1964, but couldn't get to Ryan.

Jim Brown gained 114 yards on 27 carries. The entire Baltimore club had 101 yards rushing. Unitas completed 12 of 20 passes for only 96 yards. His outstanding wide receivers, Raymond Berry and Jimmy Orr, caught only five passes for 69 yards. Ryan was 11-of-18 passing for 208 yards. Collins had five receptions for 130 yards.

The doubters had called the Browns "Laugh Champs." The Colts found nothing funny on that December day in 1964.

Paul Brown and Blanton Collier had always been best friends in the days they were making the Cleveland Browns the premier franchise in the All-America Conference and later the NFL. But Brown, Collier's old boss, didn't act like much of a chum after a 1970 preseason game in which the Bengals beat the Browns in Cincinnati. Brown was now head coach of the Bengals, a team the Browns had to play twice a year as a member of the new Central Division of the American Conference in the realigned NFL.

Collier, who took the Browns' head coaching job following Brown's firing by new owner Art Modell in 1963, walked across the field to shake hands with the man for whom he had been an assistant coach for nine seasons. But Brown chose to disappear into the Cincinnati dressing room without even acknowledging the man who had done so much to help him make the Browns the scourge of two leagues. Collier was standing alone in the middle of the field after being jilted.

Would he do it after the Browns and Bengals met for the first time in a regular-season clash, which would also be the first game Brown would coach in Cleveland since 1962? No one was sure. Brown said it was his custom to exchange greetings before a game, not after.

"Blanton knows that," Brown said. "I haven't done it since the league sent out a directive many years ago, when I was still [in Cleveland], that the practice [of walking across the field to shake hands with an opposing coach] should be eliminated. You never know when someone is going to come out and take a swing at you."

Directive or not, the action didn't sit well with Browns fans. Brown, to them, was a sore loser who should just swallow his pride and do what the rest of the league's coaches do. Some thought he would do that in Cleveland, and that he only did it before because he was on his home turf and it was only an exhibition game.

Collier and Brown met before the game. Collier said he told Brown the critical brickbats after the no-shake incident in preseason had not been instigated by him. Collier said Brown believed they were not.

The Browns won the game, 30-27, and at the moment everyone was waiting for, Paul Brown did not shake hands with Blanton Collier. The boos cascaded, deafening, throughout Cleveland Stadium. Collier claimed he understood.

"It has to do with the way he, or anyone, deals with defeat," Collier said. "He feels worse immediately afterward, and as time goes on he deals with it better. I'm the opposite. I feel badly enough at first but as time goes on it gnaws on me more and more, and I feel worse and worse."

The Browns were 10-point favorites, although it was a hard game to handicap. Cleveland's quarterback, Bill Nelsen, was suffering from a knee injury and played with a heavy bandage wrapping the injury. The starting running backs, Leroy Kelly and Bo Scott, were also suffering from minor injuries and did very little practicing during the week.

The Bengals were having real quarterback troubles. Greg Cook, who'd been the AFL Rookie of the Year in 1969, underwent arm surgery over the summer and was lost for the first part of the '70 season.

Backup Sam Wyche, who had led Cincinnati to an upset of the Raiders in the first game of the regular-season, had failed to move the Bengals' offense in the following two games and was replaced by Virgil

The Birth of a Rivalry

Browns 30
Bengals 27

Paul Brown's return to Cleveland is an unhappy homecoming as Blanton Collier's Browns prevail.

Carter, who had been acquired recently from the Chicago Bears.

In the first quarter, Cincinnati built a 10-0 lead on a 50-yard field goal by Horst Muhlmann and a two-yard touchdown run by Jess Phillips. Then Walter Johnson tackled Carter in the end zone for a safety to give the Browns their initial points.

The Bengals held a slim lead over the middle quarters. Kelly and Nelsen hooked up on a three-yard touchdown to make it 10-9. Bengals defensive end Royce Berry returned a fumble 58 yards for a TD and Nelsen found Milt Morin on a four-yard scoring pass to make the score 17-16 Bengals at halftime.

Muhlmann added another field goal in the third quarter, the only scoring of that period, but also missed a 39-yard attempt in the third. Meanwhile, the Browns' defense, shaky in the first quarter, was starting to assert itself. The Bengals' offense scored three points in the middle quarters and saw Carter sacked five times.

Kelly finally gave the Browns the lead on a one-yard TD run in the fourth quarter. Erich Barnes then intercepted Carter's pass and returned it 20 yards to the Cincinnati six. Two plays after that, Bo Scott ran into the end zone from a yard out.

Carter brought the Bengals back with a 16-yard TD pass to Speedy Thomas. The Browns were faced with third down and three on their 38-yard line with 1:50 to play — plenty of time for the Bengals to get Muhlmann in position to kick a tying field goal — but Gary Collins caught Nelsen's sideline pass and stepped out of bounds at the Cleveland 46, enabling the Browns to run out the clock for a 30-27 triumph.

Nelsen, despite his injured knee, completed 17 of 29 passes for 226 yards as the Browns outgained the Bengals 346-236. Cincinnati had virtually nothing on the ground (54 yards rushing, 20 attempts), but Virgil Carter solidified his hold on the starting quarterback job by completing 20 of 28 passes for 218 yards.

The victory gave the Browns a 3-1 record and made the Bengals 1-3. The Bengals won the rematch in Cincinnati on Nov.

15, 14-10. The narrow point margins of both games foretold a pattern of tight, hard-fought contests that would characterize the Browns-Bengals rivalry.

In the Bengals' locker room after the game, Paul Brown was visited by three of his former Cleveland stars: Otto Graham, Dante Lavelli and Tommy James. He said he was proud of both of *his* teams, praising the Bengals and Browns equally. "It looked as if it might have been an intra-squad game," he said. "We both knew each other's styles. We've used the same numbering system and much of our football is the same."

The Bengals would go on to capture the 1970 AFC Central Division title in only their third year of existence. Clearly Paul Brown's coaching genius was now at work in southern Ohio.

After failing to shake Blanton Collier's hand after the game, Bengals Coach Paul Brown exited the Cleveland Stadium field to a chorus of boos.

Cincinnati Bengals general manager Paul Brown and his head coach, Forrest Gregg, could have gotten some personal satisfaction with a Bengals victory over the Browns on the last day of the 1980 season. Both men had been fired by Browns owner Art Modell, and there was little doubt both would have enjoyed a pay back.

The Browns had a 10-5 record and a 7-4 conference mark when they visited Cincinnati's Riverfront Stadium. A victory would not just get them their first playoff berth since 1972, but would give them their first AFC Central championship in nine years. The Browns and Oilers each had 10-5 records going into that day, but the Oilers were done with their conference slate, having compiled a 4-2 record in their division, 7-5 in the AFC.

A win would have left the Browns 4-2 in the Central Division, but a game in front of Houston conference-wise. A defeat and Cleveland was facing elimination as the Steelers, also 4-2 in the Central, were playing San Diego in a Monday night game. Pittsburgh was 9-6 at the time, while the Chargers were 10-5 and in need of a victory to rule the AFC West over the Raiders.

The Steelers were obviously in the most unenviable situation, having to battle an opponent with a division title on its mind at their place. The Oilers were meeting the Vikings, who had already clinched their divisional crown. The Browns were meeting a team with a 6-9 slate that had fallen 31-7 four weeks earlier in one of only two lopsided victories for the Browns that season.

But Cleveland had to be leery of playing away from home against an opponent led by men for whom there was no love lost between them and Art Modell. For the Bengals, last place in the Central Division would have been easier to deal with had they thrown a monkey wrench into the Browns' playoff plans.

But this was the season of the "Kardiac Kids" and, as was the rule in 1980, the outcome wasn't decided until the closing moments. Don Cockroft kicked a field goal with 1:25 to play to snap a 24-24 tie, and defensive back Ron Bolton halted the final drive by tackling Bengals receiver Steve Kreider in bounds at the Cleveland 14 with time running out.

"I could have intercepted the ball, or even knocked it down," Bolton said. "But I didn't want to take any chances. If the pass had been incomplete, [the Bengals] would have had another play. I knew if he caught it and I could keep him in bounds, the game would be over."

The Bengals had used all of their time outs, and could neither set up a field goal try nor run another play from scrimmage. The game ended 27-24 Browns, giving the Clevelanders their Central Division title. Houston had downed the Vikings, making the triumph that much more essential.

It looked as though it would never happen at first. The Bengals' Jim Breech kicked a 42-yard field goal and backup quarterback Jack Thompson scored on a 13-yard run to make it 10-0 Cincinnati. Brian Sipe, the Browns' quarterback, had fumbled to set up Thompson's TD with 10 minutes to go before halftime.

Sipe came back and threw a 42-yard scoring pass to Reggie Rucker, then Dino Hall's recovery of a fumbled punt return set up Cockroft's 26-yard field goal with 14 seconds left in the first half. Halftime score: Browns 10, Bengals 10.

In the third quarter, Ray Griffin intercepted Sipe and returned it 52 yards for a

Palpitating Performance

Browns 27
Bengals 24

The Kardiac Kids win the AFC Central Division with one more heart-stopping finale.

TD to put the Bengals ahead 17-10, but the Browns came back with two touchdowns on 35- and 34-yard passes from Sipe to Ricky Feacher, who played for injured starter Dave Logan, to grab a 24-17 lead.

Bengals receiver Pat McInally, who lay on the field for about 10 minutes in the first quarter after being clobbered by Browns free safety Thom Darden, gained revenge when he caught a 59-yard third-quarter TD pass from Thompson to tie the game for the third time. McInally had been carried off the field on a stretcher, but returned to grab three passes for 86 yards.

The Browns' winning drive began at their own 46-yard line and 6:04 remaining. The running game, which had been ineffective against the Cincinnati defense, suddenly became the primary weapon. Mike Pruitt got most of the calls and finished the game with 51 yards to end the season with 1,034, the second of three straight years the Browns' fullback would surpass 1,000 yards rushing.

The Browns were at the three-yard line on third and goal when Sipe called what Head Coach Sam Rutigliano called a "feast or famine" bootleg. The quarterback elected to keep the ball rather than pitch it to Cleo Miller. The play fooled everyone except Cincinnati cornerback Ken "The Rattler" Riley, who came up to nail Sipe behind the line of scrimmage.

Not to worry. The Browns still had Cockroft, who had been kicking for them since 1968. Cincinnati called a time out to unnerve Cockroft, but to no avail as the veteran made it perfect and the Bengals' use of a time out came back to haunt them when they had none for the final possession.

Cockroft had gone through a trying season, having been bothered by a sciatic nerve injury since the second regular-season game. It would be his final pro season.

"The Bengals were only 6-9, but they wanted to salvage something, and they almost did," offensive tackle Doug Dieken remarked after the game. "And because they had nothing to lose it was a defensive lineman's holiday."

Ricky Feacher is hoisted by Willis Adams following one of Feacher's two TD catches. Joe DeLamielleure (64) and Robert E. Jackson (68) join the celebration.

The Bengals still had 1:18 to move from their own 32-yard line into field goal range. Ken Anderson, who would lead Cincinnati to the Super Bowl a year later, moved the Bengals to the Browns' 34. He then threw out of bounds to stop the clock. Finally, his 20-yard pass to Kreider was complete at the 14, but Bolton tackled Kreider in bounds and time expired. The Kardiac Kids had won the Central with another palpitating performance.

Sipe had 308 yards passing that day to conclude the year with 4,132 yards, still a club record in 1995. At the time it was only the fourth time in league history a quarterback had thrown for more than 4,000 yards. His effort would be recognized with the NFL's Most Valuable Player award.

L ittle did Browns fans realize after their favorites upset the mighty Dallas Cowboys, 38-14, on Dec. 28, 1969, that it would be another 17 years before the Browns would again see victory in a playoff game. Cleveland had landed in the playoffs five times between that 1969 conference playoff game with Dallas and their divisional tilt against the New York Jets in Cleveland Stadium on Jan. 3, 1987, but had always departed early.

The 1986 season was different, however.

The Browns posted a 12-4 regular-season record, the best in the AFC, and were rolling. They had flattened the San Diego Chargers by 30 points in their final game. The week before that they'd handed the Cincinnati Bengals, who had defeated them earlier in the season, a 34-3 walloping in Riverfront Stadium.

The Browns had won their last five games and eight of their final nine. They had even defeated the Steelers in Pittsburgh for the first time since 1969, the same year they had last won a playoff contest.

But there were low spots that season. The Browns lost at home to the then-winless Green Bay Packers in Game 7, after leading 14-3 at halftime. They were lucky to escape Houston and Minnesota with 23-20 victories. They needed overtime to beat the Steelers and the Oilers in Cleveland. While the Browns were impressive, they were hardly a juggernaut.

Dramatic Win in Double OT

Browns 23
Jets 20

A Kosar-led comeback, an undaunted defense and Moseley's kicks give the Browns a thrilling victory.

The Jets weren't either, although they had looked like one when the 1986 season commenced. Head Coach Joe Walton's team enjoyed the best record in the league with a 10-1 record. Quarterback Ken O'Brien, who had thrown for 3,888 yards with 25 touchdowns and only eight interceptions the year before, was lighting up the passing lanes via a 62.2-percent completion rate. Al Toon was catching 85 passes and Freeman McNeil, who had 1,331 yards rushing in '85, was on his way to another four-digit season.

Then came the crash. The Jets lost their next five and barely made it past Seattle and Cincinnati to be one of the two wild-card playoff entries.

But just when New York was given up for dead, No. 2 quarterback Pat Ryan, who Walton started over O'Brien in hopes of giving the Jets a psychological lift, completed 16 of 23 passes, with three touchdowns and no interceptions, in a 35-15 smashing of the Kansas City Chiefs in the wild-card game. Suddenly the Browns were facing a team that had again found its confidence.

It found more than that in the second half. With the Jets leading 13-10 in the fourth quarter, Browns quarterback Bernie Kosar moved the team to the Jets' two-yard line. But Kosar, in his first full season as a starter, tried to force a pass to Webster Slaughter in the end zone as Slaughter was double-covered. Russell Carter intercepted.

It was the first interception Kosar had suffered since November, but it would be the first of two that quarter. After the defense held and the Browns took possession at their own 17, Kosar was picked off by Jerry Holmes. Kosar had never thrown two consecutive interceptions before that.

Freeman McNeil, who didn't get his 1,000-yard season but had burned the Chiefs for 135 yards and two TDs the week before, then went 25 yards around the right side for a touchdown and a 20-10 Jets lead. It forced many of the 78,106 fans to get up and leave. Only 4:08 was on the clock and suddenly visions of the 1980 playoff loss to the Raiders, which ended on an interception in the end zone, and the previous year's loss to Miami, in which the Browns squandered a 21-3 lead at halftime, were haunting the long-suffering Browns supporters.

Kosar, however, would reward them for their persevering faith. Mark Gastineau was called on a roughing-the-passer penalty on the first play, which so obviously occurred after Kosar released the ball that many believed it cost the Jets the victory, to put the ball at the Cleveland 33-yard line.

Kosar then fired five completions to Reggie Langhorne, Brian Brennan (two each) and Curtis Dickey to get the Browns to the one-yard line at the two-minute warning. Fullback Kevin Mack plunged in for the touchdown on the next play. It was now 20-17, Jets.

The defense held the Jets without a first down, and the Browns took over at their own 33 with 51 seconds to go. A 25-yard pass interference penalty and a Kosar-to-Slaughter completion got Cleveland to the Jets' five-yard line where Mark Moseley hammered home a 22-yard field goal to put the game into overtime.

The 38-year-old Moseley, a former Washington Redskin who once kicked a then-NFL-record 23 straight field goals over a two-season span (1981-82), had been signed by Cleveland in the last week of November after a leg injury to Matt Bahr.

Moseley, however, would miss a 23-yard attempt in the first overtime, but the Browns' defense then smothered the Jets. The feeling that Moseley would have another chance was so strong the players could taste it. "We thought if we could keep getting the ball in Bernie's hands, we'd win," defensive end Carl Hairston said.

Cleveland took over for the final time at its own 31 with 2:38 to play in the second extra period. Kosar went to the ground, especially to Kevin Mack, who gained 44 yards on the effort. Receiver Brian Brennan, however, might have been the biggest hero as he broke up what looked to be a certain interception at the Jets' 42.

The Browns were at the nine-yard mark when Moseley came onto the field again. This time, he made good from 27 yards away, the Browns took a 23-20 victory with 12:58 to go in the second overtime and

Moseley won the fifth overtime game of his long career.

Kosar threw a playoff-record 64 times with a record 33 completions for a record 489 yards. Jets punter Dave Jennings was called to duty a record 14 times.

The win was likely the most stirring comeback the Browns had seen since their 1950 championship game, a 30-28 victory over the Rams. The 1980 Browns were supposed to be the Kardiac Kids, but that Jan. 3, 1987, double-overtime triumph had too

many fans' hearts pounding much too quickly.

"Bernie comes in the huddle and says 'We're going to take this game.' It was incredible the way he brought us together one play at a time," offensive tackle Paul Farren said about the last minutes of the final quarter.

"There were people going home in their cars who wish they'd stayed for the finish," linebacker Scott Nicholas said. You have to wonder if they were at least listening to the thrills on the radio.

Mark Moseley kicked one field goal to put the game into overtime, then kicked another (above) to win it in the second overtime. Jeff Gossett is the holder.

Things looked pretty dismal for the Cleveland Browns between Dec. 4 and Dec. 10, 1994. What was up until then a sparkling season, their first winning one since 1989, appeared to be going downhill. Cleveland had lost to the New York Giants, a decidedly average outfit, on Dec. 4.

The Browns had fallen out of first place for the first time all season, held a record of 9-4 and now had to visit the home field of the Dallas Cowboys, the two-time defending Super Bowl champions. The Cowboys were awesome. Their record at the time was 11-2, tied for the best in the league with the San Francisco 49ers. One of their losses had been to the Niners, and those clubs were in a heated race for the home-field advantage through the playoffs.

The Cowboys certainly were not about to take anybody lightly through the rest of the 1994 season, let alone the Browns, a team that had allowed the fewest points in the NFL through 13 games (164).

The main criticism the Browns had to endure through the '94 season was that their schedule was full of patsies. By the time of the 14th game, Cleveland had only beaten one team with a winning record, the 8-6 Patriots, and had lost to the two other winners on the slate, the Pittsburgh Steelers and Kansas City Chiefs.

The Browns, however, had been given credit for avoiding being upset, but that was prior to the Giants surprising them, 16-13, in Cleveland Stadium. "We don't make the schedule," safety Eric Turner said. "We just play it."

"I can't say those who were skeptical about us were not justified," linebacker Carl Banks added. "We have been inconsistent at times."

Skeptics became believers on Dec. 10. The Browns beat the Cowboys 19-14 in Texas Stadium to lock up a playoff berth for themselves and throw a serious roadblock into Dallas' plans of home-field advantage in their march to an unprecedented third straight Super Bowl championship.

As with most upsets, a little bit of luck played a big part in this one. It looked as if the last play of the game was going to be a game-winning six-yard touchdown pass from Dallas quarterback Troy Aikman to his All-Pro tight end, Jay Novacek. Browns linebacker Mike Caldwell overran the coverage of Novacek, and Aikman saw him alone over the middle.

But as the Dallas tight end was making his turn to waltz into the end zone, he slipped on the AstroTurf and hit the deck. He was immediately covered by Eric Turner, who was playing the game despite an injured shoulder.

The play started with 10 seconds on the clock and it ended with time expired and the ball no more than three inches from the goal line.

A smaller piece of luck occurred earlier on the Cowboys' potential game-winning drive when wide receiver Michael Irvin failed to step out of bounds and stop the clock after catching a pass at the Browns' 25-yard line.

Irvin, according to the Browns, had gotten away with a pass interference on cornerback Don Griffin, who was knocked to the carpet by Irvin as the latter ran his route. With Griffin fallen, Irvin suspected he might be able to score. But Griffin recovered and Browns safety Stevon Moore came over to help as Irvin was tackled in bounds at the 21.

Aikman spiked the ball to stop the clock with 28 seconds to go, but a few precious

Number 10
December 10, 1994

How 'Bout Them Browns!

Browns 19
Cowboys 14

The improving Browns get a little respect in Big D from the defending Super Bowl champs.

ticks had gone off before the Cowboys could line up and down the ball.

Kevin Williams caught a 15-yard pass from Aikman over the middle to get the Cowboys to the six-yard line. Aikman again spiked the ball to stop the clock, this time with 10 seconds left. The Browns called time out to discuss their defense, and decided to try a matchup zone rather than risk blitzing a high-powered offense like the one Dallas possessed.

"If one guy gets beaten, that's the game," Browns defensive coordinator Nick Saban said. "You have a greater chance to make a big play (when you blitz), but you're also more susceptible to getting beaten."

The Browns were beaten, but a fortuitous slip saved the day. It was as if fate had thrown an invisible banana peel in Jay Novacek's path to the end zone.

But there was plenty of bad luck on the Browns' side, too. Defenders, for example, dropped five sure interceptions. And running back Leroy Hoard seemed to have a clear path to the end zone on the Browns' first series, but All-Pro Charles Haley, who'd been blocked to the ground as he rushed quarterback Vinny Testaverde, recovered, chased down Hoard from behind and knocked the ball loose at the Cowboys' two-yard line. The ball was recovered by Dallas in the end zone for a touchback.

The Cowboys took advantage of the break and went 80 yards on 13 plays to take a 7-0 lead. Emmitt Smith, who had won three straight NFL rushing titles, scored on a pass from Aikman from seven yards out.

The Browns answered on their next series when wide receiver Michael Jackson caught Testaverde's pass from two yards away to tie the score, 7-7, as time ran out on the first quarter.

Three possessions had produced three impressive drives, and it looked as if the game might be high-scoring. Not so. The Browns stifled the Cowboys at every turn. Griffin and Turner intercepted Aikman and the Browns recovered two Dallas fumbles. They could manage no touchdowns them-

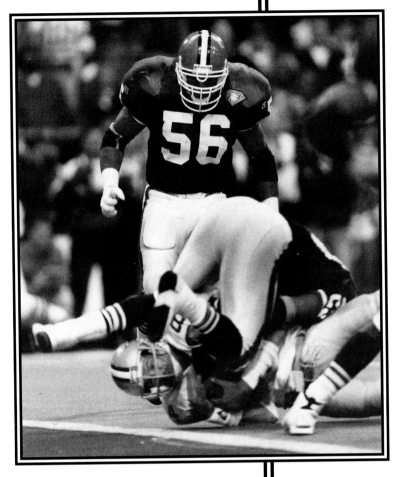

selves, but got close enough for Matt Stover to kick field goals of 34, 32 and 43 yards and make it 16-7 with 12:44 to go.

The Cowboys then followed Stover's third field goal with a 12-play, 78-yard 6:23 scoring drive. Smith did the honors on a four-yard TD run.

Jay Novacek's shoulder lands just short of the goal line on the game's final play. Eric Turner covers him while Mike Caldwell (56) approaches.

Stover, who closed the '94 season with a Browns-record 20 straight field goals without a miss, made it 19-14 with a 32-yarder with 1:49 remaining. Defensive tackle Bill Johnson had recovered a Cowboys fumble at the Dallas 16. Though the Browns failed to move the ball, Stover's kick put the Cowboys in an unenviable position of needing a touchdown rather than a field goal to win.

"I don't think we need to ask for respect any more because we got it now," Eric Turner said after the victory. "We beat the Super Bowl champ so everybody has to eat their words a little bit."

FIERCE COMPETITORS: *Defensive lineman Pio Sagapolutele gets a hand on Pittsburgh quarterback Neil O'Donnell. Since 1950, the Browns-Steelers rivalry has been one of the NFL's best. Entering 1995, the Browns led the regular-season series 52-38 as both teams were contenders for the AFC championship.*

How many times have you heard Frank Gifford say this on "Monday Night Football": "These two teams just plain don't like each other very much." A major ingredient in any rivalry is good old-fashioned animosity. That does not mean a healthy portion of respect is not there. It usually is. Gifford, during his playing days in the 1950s and '60s, certainly was respected by the Browns, as were the rest of his New York Giants teammates.

Players such as Emlen Tunnell, Sam Huff, Rosey Grier, Charlie Conerly, Y.A. Tittle, Pat Summerall, Jim Katcavage and Rosey Brown were matched against the best of the Browns. The Giants provided the Browns their first

something like this: "The Browns were so much better than anyone else in the AAFC, they caused the league to fold. There simply was no competition!"

Well, that's not entirely true, although it isn't entirely fiction either. Clearly, Cleveland was better than any other team in the AAFC. They lost four games in the four years of "the All-American," as some of the players called, and still call, their league. And there was the 1948 season when the Browns were undefeated, a nearly impossible feat in pro sports.

Of the four losses from 1946-49, San Francisco inflicted two of them: 34-20 in 1946 and 56-28 in 1949. In the '48 undefeated season, the closest call the Browns had was a 31-28 battle with the 49ers in San Francisco, a game in

The Rivalries

great National Football League rivalry, as both were perennial playoff contenders into the mid '60s before the aging Giants entered a down period beginning in 1964.

Other "respected" Browns rivals have included the New York Yankees and San Francisco 49ers during the All-America Conference years; the Los Angeles Rams and Detroit Lions in the 1950-57 playoff era; the Pittsburgh Steelers from the '50s through the '90s; the Dallas Cowboys in the '60s; and, beginning with the AFL-NFL realignment of 1970, the Cincinnati Bengals and Houston Oilers. Then, of course, in the late '80s there were the dreaded Denver Broncos.

There are those who will tell you that when it came to the AAFC days, the Browns had no rivals. Conventional wisdom at the time went

which Otto Graham played with an injured knee and the Browns played on just three days rest after a Thanksgiving-Day win over Los Angeles. The 56-28 defeat in 1949, also in San Francisco, ended the Browns' 29-game unbeaten streak which had begun in 1947.

Despite the losses, the Browns maintained the upper hand, beating the 49ers seven times, including the 1949 AAFC title game. In four years, the 49ers finished second behind the Browns each season: three times in the Western Division (1946-48) and again in '49 when the league played its final season as a seven-team circuit without divisions.

The early Browns-49ers rivalry is sprinkled with storied names: Graham, Marion Motley, Dante Lavelli, Mac Speedie and Edgar "Special Delivery" Jones for the Browns; Frankie

By Jim Campbell

Albert, Norm Standlee, Johnny "Strike" Stryzkalski, Len Eshmont, Bruno Banducci and Joe "the Jet" Perry for the 49ers.

When the teams joined the NFL in 1950 and were placed in different conferences, the rivalry lost some of its intensity. But a tense moment, nevertheless, occurred in the 1953 game in Cleveland Stadium when Otto Graham rolled right, was forced out of bounds and then took an elbow in the mouth by the 49ers' Art

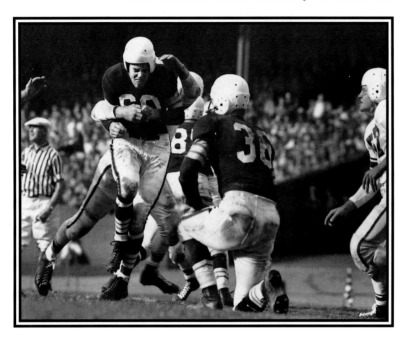

THE NINER NEMESIS: *The Browns lost just four games in their four AAFC seasons, two of which were to Western Division rival San Francisco. Otto Graham is wrapped up after a pass in their first-ever meeting, a 34-20 49er win in Cleveland Stadium on Oct. 27, 1946.*

Michalik. Graham returned in the second half with a Paul Brown-invented thin plastic bar bolted to his helmet. The device was a forerunner of the modern-day face mask.

That play in 1953 probably aggravated Brown as much as having to watch Y.A. Tittle perform in a 49er uniform. Back in 1948, Baltimore was the weakest link in the AAFC, both on the field and at the gate. Its troubles resulted in the league conducting two April "restocking" drafts for the Colts in which the seven other clubs gave up players to whom they held the rights, but would receive no compensation.

One of the two players the Browns sacrificed was Tittle, who had been a Cleveland

draftee and had just signed his first contract with the team. Brown had hoped to groom Tittle as the eventual successor to Graham, but instead watched Tittle launch a Hall-of-Fame career with the Colts, 49ers and Giants.

When it came to the AAFC championship game, the Browns were unbeatable. In the first two years they victimized the New York Yankees, then the Buffalo Bills, and finally the 49ers. The 1946 Yankees were almost the equal of the Browns. They finished 10-3-1 in the Eastern Division and had quarterback Ace Parker and tackle Bruiser Kinard (two future Pro Football Hall of Famers), plus tailback Spec Sanders and receiver Jack Russell.

The Yankees scored first in the championship game in Cleveland Stadium on a field goal, but Motley's short plunge and Lou Groza's PAT put the Browns ahead, 7-3. Sanders scored for New York, but Lou Rymkus blocked the extra point: New York 9, Cleveland 7. In the final five minutes, Graham led the Browns on a steady march, topping it off with a 16-yard TD pass to Lavelli. Groza converted and the final score stood at 14-9. Motley rushed for 100 yards on 13 carries. Graham threw for 213 on 16 of 27. Lavelli and Speedie each caught six passes.

In the 1947 rematch, this time in Yankee Stadium, the Browns scored first on a sneak by Graham. The score was set up by Motley's 51-yard dash around right end. Groza kicked the PAT. New York scored a field goal, but Special Delivery Jones blasted into the end zone from four yards in the third period. Lou Saban's PAT ended the scoring for the day: Cleveland 14-New York 3.

Although the Browns defeated the Yankees seven of the eight times they met in the regular season, that one non-victory, a 28-28 tie in 1947, serves as one of the greatest comebacks in Browns history. The game was played in Yankee Stadium on Nov. 23, 1947, before the largest New York pro football crowd (70,060) to that date. The Yankees worked especially hard on film study and Browns play diagramming, and felt they could snap the Browns' four-game

COMEBACK: *Tom Colella misses, but Marion Motley, playing linebacker, is on target to tackle Buddy Young in the first quarter of the Browns-Yankees battle in Yankee Stadium on Nov. 23, 1947. The Yankees built a 28-0 first-half lead before the Browns, in one of their greatest comebacks, erased the deficit for a 28-28 tie. Motley scored twice: on a 12-yard catch and a 10-yard run.*

winning streak in the series. At first, it looked as though Coach Ray Flaherty's off-field prepping would pay off. The Yankees were ahead, 28-0, after only 23 minutes of play.

Then Otto Graham went to work! First he connected with Bill Boedeker for a 34-yard scoring pass late in the second quarter. Late in the third, Graham found Marion Motley for a 12-yard TD strike. This score was set up when the Browns' defense stopped New York a yard short of the goal line. Then, throwing from his own end zone, Graham collaborated with Mac Speedie for 82 yards.

Three minutes later, Motley scored again, this time on a 10-yard run. In the final minutes of the fourth quarter, Graham's passing set up Jim Dewar's four-yard quick-opening touchdown thrust. As he did three previous times, Lou Saban, filling in for an injured Lou Groza, was true on the fourth and tying PAT. Browns 28, Yankees 28. But the game was not over yet! With 1:30 to play, behind the running of

Sanders and Buddy Young, New York drove 50 yards to the Cleveland 30. But time expired as the Browns' defense covered all receivers and Sanders couldn't unload to stop the clock with an incompletion.

Writing in the *New York Times*, Louis Effrat called the Browns' comeback "one of the greatest, most spectacular comebacks in many a year." While "only a tie," the game proved that no lead was safe against the powerful Browns.

When the AAFC merged with the NFL in 1950, a draft was held to redistribute players from the defunct AAFC franchises. As part of the maneuvering, the New York Giants were given first choice of players from the Brooklyn-

New York Yankees (the Yankees had merged with the Brooklyn Dodgers for the AAFC's final season in '49).

Although many of the ex-Yankees became members of the NFL's newly-formed New York Yanks in 1950, the Giants took some of the very best, including defensive backs Tom Landry, Harmon Rowe and Otto Schnellbacher, plus future Hall-of-Fame defensive tackle Arnie Weinmeister.

A GIANT DEFEAT: *Most Browns-Giants games in the early '50s were tight, low-scoring contests. This one in 1953 was not. Ken Carpenter lands over the goal line for six more points in the Browns' 62-14 victory in Cleveland Stadium.*

Landry, Rowe and Schnellbacher became three of the four spokes in the Giants' "Umbrella Defense," designed by Head Coach Steve Owen and featuring an arc of linebackers and defensive backs geared to stopping Otto Graham's passing efforts. The scheme worked to near perfection as the Giants beat the Browns twice in the 1950 regular season. New York shut out the Browns in Cleveland (6-0), then held them in check three weeks later at the Polo Grounds (17-13). Both teams finished 10-2 and a playoff was needed to determine the American Conference title.

The game was played on Dec. 17 in 10-degree weather in Cleveland Stadium. Only 33,054 fans braved the wind chill factor to see what would become typical of the series: a hard-fought, low-scoring game. Browns and Giants alike wore sneakers to get a foothold on the frozen field, except for Lou Groza, who wore a sneaker on his left foot and a football shoe (minus cleats) on his right kicking foot.

Going into the final quarter the Browns were ahead, 3-0. Then the Giants nearly scored when halfback Gene "Choo-Choo" Roberts broke free and headed for a touchdown. But suddenly, in one of the most memorable plays in Browns history, Bill Willis, the Browns' cat-like middle guard, made up 20 yards on Roberts and caught him at the Cleveland four-yard line. The Browns' defense held, actually pushing the Giants back to where Randy Clay kicked a tying field goal to match Groza's.

In the final minute, Groza broke the tie with his second field goal. Then, shortly thereafter, Willis broke through to sack Charlie Conerly in the end zone for a safety and an 8-3 victory for the Browns.

For the next six seasons, the Browns held the edge in the rivalry, going 8-3-1 against the Giants from 1951-56. But as the Browns were winding down their streak of six straight NFL title games, the Giants were gearing up as their successor, winning the NFL championship in 1956, the Browns' first year without Otto Graham leading the offense.

Then, in 1957, came Jim Brown! The newfound rivalry within a rivalry (fullback Brown vs. middle linebacker Sam Huff) became the stuff of which legends and TV documentaries are made. Shielded from Browns blockers by his front-four, Huff was free to "dog" Brown on nearly every play. He did more than today's "spies," he simply tackled Brown whether or not he had the ball. Mostly he did. An example of the effectiveness of this strategy was the 1958 Eastern Conference playoff. The Giants won the right to face the Colts in the Sudden Death championship game by defeating the Browns, 10-0. Huff and friends held Brown to eight yards on seven carries. But there was a toll

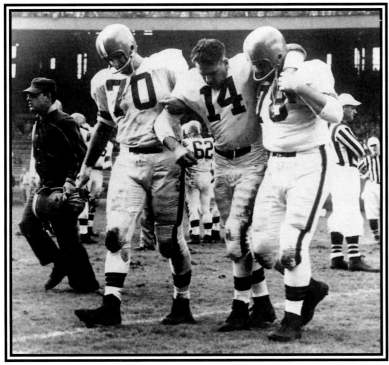

FIFTIES BATTLES: *Top: Marion Motley gains 11 yards in the 1950 playoff game. Left: Don Colo (70) and John Sandusky (78) help Otto Graham leave the field after he was knocked out of the game in 1955. Right: Rosey Brown (79), Dick Modzelewski (77) and Don Colo (70) have harsh words in '56.*

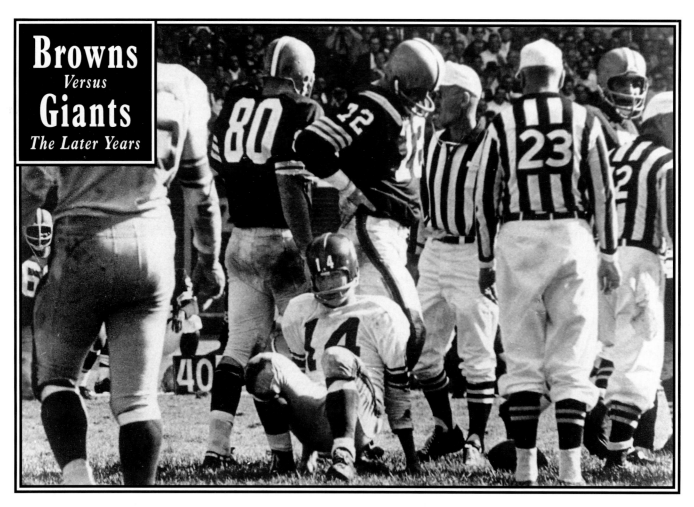

DEFENSIVE MANEUVERS: *Top: Bill Glass (80) and Floyd Peters (72) walk away after putting Y.A. Tittle in a down mood in 1962. Left: Sam Huff (70) and four other Giants take their best shot at Jim Brown in 1963. Right: The Browns' defense puts the pressure on Charlie Conerly in 1959.*

charge. Huff said, "Tackling Jimmy Brown was like running into an oak tree in the dark."

From 1958-63, the Giants won the Eastern Conference championship five times while the Browns finished second or third each season. By the mid-'60s, the Giants' dynasty had ended and the Browns gained the upper hand, keeping it until the merger reduced the frequency of the once titanic struggles to that of a presidential election.

During the early years of the 1950s, the Los Angeles Rams, a team that won the 1945 NFL title as the Cleveland Rams before relocating to the West Coast in '46, were one of the few teams that could match the Browns' offensive firepower with Bob Waterfield, Norm Van Brocklin, Tom Fears, Deacon Dan Towler, Elroy "Crazylegs" Hirsch and Paul "Tank" Younger. But their defense didn't quite match that of the Browns.

The teams met in the 1950 NFL title game. On the first play from scrimmage, Waterfield threw an 82-yard touchdown pass to Glenn Davis, "Mr. Outside" of Army fame. Graham countered shortly thereafter with a 31-yard scoring strike to Dub Jones. He also threw later scores to Lavelli twice and Rex Bumgardner. But in the end it was Groza's educated toe that spelled victory. His 16-yard field goal with 28 seconds to play lifted the Browns to their fifth league title in five years and their first in the NFL, 30-28.

As often happened in the pre-free agency days, there was a title rematch in 1951. This time the Rams won, 24-17, in the Los Angeles Coliseum. The back-breaker was a 73-yard pass to Fears from Van Brocklin, one of two Hall-of-Fame quarterbacks (Waterfield was the other) who alternated at the position for the Rams. It broke a 17-17 tie.

With Graham coaxed back for another year after announcing his retirement in 1954, the Browns defeated the Rams, 38-14, in the 1955 championship. Graham threw two TD passes (Lavelli, 50 yards and Ray Renfro, 35 yards)

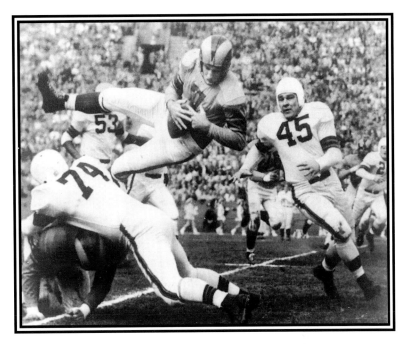

and ran for two scores, but equally important were six Cleveland interceptions. The Browns generated 24 points — the margin of victory — from the turnovers. Don Paul set a championship record with his 65-yard interception return for a touchdown.

What more could a fan ask for than a matchup of Hall-of-Fame quarterbacks: the Lions' Bobby Layne and the Browns' Otto Graham? If you're a Browns fan, and we assume you are, a lot more. The Lions and the Browns only play about every three years now, but in the '50s it was another story.

In 1952, 1953, 1954 and 1957 the two teams met for the NFL championship. In the first three, it was Layne vs. Graham, with Layne winning in '52 and '53. Buddy Parker was about the only coach to get the best of Paul Brown in head-to-head competition. It must have been particularly galling to Brown since Parker's use of football's renegades was the opposite of Brown's emphasis on players with character.

The Lions won both the regular season (17-6) and league championship game (17-7) in 1952. They repeated in the 1953 title game (17-16) when Layne engineered a long, late drive

RAM RIVALRY: *A year after the Browns beat the Rams for the 1950 NFL title, quarterback Bob Waterfield goes airborne in the '51 title game in the L.A. Coliseum, won by the Rams, 24-17. Browns pictured are Tony Adamle (74), Len Ford (53) and John Kissell (45).*

for a score (the payoff being a 33-yard touchdown pass to Jim Doran, who had been used as a defensive end for much of the season) with what was to become Layne's signature, the two-minute drill.

Graham, with assistance from flanker Ray Renfro, avenged the two prior championship defeats in 1954. He scored three times on short QB sneaks and threw twice to Renfro and once to Pete Brewster for touchdowns as the Browns trounced the Lions, 56-10. Graham said beforehand, "This is my last game." It wasn't.

The Lions and the Browns gave it a rest for two years, but went at it again in 1957. With Graham's successors Tommy O'Connell and Milt Plum playing with injuries, and Layne on the injured reserve list, Tobin Rote dismantled the Browns, 59-14. The closest the Browns could get was 17-7 on rookie Jim Brown's 29-yard scoring run. Then the wheels came off.

In a strange twist of fate, the Browns' Hall-of-Fame center Frank Gatski played on the winning team in both title blowouts: for the Browns in 1954 and for the Lions in 1957. After 11 years in Cleveland, he was traded to the Lions before the '57 season and was the starting center in the 59-14 game.

FRIENDS TO FOES: *Bill Cowher and Chuck Noll are former Browns linebackers who later coached the Steelers. A Brown from 1980-82, Cowher (above) succeeded Noll at the Pittsburgh helm in 1992.*

There is an old saying that "familiarity breeds contempt." Maybe it is the closeness (only a hundred miles by turnpikes). Or the similarity (both traditionally blue-collar, working-class cities). Whatever the reason, the rivalry between Cleveland and Pittsburgh is as heated and lengthy as any in the NFL. Going into 1995, the Browns led the regular-season series, 52-38. However, the early Pittsburgh teams, with their single-wing attack and hard-bitten players, once led Tom Landry of the Giants to remark, "We'd rather play the Browns twice than the Steelers once."

The Browns won 16 of the first 20 games. The Steelers never won until they ambushed the Browns in Forbes Field in 1954, 55-27. The Browns did not lose in Cleveland Stadium until 1956, 24-16. Pittsburgh never swept the two-game series until 1959. Mostly Cleveland would win in Cleveland and Pittsburgh would win in Pittsburgh. Nothing illustrates this better than the years 1970-1985 when Cleveland couldn't beg, borrow or steal, although they tried most of these tactics, a win in Three Rivers Stadium, regardless what they did.

Even when games went into overtime, the Steelers of Terry Bradshaw, Joe Greene, Jack Ham, Jack Lambert, Franco Harris, Lynn Swann, Mel Blount, Rocky Bleier and John Stallworth would come up with a gadget play to win. Changing hotels and travel itineraries, even pre-game meals, didn't help.

The Browns didn't leave Three Rivers with a victory until 1986 when they won, 27-24, behind Gerald McNeil's 100-yard kickoff return and Earnest Byner's late touchdown. Winning coach Marty Schottenheimer said, "I'm proud of the whole team. We set our goals in practice during the week and accomplished them on Sunday."

Adding to the warmth of the rivalry is the fact that Cleveland native and former Browns guard and linebacker Chuck Noll coached the Steelers from 1969-91. When Noll wasn't too far into his regime, he said, "When I first came here, there was always more feeling for the Browns game than any other."

Noll's successor in 1992, Bill Cowher, likewise played for the Browns as a linebacker from 1980-82. Cowher's Steelers put plenty of sting back into the rivalry in 1994 when Pittsburgh defeated the Browns three times, including the Browns' first playoff game in five years.

Since 1985, the Browns have recaptured the series advantage, winning 11 of 18 regular-season games from 1986-94. The late 1990s promise to provide additional excitement in

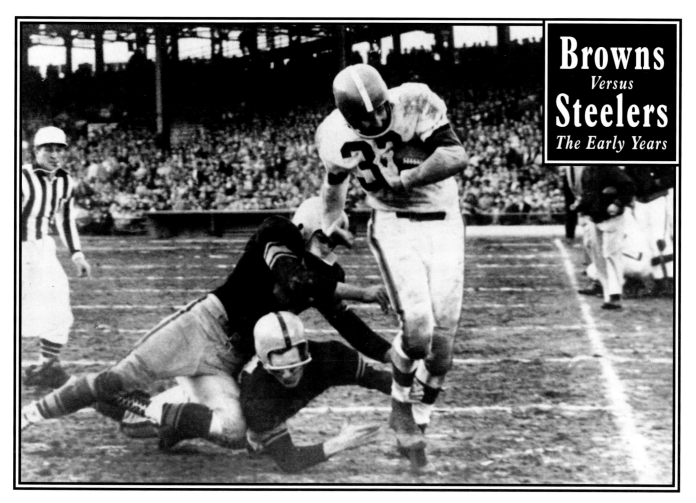

HOT PURSUIT: *Top: Richie McCabe loses his helmet as he and Marv Matuszak dive for Curly Morrison in a 1955 Browns victory. Left: Chet "the Jet" Hanulak breaks through for a TD in 1954. Right: John Baker (78), Gene Breen (52) and Ken Kortas (75) gang up on Jim Brown in 1965.*

TAKING A HIT: *Top: Boyce Green stiff arms Donnie Shell. Left: Richard Brown and Frank Minnifield wrap up Warren Williams. Above: Dick Ambrose trips up Franco Harris.*

142

the rivalry as both the Browns and the Steelers were Super Bowl contenders entering 1995.

The rivalry's most memorable game in recent years occurred in Cleveland Stadium on Oct. 24, 1993, when Eric Metcalf nearly beat the Steelers singlehandedly. Speed was the big reason Metcalf was the Browns' No. 1 draft choice in 1989. Perhaps never did that decision pay a bigger dividend than against the Steelers on that day. Metcalf equaled a National Football League record for punt returns for touchdowns in one game with two. His first return was 91 yards in the second quarter to give the Browns a 14-0 lead. It broke the old team record for longest punt return, set in 1986 by Gerald McNeil against the Lions.

The second return was a 75-yarder with 2:05 to play that put Cleveland ahead 28-23. The Steelers held the ball with 3:19 to play and a 23-21 lead, needing just one first down to run out the clock. James Jones stopped running back Barry Foster one yard short of the first down, and Pittsburgh was forced to punt.

Mark Royals got off a 53-yard punt to send Metcalf back to the Browns' 25. The blockers didn't hold anyone up at the line of scrimmage, but let the Steelers come downfield while a wall was being set up for Metcalf. Key blocks by Ron Wolfley, Stevon Moore and Terry Taylor permitted Metcalf to sail down the right side to the open end of Cleveland Stadium.

The score remained at 28-23 as Pittsburgh's final drive failed when strong safety Moore pulled the ball from the hands of wide receiver Dwight Stone, and linebacker Mike Caldwell recovered for the Browns.

Otto Graham had this to say *before* the first-ever game the Cleveland Browns played against the Cincinnati Bengals in the 1970 preseason: "We can expect a typical Browns-Bengals game." If ever there was a natural rivalry, this is the one. Instate, intra-division and intense!

Two teams with the same founder and first coach. Even the uniforms looked alike: Cincinnati's Paul Brown-designed orange and black

uniforms greatly resembled the Paul Brown-designed orange and brown Cleveland togs.

When the 1970 merger came about, Paul Brown lobbied to be able to play the Browns on an annual basis. Among other things, P.B. knew about rivalries. From the first year, both teams winning at home (Cleveland, 30-27; Cincinnati, 14-10), through Sam Wyche's ill-advised "You don't live in Cleveland" remark, there have been a lot of sparks flying. Only with the

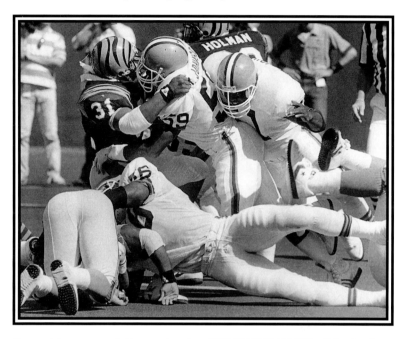

Bengals' recent fall on hard times have the Browns been able to pull ahead in the series, 25-24, going into the 1995 season. The point total is also close for the 25-year series: Bengals 1,017, Browns 997. Individual games likewise reflect the closeness with scores such as 30-27, 14-10, 27-24, 31-27, 10-7, 13-10, 28-27, 20-17, 12-9 and 14-13.

NO PUSHOVER: *Linebacker Mike Johnson stops Ickey Woods short of the goal line in a late 1980s game. Beginning with a 30-27 Cleveland victory in 1970, the Browns-Bengals rivalry has never been short of close, hard-fought games and as much intensity as any in the National Football League.*

The feelings of Paul Brown toward beating the Browns in the early '70s were said to equal those toward the Eagles in 1950: He had something to prove. Other coaches on both sides of the field in succeeding years seconded Brown's emotions. Whether it was Brian Sipe hitting Ozzie Newsome on a key 18-yard pass to set up Don Cockroft's game-winner in OT in 1978

(13-10), or Eric Thomas blocking Matt Stover's final-play field goal attempt to preserve a 1991 Bengal win (23-21), fans of both teams seem to always get their money's worth.

Ask any recent Browns player or Browns fan how much they like the Denver Broncos' John Elway and you'll likely get "not much" as the most publishable response. Ask how much they respect him and his many abilities and a likely

SWEET REVENGE: *Guard Dan Fike congratulates Matt Bahr after the Browns' kicker booted the game-winning field goal versus Denver at Cleveland Stadium in 1989. After AFC title-game losses in 1986 and '87, and a regular-season defeat in '88, the Browns had finally beaten their longtime nemesis.*

answer could be "plenty." In the 1980s, the rivalry between the Browns and the Broncos was as intense as the Browns vs. the Steelers or the Browns vs. the Bengals. Think Browns and Super Bowl and you also have to think Broncos and jinx.

More times than the team and its fans care to remember, the Broncos have dashed the Browns' high hopes, and a fair amount of the dashing has been done by Mr. Elway. Can anyone forget, or completely recover from, "the Drive"? In the 1986 AFC championship game at Cleveland, behind Bernie Kosar, the Browns were leading, 20-13. Elway started a drive in the closing minutes at his own two. With 1:47

to play and the down and distance third and 18 at the Cleveland 48, Elway connected with Mark Jackson for 20 yards and a first down. Five plays later he hit Jackson again, in the end zone, to send the game into overtime. In overtime, Elway completed several key passes to set up Rich Karlis' game-winning, heartbreaking 33-yard field goal. The final: 23-20 Denver.

The next year, in the AFC title rematch in Denver, Elway and Co. prevailed again, 38-33. This game would be remembered for "the Fumble." Browns running back Earnest Byner had been outstanding all day. He caught seven passes for 120 yards. He picked up 67 on the ground and scored twice. Kosar had been matching Elway big play for big play. Battling from 18 points down, the Browns had tied the game at 31-31. Then Elway took Denver on a five-play, 75-yard drive to go up, 38-31.

But the Browns weren't done. Kosar was Elwayian in driving the Browns goal-ward. He quickly had the team at the Broncos' eight on second down. He handed off to Byner who burst over left guard and headed for the end zone. He almost made it. At the two, he tried to knife between two Broncos defenders. Jeremiah Castille stripped him of the ball.

After a sabbatical in 1988, the Browns and Broncos were right back at it in 1989. The AFC championship was played in Mile High Stadium. To show that they were not snake-bitten, or that the rivalry was one-sided, the Browns had seemingly broken the Broncos' jinx with a 16-13 win in a regular season game when Matt Bahr slipped a field goal over the crossbar in the final two minutes to climax Kosar's 62-yard version of "the Drive."

But now it was the AFC title game again. The Broncos had a 10-0 lead at halftime. The Browns scored first in the third quarter when Kosar connected with Brian Brennan. Denver answered with two TDs, but then Cleveland came back with a pair to close to 24-21. Then Elway used a six-play, 60-yard drive to put the Broncos up, 31-21. The Browns couldn't score in the final period, but the Broncos added two field goals to make the final, bitter score, 37-21.

CLUTCH PLAYS: *Top: Linebackers Clay Matthews (56) and Tom Cousineau sack Bengals quarterback Turk Schonert. Left: Wide receiver Ricky Feacher cradles a critical catch. Right: Running back Kevin Mack charges past the grabbing efforts of Bengals linebacker Leo Barker.*

Winning championships in professional football has always required coaching expertise, skilled players, blue-chip draft choices, team chemistry and a healthy measure of "intensity." But to develop a consistent contender, there must also be a willingness to use all the tools available to build a winner, and that includes making trades.

From the beginning, the Browns have been willing to "pull the trigger" on major deals to improve the team. Although a few may have backfired, the fact is that some of the greatest players in team history have joined the Browns via trade. The following is a look at a few of the more memorable trades in Browns history:

ie. His start with the Browns was slow as he caught only nine passes and carried 33 times in '48. He increased his carries to 77 for 344 yards and four touchdowns in 1949.

"Dubber" really broke out in the '50s after the Browns joined the NFL. He had 104 receptions in the first three years of Cleveland's membership with that league and led the club in rushing with 492 yards in '51. Jones scored 11 touchdowns in 1950 and 12 the following year. He finished his career in 1955.

1953: The largest trade in NFL history saw the Browns send 10 players to the Baltimore Colts in exchange for five. It might have appeared the Browns were being shortchanged, but one of the men they received was Mike McCormack. The Browns acquired McCorma-

All the Right Moves

By Steve Byrne

1948: Paul Brown was looking for a defensive back in 1948 to replace Don Greenwood. He decided a star defensive halfback for the Brooklyn Dodgers, William (Dub) Jones, was the guy he wanted. The price to get Jones was considered high – the draft rights to Michigan All-America halfback Bob Chappuis. But Paul Brown was never one to sign a player simply because he was a big name. The Browns' coach was more than willing to give Chappuis to Brooklyn for Jones.

Chappuis played only one season for the Dodgers. Jones, on the other hand, played eight for the Browns (1948-55). Oddly, it was not on defense. Jones played in the secondary through the '48 preseason, but was shifted to offensive halfback when the regular season began.

It still ranks as one of the best deals the Browns ever made. Jones was skilled as both a ball carrier and pass catcher, providing an ideal complement to Dante Lavelli and Mac Speed-

ck, defensive tackle Don Colo, linebacker Tom Catlin, guard Herschel Forester and halfback John Petitbon in exchange for quarterback Harry Agganis, defensive backs Don Shula, Bert Rechichar and Carl Taseff, ends Art Spinney and Gern Nagler, guards Ed Sharkey and Elmer Wilhoite, and tackles Stew Sheetz and Rich Batten.

The trade was beneficial to both teams. The Colts were opening their first season in Baltimore after the remains of the defunct Dallas Texans were relocated there. (The previous Colts franchise had disbanded after the 1950 season.) The "new" Colts needed new players. Rechichar, Taseff and Spinney became starters on Baltimore's NFL title teams of 1958-59.

Meanwhile, the Browns were rebuilding an aging roster in the midst of their 10-year run of title-game trips. McCormack, Colo, Catlin and Forester became starters over the next several seasons.

ROLE REVERSAL: *Dub Jones was acquired in 1948 by Paul Brown as a defensive back. But after switching positions to halfback-receiver, Jones caught a few opposing defensive backs out of position (above) during his eight-year Browns career.*

McCormack was a member of the New York Yanks as a rookie in 1951, then spent two years in the military before succeeding the retired Bill Willis at defensive middle guard in 1954. In 1955, he took over for John Sandusky at right offensive tackle, remaining there until his retirement in 1962. McCormack made the Pro Bowl six times, once with the Yanks and five times with the Browns. He was elected to the Pro Football Hall of Fame in 1984.

1962: It looked like a simple swap of quarterbacks. Five-year veteran Milt Plum, who was not happy with the Browns and vice versa, was traded to Detroit for Jim Ninowski, the Lions' starter. Ninowski had been Plum's backup in 1958 and '59, but won out over Earl Morrall for the Lions' job in 1960-61. He was expected to return to Cleveland as a starter.

But a separated shoulder and broken collarbone Ninowski suffered in the seventh game of the 1962 season made the Browns turn the job over to Frank Ryan, who was acquired from the Rams as quarterback insurance in the event Len Dawson jumped to the AFL. (He did.)

Ninowski never got his job back. Ryan, who had backed up Bill Wade for three seasons and

Zeke Bratkowski for one in Los Angeles from 1958-61, became No. 1 in Cleveland through 1967, guiding the Browns' offense through five winning seasons and the 1964 NFL title.

1964: There wasn't much more that Dick Modzelewski could do for the New York Giants. He had been a starting defensive tackle on the Giants teams that won the Eastern Conference six times over an eight-year stretch from 1956-63. But Head Coach Allie Sherman was in a housecleaning mood in 1964, particularly with regard to his aging defense.

The Browns, on the other hand, had a talented, but inconsistent defense that needed someone to show their youngsters how to win. Modzelewski, 33, was the one and the Browns did not care about his age. "Mo" was a winner.

Modzelewski, acquired for receiver Bobby Crespino, was originally to be a swingman, but an injury to Frank Parker forced Head Coach Blanton Collier to use him full-time. It paid off. Not only did Modzelewski hold his own in 1964, but he was credited with helping the development of the other starting defensive tackle, young Jim Kanicki, and with instilling a winning spirit so vital over the course of that championship season.

1971: One of the better trades the Browns ever made sent a native Clevelander to Chicago so the club could draft a native Chicagoan. Doug Dieken, who grew up in the Chicago suburb of Streator, Ill., was an All-Big Ten tight end at the University of Illinois. He was drafted in Round 6 of the 1971 draft, after the Browns acquired the pick from the Bears for wide receiver Eppie Barney, a two-year veteran and a graduate of Cleveland's Collinwood High School. Barney never played for the Bears. Dieken was switched to offensive left tackle in 1971 and held the job through '84, setting team records for consecutive games (203) and consective starts (194).

1978: Mike Phipps, the Browns' top draft pick in 1970, never became the star quarterback everyone thought he would be. So when Brian Sipe took over early in 1976 and proved his abilities, Phipps became expendable.

He was traded to the Bears in 1977 for their first-round draft pick in 1978. The Browns then traded that selection and a fourth-rounder from Washington to Los Angeles for the Rams' No. 1 draft choice. They used it to take Alabama wide receiver Ozzie Newsome.

Newsome played for the Browns for 13 seasons and finished first on the club's all-time list of receptions (662) and yards (7,980). Moved to tight end in the NFL, Newsome was a three-time Pro Bowl choice. Phipps played five seasons with the Bears, but only one as a starter (1979).

1979-80: The Kardiac Kids were not just Brian Sipe, Doug Dieken, Mike Pruitt and the other veterans who had been drafted by the Browns in the 1970s. Many of the players who helped Cleveland to the 1980 AFC Central title had been groomed in other organizations. Two of them, defensive end Lyle Alzado and guard Joe DeLamielleure, had been perennial All-Pros elsewhere. Alzado was All-Pro in 1977 and '78 for the Denver Broncos and DeLamielleure made it five times with the Buffalo Bills.

Alzado was acquired in 1979 for second- and third-round draft choices and tied Jerry Sherk for the team lead in sacks his first season with 10 1/2. He played three seasons with the Browns and registered 28 sacks.

DeLamielleure also cost the Browns future draft choices in Rounds 2 and 3 when they traded for him in training camp of 1980. He became a starter in Game 4 and ended the season being named to his sixth straight Pro Bowl.

1984-85: The Browns went to extremes in the supplemental draft two years in a row and landed two players who were instrumental in the club making the playoffs five consecutive years and winning four AFC Central titles. In each case the team had to swing a deal to get their man. The first blockbuster came in 1984, when the Browns gave the Chicago Bears their last four draft choices, in rounds 9-12, for the Bears' choices in the supplemental draft. They used it to get Kevin Mack with their first pick.

Mack, a slashing runner who played for the Los Angeles Express in the United States Football League in 1984, joined the Browns on Feb. 1, 1985, the day after being waived by the Express. He went on to play nine seasons with the Browns and lead them in rushing six times. In 1985, his rookie year, Mack gained 1,104 yards on 222 attempts (five yards per carry). Entering 1995, he was fifth on the Browns' list with 5,123 yards rushing and 54 touchdowns in his career.

In 1985, the Browns gave the Buffalo Bills a ton to land quarterback Bernie Kosar from the University of Miami. Kosar said that he would leave Miami after his junior year of eligibility if he could play for the Browns, the team he followed as a youth in Boardman, Ohio. The Bills had the first choice and were likewise in need of quarterbacking. They held the rights to Kosar's Hurricanes predecessor, Jim Kelly, but Kelly was playing for Houston of the USFL.

To bring Kosar to Cleveland, the Browns gave Buffalo their top draft picks in 1985 and '86, a third-round selection in '85 and a sixth-round choice in '86. Kosar led the Browns in passing seven of his nine years with the team. He led the NFL in completion percentage in 1987 (62 percent) and had the best quarterback rating in the AFC (95.4).

NOT BILLED: *Bernie Kosar could have been the quarterback to lead Buffalo to four Super Bowls. The Browns, however, sent four draft choices to the Bills in 1985 to acquire Kosar in the supplemental draft.*

Actor, comedian and Browns fan Martin Mull drove to his favorite pizza place near his home in Los Angeles one evening in the summer of 1995. He walked through the door, ordered his dinner and was about to reach into his wallet to pay when a voice from behind the counter interrupted. "How do you think we did in the draft?" the voice begged to know.

"The guy was a huge Browns fan, and he wanted to know what I thought about the draft," Mull said. "I ended up standing there in Los Angeles for quite some time

By Mark Craig

The Fans

talking to a guy I didn't even know about the relative merits of the Cleveland Browns' draft."

Mull might be the Browns' most recognizable fan. A native of Cleveland suburb North Ridgeville and a former place-kicker at nearby North Olmsted High School, Mull grew up a Browns fan. He savors that love today, even though he's moved away and become a successful actor-comedian.

"The thing that attracted me to the Browns and still reminds me of my boyhood hasn't changed over the years," Mull said. "The Browns haven't gone uptown. There's a certain stainless-steel feel about teams like the Cowboys and 49ers. But the Browns are still the real McCoy."

Like most Browns fans, Mull hates artificial turf and domed stadiums. He doesn't care for pre-game and halftime foolishness, and probably doesn't object to the fact the Browns are one of only two teams (Pittsburgh being the other) that do not have cheerleaders.

Mull isn't the only southern Californian who loves the Browns. Of the 160 Browns Backers organizations, the southern California chapter tops the list with more than 3,000 members.

"If you go into a lot of the bars out here, they have the Browns' games piped in on TV," Mull said. "Most of the time, the games start at 10 o'clock in the morning. And if you get there at 10, you can't find a place to sit."

Mull said that Californians see a special quality in the Browns that they do not see around them every day.

"There's a certain warmth and a camaraderie and decency of life that exists in Ohio that doesn't really exist out here," Mull said. "The Browns are a shining example of something a lot of us can hang our memories on. When they come to town, you just run for it."

Mull is not the only celebrity who loves the Browns. Baseball's all-time home-run king Hank Aaron is an avid Browns fan. He grew up watching the Browns' national television network, and admired the Browns for being the first All-America Football Conference team to sign black players.

Aaron admits to showing up one Sunday afternoon in the "Dawg Pound," which until the mid-1980s was simply known as the bleacher seats at the open end of Cleveland Stadium. Aaron said he wore a disguise and told no one who he was.

As the Browns were beginning to come out of their four-year non-playoff slumber in 1994, Aaron could sense the Browns' turnaround from 7-9 in 1993 to 11-5 in '94.

"I live and die with the Browns every year," he is quoted as saying in the 1994 Browns media guide. "They're going to come back, you watch."

Mull and Aaron certainly aren't the typical Browns fan. The typical Browns fan is more like Wooster, Ohio's Vince Erwin, one of the first "Dawg Pound" fans to pull on a dog mask and bark for the cameras.

Erwin is in his '30s, has a wife named Lisa and three young children: Logan, Meghan and Cooper. On a typical fall Sunday, Erwin gets out of bed at 4 a.m. and

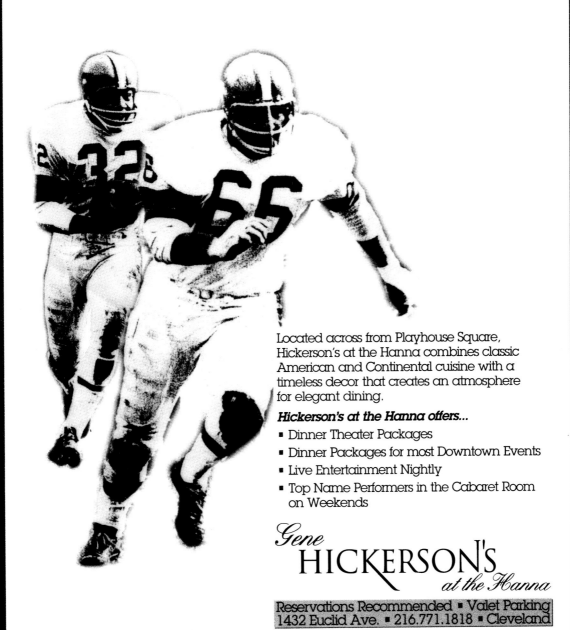

Browns fans are everywhere, including Tampa Stadium in 1989. More than 800 watched Lawyer Tillman score this TD.

four-year stretch (1991-94) of road games to Indianapolis, the Browns had a hard time checking into their hotel because the lobby was filled with boisterous Browns fans.

"I belong to the Wayne County-Holmes County Browns Backers, and there's 225 of us," Erwin said. "Every year, we get together with a lot of the other Browns Backers organizations and go to one road game.

"In 1989, we went to Tampa Bay, and it was the most unbelievable thing I've ever seen," Erwin remembered. "There were 800 people in our group. We started out in a park near the stadium. We left for the game and as we passed people, they began packing up their tailgate parties and joining us. By the time we got to the stadium, I swear there were 3,000 of us walking together. They had to block off the traffic for a long time so we could get to the stadium."

According to the Browns' management, there are more than 55,000 members in the 160 Browns Backers organizations throughout the world. There are two chapters in California, two in Texas and one based in, believe it or not, Germany. "It's gotten to the point where we sort of have to hide on the road," Byrne said. "It can get pretty wild no matter where we go."

have had fewer fan control problems as the base of season tickets has grown in the Dawg Pound. In 1985, only 2,000 of the 10,000 seats in the Dawg Pound belonged to season-ticket holders. By 1993, that number had grown to 6,000. "It's not the season-ticket holders you have to worry about," Byrne said. "They take care of themselves."

The players in the 1980s and '90s have grown attached to the fans in the Dawg Pound. "I know a lot of people who meet you and the first thing they say is, 'Hey, I'm a season-ticket holder, and you know what? I'm in the Dawg Pound,'" said Browns running back Leroy Hoard. "Forget that those are the worst seats to watch a game. The fans don't care. They're in the Pound."

Occasionally, the Dawg Pound travels with the Browns. Erwin and fans like him often show up on the road dressed in their game-day outfits. In 1991, the Browns beat the Chargers in San Diego in overtime as thousands of Browns fans roared throughout Jack Murphy Stadium. And during a

Browns fans are dedicated and they always have been, going back to the early days when large crowds would pack Cleveland Stadium to watch the Browns dominate the All-America Football Conference. Prior to the 1995 season, there had been 65 crowds in excess of 80,000 for Browns games in Cleveland Stadium. Today's seating capacity is 78,512.

Even when Browns fans can't be there in person, they're still dedicated watchers. Erwin, for instance, remembers the time when he almost missed a Browns game. He shudders at the thought. "On Nov. 22, 1987, my first child was born," Erwin said. "The Browns played in Houston that day. My wife had the baby and then we watched the Browns on TV in the recovery room. It was a good game, too." (The Browns won 40-7.)

During the spring of 1995, Erwin was thrilled when the Browns used him in a TV

The bond between the Browns and their fans is never more evident than after a touchdown near the Dawg Pound. Receiver Webster Slaughter celebrates with Pounders after a TD catch in the late '80s.

3 DOWN 11 TO GO BALL ON 47 PITT | 88 RUSH / 106 PASS / 1 TURNOV

commercial to promote season-ticket sales. Erwin, wearing his famous mask, appeared in the commercial with Mull, Browns Head Coach Bill Belichick, Leroy Hoard, linebacker Pepper Johnson and quarterback Vinny Testaverde. "I love the Browns," Erwin said. "They're a meat-and-potatoes team from the old era of pro football. They're a blue-collar team in a blue-collar town."

Players over the years have appreciated the support people like Erwin have provided. Wide receiver Paul Warfield once said one of his most memorable moments in sports was the time he received a standing ovation from the 72,070 fans in Cleveland Stadium before a Monday night game in 1973. And that's saying something considering Warfield played on the Browns' 1964 NFL championship team, back-to-back Super Bowl champions in Miami and was enshrined in the Pro Football Hall of Fame.

Warfield, a native of nearby Warren, Ohio, was playing for Miami that Monday night in 1973. It was his first game in the Stadium since the Browns traded him in 1970 for the draft choice that allowed the Browns to pick quarterback Mike Phipps.

In 1993, Browns rookie center Steve Everitt looked around Cleveland Stadium and was amazed at the energy that poured out of the stands and onto the field. And Everitt played college football at the University of Michigan, a school that routinely plays its home games in front of capacity crowds of 105,000 fans.

"Michigan has a great crowd, but this crowd is wild," Everitt said. "The noise level isn't even close. It's crazy here. I'm going to like playing in this place."

Just how loud would Cleveland Stadium get if the Browns were to host an AFC championship game, and win it? "I think not only would the Stadium go crazy, but the entire country would go absolutely nuts," Erwin said. "It'd be even bigger than what the Indians are doing now (in 1995)."

Mull gets excited at the mere mention of the words Super Bowl champions and Browns. "If that were to happen, I think I would have to go jump off a bridge. There would be nothing left to live for," he said. "OK, so I wouldn't jump off a bridge. No, I guess the minute that happens, the first thing I'll think of is repeat. Then three-peat. Then ..."

Game Time
At Cleveland Stadium

Familiar action, past and present, that makes Cleveland Browns football one of the great traditions of professional sports.

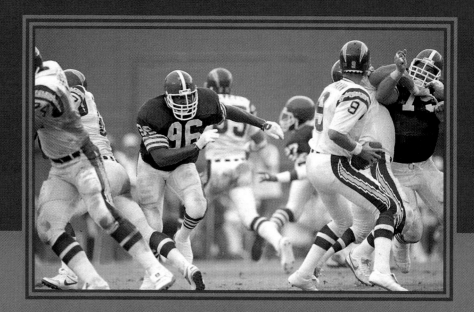

Game Time

Above Right: *Reggie Camp chases a Charger.* **Above:** *Bob Dahl blocks a Bengal.* **Right:** *Bernie Kosar sets up in the pocket against Pittsburgh.*

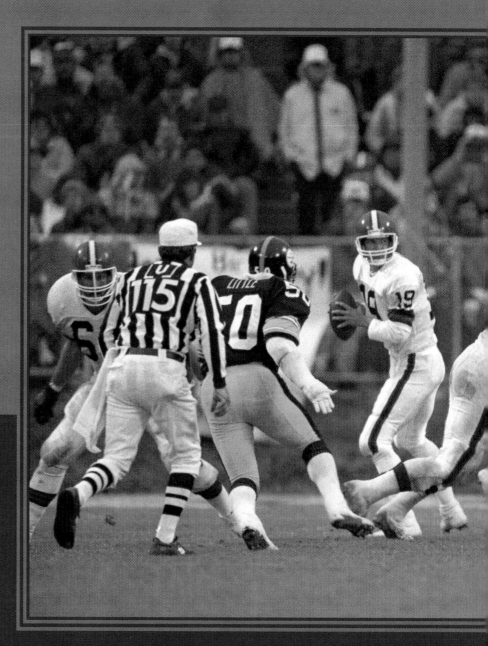

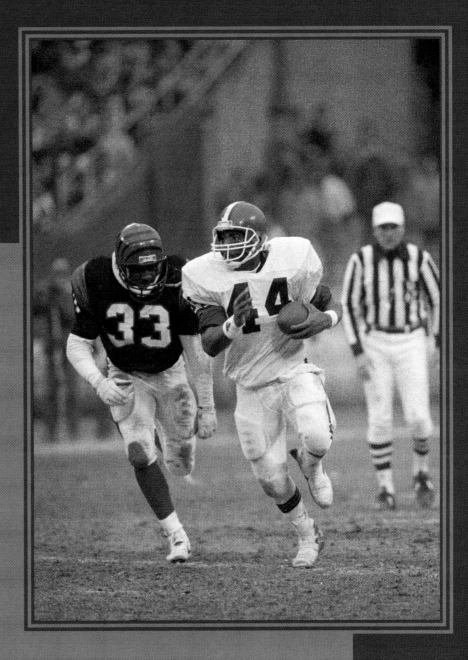

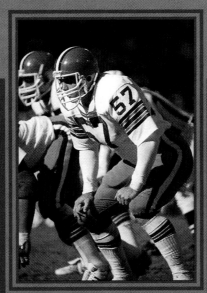

Above: *Earnest Byner sheds a Cincinnati Bengal and heads toward the closed end of the Stadium.*
Left: *Clay Matthews prepares to pursue.*

159

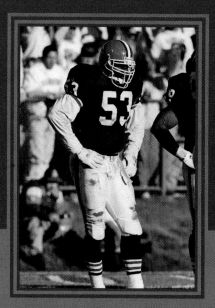

Game Time

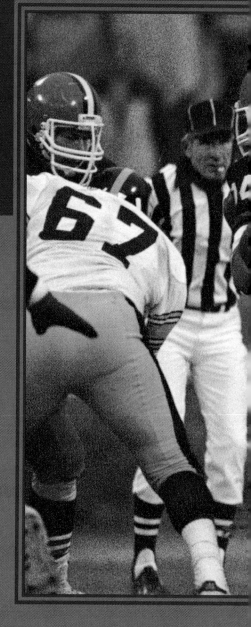

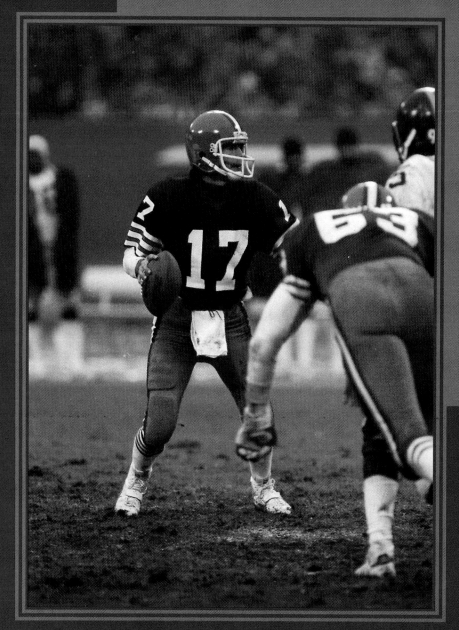

Above Left: *Pepper Johnson maintains his intensity between plays.* **Left:** *Brian Sipe spots a receiver while Cody Risien clears out a Steeler.*

160

Above: *Paul Farren (74) and Doug Dieken (73) open a hole.* **Left:** *Jim Brown sweeps left behind Gene Hickerson (left), and Dick Schafrath (77).*

Game Time

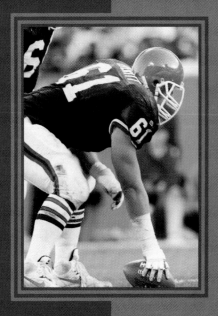

Above: *Steve Everitt sets up to snap.* **Above Right:** *Bob Golic gains ground on a Steeler.* **Right:** *Gerald "the Ice Cube" McNeil slips away from lunging Lions.*

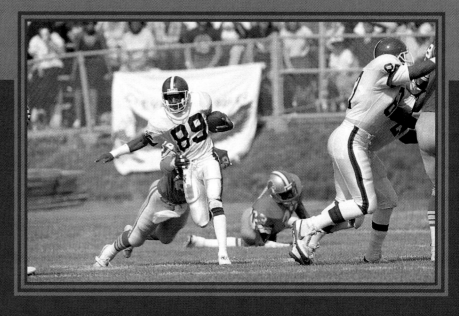

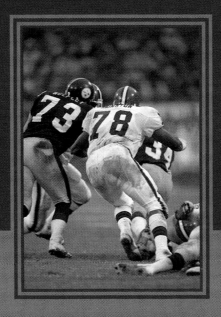

Above Right: *Carl "Big Daddy" Hairston smothers a Steeler ball carrier.* **Right:** *Ozzie Newsome outreaches a Raider to make one of his 662 career catches.*

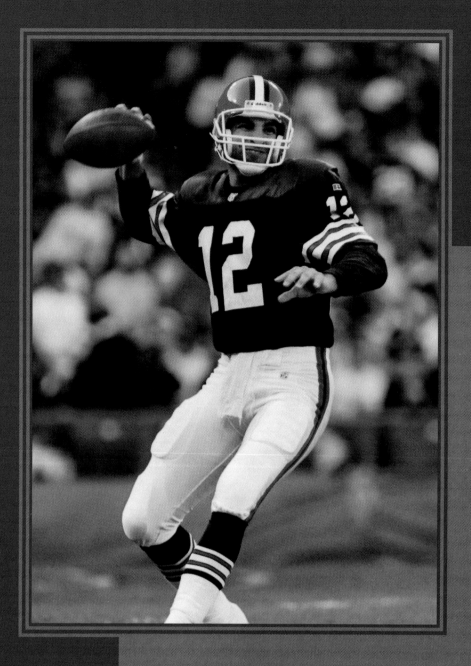

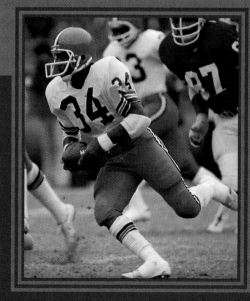

Above: *Vinny Testaverde aims downfield.* **Above Right:** *Dick Ambrose focuses on the play.* **Right:** *Greg Pruitt rolls left and outraces the Falcons.*

Game Time

The Legends & Legacies

Behind every great pro football franchise is great personnel. For the Cleveland Browns, that means a 50-year tradition of excellence, innovation, stability and longevity: both on and off the field. Browns management, coaches and players have combined to make the Browns one of the all-time leaders in victories, winning percentage and playoff appearances.

Off the field, it means management led for 35 years by Art Modell, an owner concerned not only with the success of his team, but with the long-term health and prosperity of professional football.

On the sidelines, it means just 10 head coaches in 50 seasons, seven of whom guided the Browns to the playoffs. From the legendary Paul Brown to current coach Bill Belichick, it is a record of stability unmatched in the post-World War II NFL.

On the field, great personnel means 12 Pro Football Hall of Famers, including the running back legacy of Marion Motley, Jim Brown, Bobby Mitchell and Leroy Kelly. It also means longevity at key positions such as left tackle and place-kicker. And it means a tradition of excellence on offense, defense and special teams, as Browns performers continually make contributions to the success of the team, and to the development and evolution of the game.

Jim Brown

Art Modell

By Mark Craig

Art Modell leaned across his desk and pointed to his favorite picture hanging in his spacious office in Berea, Ohio. "You see that picture?" he asked. "That's my father and his brother standing in front of the family store in 1915. My father, what a guy. He was my pal."

George Modell owned a pawnbroker store in New York City. He was a very wealthy man until Oct. 29, 1929, the day the stock market crashed. "We were wiped out," said Art Modell, who was four years old at the time. "Every nickel my father had, he lost. He lost the business. Then he had to cash in all his insurance. When he died, he left us with no insurance. He cashed it all in to keep us going."

George Modell died May 18, 1939. He left behind a wife, two daughters and 14-year-old Arthur. "He died 56 years ago last week," Modell said in May of 1995, sounding as if it had

just happened. "I still think of him quite often. He had a great sense of humor, very dapper. He had great style."

When George Modell died, Art became the man of the house. And since the family still had not recovered from the Great Depression, Art's life changed forever. "His death left a terrible scar with me," Modell said. "But I became a man overnight."

Modell dropped out of high school and went to work as an electrician's helper, cleaning out the hulls of ships in a Brooklyn shipyard. "Bethlehem Steel Shipyard, I pulled cable," Modell recalled. "I got into the hulls of those ships in 120 degrees of heat."

Meanwhile, Modell went to high school at night. After he graduated, he joined the Air Force at the age of 18 in 1943. He was stationed in Kansas where he continued the breakneck pace in an effort to support his family.

"In addition to working for the Air Force, I worked for the Chicago Rock Island Pacific Railroad from midnight to eight in the morning," Modell said. "I was an oiler. My supervisor was a man named Lou Paley. He would inspect the old journal boxes that were right over the bearings of the wheel. If the box needed oil, Lou would mark an 'X' on the box and I would oil it. We always knew from the arrivals on the blackboard that the trains coming from the West going east would be heavy because they were loaded down with wheat. That meant more pressure on the wheel, and they would need more oil. It was a fascinating experience. Absolutely fascinating."

Modell worked on the railroad for about nine months until the Air Force medical officers ordered him to stop because he was a physical wreck. "In those days, if you were able to send $28 a month home, the government would add $22 dollars to it," Modell said. "So my mother got $50 a month, plus what I was able to earn at my other jobs."

When he left the service, Modell took advantage of the G.I. Bill, enrolling in televi-

sion school in New York City. "I didn't want to go to college," Modell said. "I wanted to go into something that I might make my profession.

"Now I can't tell you what I had for breakfast yesterday, but I sure can remember things from those days. The instructor's name was Byron McKinney. We had a class of kids just out of the war, boys and girls, and we were learning television."

CLOSE BOND: *Blanton Collier (left) coached the Browns to four NFL championship games in the 1960s. "Blanton was my all-time favorite," said Modell (right). "I loved him dearly. He was a great human being and I also think one of the greatest football minds of all time."*

Television in those days was much different than it is today. In fact, there were only about 5,000 television sets in the entire New York area. Modell eventually produced some of the first daytime television in the United States. "We had 12 hours of programming a week," Modell said. "You name it, we had it. Interviews, music, dramatic vignettes, cooking, dance."

In 1954, Modell joined the advertising business and became a partner for the L.H. Hartman Company. Meanwhile, his love for professional football had begun to grow. He was one of the first New York Giants season-ticket holders in the Polo Grounds.

In late 1960, Modell heard from friend Vince Andrews, a theatrical agent and business acquaintance, that there was a pro football team for sale. Andrews had learned the Cleveland franchise was for sale from Curly Morrison, a Browns fullback from the mid-1950s. Morrison was working for the Columbia Broadcasting System at the time. When Modell discovered the team for sale was the Browns, he said, " Where do I go and who do I see?"

On March 21, 1961, Modell bought the Browns from David Jones, Ellis Ryan and Bob Gries for a then-outrageous sum of $4 million. Modell was 35 at the time.

"I was in dreamland. Wow! Owner of the Cleveland Browns," Modell said. "I went into hock. I didn't have $4 million, but the banks trusted me." Modell put up $250,000, which he borrowed with a personal signature from a bank in New York City.

When Modell first purchased the team, he said the greatest asset he bought was Head Coach Paul Brown. But by the 1962 season, the Modell-Brown relationship had deteriorated so badly that Modell fired Brown following the 1962 season.

Brown called the 1961 and '62 seasons "the darkest period of my life." He resented Modell's lack of football background, his grandiose predictions and accused him of purposely undermining his authority and trying to discredit him and his coaching methods. Modell also socialized with the players, which Brown did not approve.

"I don't think Art did anything deliberately to undermine Paul," said Chuck Heaton, who covered the Browns at the time for the *Cleveland Plain Dealer*. "Art was a fan. He wanted the players to like him."

Hal Lebovitz, a former Browns beat writer, *Plain Dealer* sports editor and a close friend of Modell's, said the Browns' owner has always been very charitable. "People like to say he's cheap, but nothing could be further from the truth. He's one of the most magnanimous own-

ers in the league," Lebovitz said. "I see the things he's done for players. He's loaned them money and helped take care of them."

Ken Coleman, the former radio and television voice of the Browns, said Modell never gets the credit he deserves when it comes to being a caring owner. "The thing I will always remember about Art was a scene one night in his office at Cleveland Stadium," Coleman said. "It was about five o'clock one evening and he was in his office alone. I was down at the stadium to cover the Indians game that night and I walked into Art's office just to say hello, and he was sitting at his desk crying.

"I looked at him and I said, 'What is going on here? What's the matter?' He said I just got a call from the College All-Star camp and they told me Ernie Davis has leukemia. Art had been negotiating Ernie's contract and had become very close and friendly with Ernie and his family. Arthur wasn't crying that day because he had just lost a running back. He cried because he cared about the guy."

Davis, a big fullback who broke most of Jim Brown's records at Syracuse, never played for the Browns after they acquired his rights in a trade with Washington in 1962. The Browns gave up future Hall of Famer Bobby Mitchell and their second first-round draft pick, running back Leroy Jackson, for Davis, who was the first pick in the draft that year. Some argue Davis' condition is what caused Modell to fire Brown. Modell, on the advice he said he got from the doctors who were treating Davis, felt Davis should have suited up if for nothing more than to help his morale.

Brown, on the advice of his medical consultants, refused to play Davis out of fear that an injury would worsen Davis' condition. Brown, however, won the standoff and later said his relationship with Modell went into a "deep freeze" from that point.

Modell still says that firing Paul Brown was "the most unpleasant task of my entire life." Although Brown's bitterness toward Modell softened through the years, it never totally disappeared. "It was a terrible

When discussing the history of the Cleveland Browns, the various eras comprising their first 50 years are defined by the head coaches who guided them through those eras. First there was Paul Brown — the organizer, innovator, taskmaster and Hall of Famer — who took the team to 11 title games in the first 12 seasons of his 17-year tenure. Then there was Blanton

Head Coaches

By Mark Craig

Collier, Brown's longtime former assistant who calmly led the team to four more title games in the 1960s. Later there was Sam Rutigliano and Marty Schottenheimer, the successful guiding forces behind the Kardiac Kids and the Kosar-led contenders, respectively, of the 1980s. In 1995, there is Bill Belichick, the most recent man in charge of pursuing the Super Bowl.

In the midst of their 50th season in 1995, the Browns have employed only 10 head coaches. And for most of those seasons, the words "stability," "longevity" and "success" could be applied to the team's coaching fraternity. It all began with Paul Brown.

By the fall of 1948, the Browns were the ill-respected All-America Football Conference champions. It would take another two years before they were able to reach into the hearts of

Coach Greasy Neale's Philadelphia Eagles and rip out the NFL's respect. To some, that might have seemed like an impossible dream in 1948. But to Paul Brown, it was a reality for which he had already begun planning.

One of pro football's great visionaries, Brown not only knew the AAFC-NFL merger was imminent, he knew which team the NFL would throw at the Browns once they joined the established league.

"Paul would say to us in those early days, 'We'll be so good, we'll make 'em take us,'" said former Browns right guard Lin Houston in a May 1995 interview. "And by God, that's what happened."

Houston, an original Brown who played from 1946-53, died at age 74 at his Canton, Ohio, home in September 1995, eight days before the 45th anniversary of the Browns-Eagles matchup on Sept. 16, 1950.

The Browns went 52-4-3 and won all four AAFC titles from 1946-49. Meanwhile, off the field, Brown already had his eyes fixed on Philadelphia. The Eagles won the NFL title in 1948 and 1949. Brown had studied them every step of the way. He had scouts at their games, he analyzed films of their games, and even went so far as to work on the Eagles in practice as early as 1948.

Brown was leaving nothing to chance. His team had been taunted and teased relentlessly for playing in the "inferior league," and for its wide-open style of offense. Even NFL Commissioner Bert Bell had joined in the criticism.

"This was a league that was laughed at by the NFL for four years," said Joe Horrigan, curator at the Pro Football Hall of Fame in Canton. "The NFL sort of patted them on the head and said, 'Go get a ball and we'll play you.'" Brown's rage burned inside all the while. But on the outside, he was cool as usual.

"Paul was smart," Otto Graham remembers. "He never said a word. He'd just pin all those negative articles on the bulletin board so we had a chance to read them every day."

When Brown discovered his team would open its first NFL season in Philadelphia, he wrote letters to each of his players. He told them to come into training camp in shape, and explained why. "When we found out we were playing the Eagles in that first game in Philadelphia, everybody said we'd get beat 40-0," Houston said. "We said the heck we will."

In May of '95, Houston smiled at the memory of that Saturday night in 1950. He still wore the NFL championship ring he earned in the Browns' 30-28 win over the Rams that season, but it's the stunning 35-10 rout of the Eagles that he remembered most.

"If you ever saw a personality fit a situation perfectly, it was Paul Brown and that game," Houston said. "He had us so high for that game. I don't think any team in the country, as good as there ever was, would have beaten us that night. I had never seen perfection until that game, or after that game. But in that game, it was perfection."

Graham agrees. "I guarantee no team was ever, ever more emotionally ready for a football game than we were that day," said Graham, whose passes to Dante Lavelli, Mac Speedie, Dub Jones and Rex Bumgardner frustrated the famed "Eagle Defense" for three quarters while setting the stage for powerful fullback Marion Motley to grind out the final quarter.

"After hearing everyone bad-mouth us for four years, we would have played those guys for a keg of beer, or in my case a chocolate milkshake," Graham added. "We just wanted to prove we were a good football team."

After the game, Greasy Neale was less than gracious in his remarks on the Browns. Steve Van Buren, the NFL's leading rusher in 1945 and 1947-49, missed the game with a foot injury, and speedy halfback Bosh Pritchard was out as well. "Why, all [the Browns] do is pass and trap," Neale said. "They're like a basketball team the way they throw the ball around."

Brown loved it, especially when Bell came into the Browns' dressing room after the game and called the Browns "the greatest team ever to play the game." In his autobiography, *PB:*

The Paul Brown Story, Brown wrote, "I knew we had embarrassed the National League, and I was quite pleased."

Brown led the Browns to another six NFL title games after the 1950 season, winning two more before being fired by owner Art Modell following the 1962 season. His record with the Browns was 167-53-8 (.759), including records of 14-0 in 1948 and 11-1 in 1951 and 1953. Brown's only losing season in 17 years with the Browns was 1956 (5-7).

"Paul Brown took a part of what America was all about at the time and capitalized on it," Horrigan said. "He took a lot of young, disci-

Paul Brown
1946-62

Brown taught new strategies that overwhelmed the AAFC and defeated the champion Philadelphia Eagles in the Browns' first-ever NFL game in 1950.

SIDELINE SCENE: *Paul Brown watched his team win four straight AAFC championships, including the 1947 title (above) over the New York Yankees, 14-3, in Yankee Stadium.*

plined men who were goal and task oriented, most of whom had been in the service, and won a lot of games with his structure and preparation."

Brown was the first to hire a full-time, year-round coaching staff and the first to use notebooks and classroom techniques extensively. He was the first to use intelligence tests and the first to do statistical film-clip studies and grade his players from individual film clips.

"George Halas was a real taskmaster and a big believer in game film before Brown was, but Brown brought classroom to the game of football in the strictest sense," Horrigan said. "Like the great ones, Paul took a lot of existing ideas and retooled and improved on them."

Brown also invented the first single-bar face mask and was the first to create the messenger-guard system so he could call plays from the sidelines. He also invented or refined many of the standard plays in today's game, such as the screen pass, the draw and the trap plays.

"Paul Brown could anticipate the answer before you asked the question," said Houston, who was with Brown at Massillon Washington High School, Ohio State and the Browns. "He was just that kind of guy."

Brown tried to instill that quality in his players. Each year, he made his players write out their assignments and keep them in a notebook. The notebook then became a player's most treasured possession, if he knew what was good for him.

Sportswriter Hal Lebovitz remembers the day punter/wide receiver Horace Gillom didn't have his notebook in order: "Paul was very tough and he'd look at you steely-eyed," said Lebovitz, who was sports editor of the *Cleveland Plain Dealer* at the time. "He looked at Gillom and said, 'Horace, you're like an apple on a tree. You get too ripe, you'll fall off.'"

Ken Coleman was hired to do the Browns' radio play-by-play in 1952. Brown was the man who hired him, and the man who told him what his duties would be.

"Part of my contract said I had to be at Hiram College and stay there for the entire training camp," Coleman said. "I had complete access to all the coaches meetings, and I'll never forget the detail and sophistication that Paul Brown brought to the game."

Coleman also remembers the day Brown took his knack for detail to an unheard of level. "During his opening day speech at Hiram, he said, 'Just so you know, since we're using pencils, the pencil sharpeners are located by rooms 102, 125, 155, whatever,'" Coleman said. "He had gone down the halls to see where the pencil sharpeners were."

There was nothing the Browns did that Paul Brown didn't have a hand in. He even distributed the players' game tickets because he didn't want the wives and girlfriends sitting next to each other.

"We had great chemistry on our team, and Paul wouldn't let anything get in the way of that," Graham said. "We'd get two tickets for each game, and they were scattered all over the stadium because he didn't want Lavelli's wife or Speedie's wife sitting up there with my wife complaining because I wasn't throwing the ball to their husbands."

Brown's policies began to rub some players the wrong way as his tenure reached the 1960s. That, coupled with his crumbling relationship with Modell, led to his firing.

Wide receiver Gary Collins, a rookie in Brown's final season, said he was one of the players who felt Brown was tough, but fair with the players. "He's probably what's lacking in today's world across the board," Collins said. "He demanded discipline in the job and discipline in the family."

Like Houston, former Browns cornerback Tommy James first met Brown at Massillon, where Brown posted an 80-8-2 record and outscored opponents 3,202-339 from 1932-40. "I was 14 years old and I looked at him in total awe," said James, who also played for Brown at Ohio State. "Sometimes you absolutely hated him. But you always respected him."

Chuck Heaton covered the Browns either part-time or full-time from their inception in

1946 until 1992. He said Brown was the most cooperative coach with the media the team has ever had.

Horrigan also points out that Brown doesn't get the credit he deserves for signing the AAFC's first black players, Hall of Famers Marion Motley and Bill Willis, in 1946. That was the year before Jackie Robinson broke the color barrier in major league baseball, and only a month after the Rams made Kenny Washington and Woody Strode the first black NFL players since the Chicago Cardinals' Joe Lillard and the Pittsburgh Pirates' Ray Kemp played in 1933.

"Paul Brown's willingness and open-mindedness to invite Bill Willis and Marion Motley

A PRO'S PRO: *Paul Brown brought high professional standards to the AAFC and the NFL, both on and off the field. His players were taught in a classroom setting (above) and abided by a strict dress code.*

to what was then an all-white AAFC was quite a risk," said Horrigan. "I think lost in the positive results of that move are the admirable risks Paul Brown took to bring them into the league."

Brown, however, was a remarkable judge of talent, and there was no doubt Motley and Willis were talented players. And so was Gillom, another black player, who came to the Browns in 1947. Brown also wanted to surround himself with good people, and knew Motley, Willis and Gillom would be able to

INNOVATOR: *Paul Brown's many inventions included the single-bar face mask, devised for Otto Graham (left) in 1953. The first version was a narrow plastic bar, but other styles were tested such as the one above.*

handle the challenge awaiting them in each AAFC city.

"Paul ran a high-class organization," Graham said. "He surrounded himself with high-class coaches. If a guy was a drunk or chased women, Paul didn't want him. And when it came to the players, he changed the image there too. He changed it from the big potbellied guys with big black cigars to more like a college team."

Brown wasn't an outstanding athlete, but as usual he got the most out of what he had. Born Sept. 7, 1908 in Norwalk, Ohio, Brown moved to Massillon with his family when he was 12. Despite never weighing more than 120 pounds, Brown quarterbacked the Tigers two straight

years. He enrolled at Ohio State, but transferred to Miami University (of Ohio) when it became obvious he wasn't going to play for the Buckeyes. He spent two years as an above average passer and good runner for Miami.

When he returned to Massillon as head coach and athletic director, Brown rebuilt Massillon's sports teams. His last six football teams were a combined 58-1-1 with six straight Ohio state titles. His 1940 team, arguably the best in school history, was 10-0 and outscored its opponents 477-6.

Brown then moved on to Ohio State, where he was 18-8-1 from 1941-43. His 1942 team became national champions after going 9-1.

In 1944, Brown enlisted in the Navy. He became a lieutenant and was appointed athletic officer at the Great Lakes Naval Training Center outside Chicago. As head coach of the football team, he went 15-5-2 from 1944-45. His 1945 team, featuring Motley at running back, upset Notre Dame, 39-7.

Five years after parting with the Browns, Brown resurfaced as founder and head coach of the expansion Cincinnati Bengals. Three seasons later, in 1970, the Bengals became the first third-year expansion team ever to win a division title, the AFC Central. Brown stepped down as head coach in 1975 so he could concentrate on his duties as general manager and vice president. The Bengals reached the Super Bowl twice, losing to San Francisco both times following the 1981 and 1988 seasons.

Brown, a Hall of Fame enshrinee in 1967, experienced success every step of the way by keeping things simple and working very hard on the fundamentals. He stuck by that philosophy until he died Aug. 5, 1991 at the age of 82.

Said Graham: "Paul was a great, great teacher. He stressed repetition, repetition all the time. It wasn't anything real fancy. We ran the same plays over and over and over until we ran them perfectly. He was as good as any coach in history, not because he knew more about football. He was just better organized."

Graham originally was drafted by the Detroit Lions in 1944, but chose to become the first player ever to sign with the Browns. Sometimes, he wonders what might have been had he not chosen the Browns.

"I was very lucky to have signed with Paul Brown," Graham said. "If I had signed with Detroit, you wouldn't be calling me today. And no one would have remembered who Otto Graham was."

Blanton Collier had won 79 games in eight seasons when he walked through the door into Owner Art Modell's office one day following the 1970 season. The man who replaced Paul Brown and led the Browns to an NFL title in 1964, and to within one game of the Super Bowl in 1968 and 1969, wasn't looking for a raise. No, he was coming in to tell the owner he was going to quit.

"He came in and cried," Modell remembers. "He said, 'I hate to do this to you, but I can't do it anymore.'" Collier, 64 at the time, was partially deaf. Practices and meetings had become progressively difficult. Game day was a nightmare.

"He wasn't hard of hearing," Modell said. "He had a nerve differential problem from being too close to the recoil of a rifle during World War II. It would change the meaning of everything he heard. A word like 'joy' would come out 'toy,' or 'bad' would come out 'mad.'"

"It caused quite a bit of confusion," Modell added. "I could hardly converse with him on the phone. When I would call him, I'd have Harold Sauerbrei, my business manager who lived up the street from Blanton in Aurora, go over there and accept my call so I could convey my message to Blanton. Either that, or his wife would have to interpret for me."

Modell has traditionally not allowed wives to travel to away games. But he made an exception in Collier's case, letting Mary Collier join the team to assist her husband.

"Blanton was my all-time favorite. I loved him dearly. He was a great human being and I also think he was one of the greatest football minds of all time," Modell said. "When he was head coach at Kentucky [1954-61], he had on his staff at one time Don Shula, Chuck Knox and Bill Arnsparger. He taught each and every one what it's like to be a football coach, Shula included."

Collier was a member of Paul Brown's coaching staff from 1946 until he left for the head coaching position at the University of Kentucky in 1953. He returned in 1962 and was given his first NFL head coaching opportunity as Brown's successor in 1963. Despite working with Brown at Great Lakes Naval Training Center and with the Browns, Collier's style was dramatically different from Brown's.

"Paul had the players scared," said Hal Lebovitz. "They didn't always like him, but they respected him. Blanton was more like a sweet father to the players."

Known as a kind, gentle man and one of the great teachers of the game, Collier probably spent more time on individual instruction than

Blanton Collier
1963-70

Collier coached the Browns to four NFL championship game trips, including a victory over the Colts in '64. His 1963-65 backfield featured (left to right) RB Jim Brown, QB Frank Ryan and RB Ernie Green.

any other head coach. He was as close to the players as any coach in Browns history.

"Under Blanton, there was more freedom within the locker room, more input by the players as far as strategy," said Gary Collins, who was with the Browns from 1962-71. "You could say things. Paul was an organizer and an administrator. Blanton was a teacher."

As an assistant coach under Brown, Collier focused on defensive strategy, particularly pass defense. But he also helped refine the skills of

Nick Skorich
1971-74

quarterback Otto Graham, and developed a grading system based on the film study of each player's game-by-game performance. Each off-season, Collier would take the films home to Paris, Ky., and would analyze each player.

"Blanton was a very important man to Paul," Lebovitz said. "In fact, Paul once told me he'd rather lose his right arm than lose Blanton."

Collier's first year brought out the best in fullback Jim Brown. In 1963, Brown had 1,000 yards through eight games and finished with a then-record 1,863 in a 14-game season. The Browns were second in the Eastern Conference at 10-4, but would win the conference title four of the next seven years under Collier.

After Jim Brown dominated in 1963, Collier came back for the 1964 championship season with the team's most dangerous passing attack in years. Quarterback Frank Ryan and receivers Paul Warfield and Gary Collins frightened opponents as much as Brown.

Brown shocked the sports world in 1966 by retiring at age 30, but Collier's offense never slowed as Leroy Kelly rushed for 1,141 yards and Ryan threw an NFL-high 29 TD passes.

But in 1968, Collier benched an ineffective Ryan after the team lost two of its first three. He turned to former Steeler Bill Nelsen and the Browns won eight straight en route to the Century Division title. They advanced to the NFL championship game, but were shut out by the Baltimore Colts, 34-0.

The Browns again made it to the title game in 1969, but were defeated by the Minnesota Vikings, 27-7. Collier then coached his final team to a 7-7 finish in 1970, which was only good enough for second place behind the Cincinnati Bengals in the newly-formed Central Division of the American Football Conference.

Collier died March 22, 1983, of cancer. He was 76. Modell stayed within the organization when he replaced Collier, naming assistant Nick Skorich as head coach. Skorich had previously coached the Philadelphia Eagles to a 15-24-3 record from 1961-63.

In Cleveland, he coached the defensive line and later became offensive coordinator. Skorich lasted four seasons and posted a 30-26-2 record, including two playoff defeats. His first team in 1971 went 9-5 and won the Central Division before losing to Baltimore in the playoffs, 20-3. In 1972, Skorich directed the Browns to a second-place finish in the Central before losing a 20-14 playoff battle with the Miami Dolphins team that went 17-0 and won the Super Bowl that year.

Skorich's last two teams failed to make the playoffs, setting up a string of seven consecutive seasons without a playoff appearance for the Browns. The 1974 team went 4-10.

Doug Dieken, who played left tackle from 1971-84, was a rookie during Skorich's first season. He said he could feel the team slipping. "Nick took over an established team that had won a lot of games," Dieken said. "He had been a buddy to a lot of the players when he was an assistant, so when he became head coach, let's just say the inmates were somewhat running the prison."

Sensing the team needed more discipline, Modell turned in 1975 to Browns offensive line coach Forrest Gregg, an offensive tackle under the ultimate disciplinarian, Green Bay's Vince Lombardi. For Gregg, it was his first head coaching opportunity after only five seasons as an assistant.

"After reading Lombardi's book, *Run to Daylight*, and listening to Forrest, I was thinking it was dejavu, because some of his quotes were almost verbatim," Dieken said. "He was just a tough, tough guy."

Gregg was a rugged Texan only five years removed from the playing field. He was 6-foot-4, 240 pounds with a booming voice. And if that wasn't enough to convince the players they were in for the workouts of their lives, then all they had to do was read the part in Lombardi's book where he called Gregg, "the finest player I ever coached."

Gregg's practices were brutally demanding. And so was everything else in Browns camp from the day Gregg was hired until the day he was fired with one game left in the 1977 season. "He preached toughness and actually meanness," Dieken said. "If you talk to the Steelers, they still blame all the fights we had with them on Forrest Gregg. They think it was him teaching us some of the techniques that were ticking them off."

Gregg's first team in 1975 began at 0-9 and finished 3-11. When they were 0-8 and heading

Forrest Gregg
1975-77

to Oakland to play the powerful Raiders, Gregg was so distraught and concerned that he brought in a motivational speaker to preach to the team the power of positive thinking. "I'll never forget the speech," Dieken said. "It was, 'If you put your mind to it, you can do it too.' That was the guy's speech. The team thought it was just a little bit overdone. We lost out in Oakland, 38-17."

Gregg's demanding personality eventually came down hardest on running back Mike Pruitt, the team's 1976 No. 1 draft choice. "Mike Pruitt and Forrest didn't see eye-to-eye," Dieken remembers. "One time during a film session, he yelled out something about Mike Pruitt. Mike said something to him, and boom,

Sam
Rutigliano
1978-84

Players had a hard time escaping Gregg's disciplined ways. He had an 11 p.m. curfew not only on Saturday nights, but Thursdays and Fridays as well. "He and his wife would drive around to see if your car was in your driveway," Dieken said. "If it wasn't, he'd call you. If you weren't there, he'd fine you."

Dieken laughs about it as he looks back. "The thing is I got along with the guy," Dieken said. "But some guys, the ones who rejected discipline, had a lot of problems."

After that 3-11 season in 1975, Gregg drove the Browns to a 9-5 record in 1976. They still finished third in the AFC Central.

The Browns opened the 1977 season at 5-2, but lost five of six thereafter and Gregg was fired with one game remaining. Assistant coach Dick Modzelewski finished the season, coaching his only NFL game, a 20-19 loss in Seattle. A former Cleveland defensive tackle (1964-66), Modzelewski became the first of two ex-Browns players to eventually coach the team. One-time defensive back Jim Shofner (1958-63) became the other in 1990.

"Mo gave the best pregame speech I'd ever heard in the pros," Dieken said. "Mo was just a good old guy, and he just basically laid it out on the line, saying this is my only chance. He was almost in tears. You really wanted to go out and play for the guy."

Next, Modell went outside the organization for the first time in 1978 and gave 46-year-old New Orleans Saints assistant Sam Rutigliano his first NFL head coaching job. He was the antithesis of Gregg. An 11-year assistant who had spent most of his years on the offensive side of the ball, Rutigliano instantly became one of the team's most popular head coaches.

He was a gambler with a boundless enthusiasm and a fabulous personality. He was close to the players, and eventually formed the team's "Inner Circle" to help deal secretly with players' personal problems.

"Sam was a fun guy who made playing football a little more relaxing," Dieken said. "Plus

Forrest threw the projector across the room."

Speaking of projectors, Dieken remembers a time when Gregg had a defensive end by the name of Stan Lewis paged at Cleveland Hopkins Airport so he could retrieve a projector before cutting Lewis.

"In those days, the rookies carried the projectors," Dieken said. "We were getting ready to fly to Oakland, and back then we flew out of the terminal.

"There was a page at the airport for Stan Lewis to contact Gate 42 of United Airlines. Stan was a rookie and he used to carry a projector. He comes running up to the desk and says, 'Am I late?' They said, 'No, we just cut you, we need the projector.' It was pretty cold."

he utilized the personnel pretty well. He came up with the offensive schemes that allowed us to put all those points up on the board.

"Sam wasn't afraid. He was out there saying 'Let's throw it!,' all the way down to Red Right 88."

Red Right 88, the Brian Sipe-to-Ozzie Newsome pass that was intercepted in the end zone by Oakland Raiders defensive back Mike Davis, brought to a close the most exciting season in Browns history. The "Kardiac Kids" of 1980 finished 11-5 as they made fans come to expect breathtaking comeback victories.

The Browns defeated the Super Bowl champion Pittsburgh Steelers en route to the AFC Central Division title, but lost to Oakland, 14-12, on a bitterly cold afternoon in Cleveland on January 4, 1981. Sipe's interception in the waning moments overshadowed an NFL MVP season, as well as Rutigliano's banner year as NFL Coach of the Year.

Rutigliano never held back his feelings for the players. After Sipe threw the interception against Oakland, Rutigliano hugged him and said, "I love you Brian."

"I also remember Sam telling us over in Pittsburgh before a game that he loved us," Dieken said. "I'm sitting there thinking, 'Great. Jack Lambert will kick my teeth out, but Sam loves me.' But that's just the kind of guy Sam was."

Rutigliano's 1981 team flopped to 5-11. The 1982 squad slipped into the playoffs at 4-5 during the strike-shortened season. In 1983, Sipe's last year before jumping to the United States Football League, the Browns went 9-7 and missed the playoffs.

With five-year veteran Paul McDonald quarterbacking the team in 1984, the Browns opened the season at 1-7. A 12-9 loss in Cincinnati on Oct. 21 finally cost Rutigliano his job.

Modell then went back within the organization and gave the Browns' 41-year-old defensive coordinator, Marty Schottenheimer, his first head coaching opportunity. An emotional optimist, a devoted teacher of the game and a stickler for detail, Schottenheimer rested some-

where between the demanding Gregg and the more laid-back Rutigliano.

Schottenheimer led the Browns to a 4-4 finish in 1984 and back into the playoffs at 8-8 in 1985. Schottenheimer's defense, however, couldn't protect a 21-3 halftime lead over the Miami Dolphins in the opening round of the playoffs that year. Miami won 24-21.

With Lindy Infante, the new offensive coordinator, juicing up the offense in 1986, quarterback Bernie Kosar and the Browns scored 391 points and won the Central Division with a 12-4 mark, the Browns' best-ever NFL win total.

Unfortunately, Schottenheimer's teams could never make it past Denver in back-to-back AFC championship games after the 1986

Marty Schottenheimer
1984-88

Bud Carson *1989-90*

Jim Shofner
1990

and '87 seasons. "The Drive," John Elway's last-minute, 98-yard march through Schottenheimer's defense helped beat the Browns 23-20 in 1986. Then in 1987, "The Fumble," Earnest Byner's forced turnover at the goal line as he was going in for the tying score late in the game, eliminated the Browns 38-33 in Denver.

The next year, the Browns lost to Houston in a wild-card game in Cleveland. Afterward, Schottenheimer was asked to make changes in his coaching staff and give up his role as offensive coordinator, which he seized when Infante left for the Green Bay head coaching position.

Schottenheimer, who was roundly criticized for his play-calling in 1988, chose to resign rather than bend to Art Modell's pressure. He

left with a 46-31 record and three division titles in four full seasons. He was hired by the Kansas City Chiefs in 1988 and was 62-41-1 going into the 1995 season.

"It's sad the way Marty and the Browns broke up, it really is," Modell said. "He's a good man and a good coach."

After Schottenheimer's resignation, Modell went outside the organization and hired New York Jets assistant coach Bud Carson, a longtime NFL assistant who had never been given a head coaching opportunity despite having designed and built the Pittsburgh Steelers' "Steel Curtain" defense in the 1970s. At the time, Modell was thrilled to have landed what he called "a defensive genius."

"I have never been involved in a more exhaustive talent search for a coach," Modell said at the time. "We wanted to make sure we studied the whole field, and when we did, Carson became the clear-cut choice."

Modell also said he expected Carson to be the last head coach he would ever hire. After the team's self-proclaimed "Season from Hell" in 1990, Modell called the Carson hiring a mistake. "He's a nice man and probably one of the best defensive coordinators in history," Modell said. "But I'll stop at that."

Carson led the 1989 Browns to a Central Division championship and another AFC title game in Denver. The Broncos won easily, 37-21, touching off a streak of losing seasons that wouldn't end until the 1994 season.

Carson was fired the day after nearly 78,331 fans turned their backs and left the Browns following a 42-0 loss to Buffalo during the ninth week of the 1990 season. The Browns fell to 2-7 en route to a franchise-worst 3-13. Assistant Jim Shofner finished the season, watching the Browns lose six of seven games. "A nightmare," Modell said of the 1990 season. "An absolute nightmare."

Feeling the need to begin a complete rebuilding program, Modell went outside the organization in 1991 and gave yet another defensive coordinator his first head coaching opportunity. Bill Belichick, a 38-year-old who was coming off his second Super Bowl victory as defensive coordinator of the New York Giants, became the Browns' eighth full-time head coach.

Belichick, a painfully shy, no-nonsense coach, jumped headfirst into rebuilding the team to fit what he had seen succeed in New York. He began building a strong defense and an aggressive special teams unit. In 1995, he entered his fifth training camp with only four players remaining from the 1991 squad that went 6-10.

Belichick put together back-to-back 7-9 seasons in 1992-93, then returned the Browns to the playoffs with an 11-5 record in 1994. But Belichick's team went 0-3 against the Pittsburgh Steelers in 1994, including an embarrassing loss in Pittsburgh, 29-9, in the first-ever playoff game between the longtime rivals.

Bill Belichick
1991-95

Modell's continued confidence in Belichick was evident in May of 1995 when he predicted Belichick will become one of the NFL's "great, great" head coaches.

"I'm expecting very big things from him," Modell said. "He took this franchise when it was in an all-out tailspin and rebuilt it in a way that will last. The man is an outstanding judge of talent, a very dedicated man, and an extremely hard worker. I will be very, very disappointed if he does not become one of the great coaches this league has seen."

Otto Graham *1946-55*

Otto Graham awoke the morning of the NFL season opener in 1955 and decided he would change his style after nine championship games in nine seasons. No longer would he eat the team's bland pre-game food. And no longer would he worry himself to the point where he "had to go to the bathroom every five seconds."

After all, the Cleveland Browns needed him, not the other way around. Graham had retired following the 1954 NFL title game, and was back only because Head Coach Paul Brown said he couldn't find a suitable replacement. The normally nervous Graham was calm, and

The Browns then defeated the Los Angeles Rams in the L.A. Coliseum, 38-14, for their third NFL championship as Graham threw for two touchdowns and ran for two more. This time, at age 34, Graham retired for good.

In 1956, without Otto Graham — the first pro player Paul Brown ever signed — Cleveland went 5-7, its first losing season in team history. Brown couldn't coax Graham out of retirement a second time. The first time had been hard enough.

"When I retired in 1954, I told Paul I would come back for one more year if I had to, but I really didn't want to," Graham explained. "I promised him that if he lost a quarterback or

Quarterbacks

unusually hungry, the morning of the 1955 season opener. He bribed a waitress into bringing him "the biggest pre-game meal in history." Then he left the locker room without visiting the bathroom once. "I said to myself, 'I'm doing these guys a favor.' Why should I get all excited?" Graham recalled.

The 10-year veteran quarterback had hoped the new attitude would work, but it didn't. The Browns were smashed, 27-17, by the visiting Washington Redskins that day. "I played the worst game of my life," Graham said. "I realized that if you aren't afraid of getting the job done, you aren't going to be successful."

With the Graham of old back the following week, the Browns beat the 49ers, 38-3, en route to six straight victories, a 9-2-1 record and their 10th consecutive conference title.

somehow became shorthanded, that I would help him out."

Brown, of course, knew just how difficult it would be to replace his star quarterback. Graham had led the Browns to all four All-America Football Conference titles from 1946-49. He led them to a championship in their first NFL season, 1950, and to defeats in the NFL title games of 1951-53 before winning two more crowns in 1954 and '55.

"At the time, they had drafted a quarterback named Bob Freeman of Auburn in the third round," said Graham. "But the guy signed a contract with Paul Brown *and* the CFL [Canadian Football League]. They went to court and the CFL won."

So Brown then contacted Graham while the Browns were on a two-week preseason trip to

By Mark Craig

UNBEATABLE OFFENSE: *Graham throws past four New York Yankees defenders in a 34-21 win in Yankee Stadium in November 1948. The victory was the Browns' 14th straight during their 29-game unbeaten streak that extended from 1947-49.*

California. "Paul called to remind me of my promise," Graham recalled. "I said 'Paul, I still don't want to come back. While you're on the West Coast, try to get yourself a quarterback. When you come back, if you don't have a quarterback, I'll come back.' Years later, I finally realized Paul didn't try very hard."

When Graham retired permanently, he took with him a 114-20-4 record, plus nine All-League and five NFL Pro Bowl selections. With a delicate passing touch, a cool head, a running attack featuring Marion Motley and a receiving corps of Mac Speedie, Dub Jones and Dante

Lavelli, Graham's teams averaged nearly 28 points per game over 10 years. He finished with 1,464 completions on 2,626 attempts (55.7) for 23,584 yards and 174 TDs. He was elected to the Pro Football Hall of Fame in 1965.

"In 1946, we didn't think we would be that good, but we had a group that wanted to win," said ex-Browns guard Lin Houston in a May '95 interview, four months before his death in September. "Otto instilled the desire to win right there on the field."

Besides his leadership qualities, Graham had an uncanny knack to see the game in slow motion while playing it full speed, especially important in the Browns' innovative pass-oriented offense. An intelligent player with outstanding coordination, he picked defenses apart like a safecracker. When the National

Football League announced its 75th anniversary all-time team in 1994, Graham was on the roster with Sammy Baugh, Johnny Unitas and Joe Montana. "My wife says Joe Montana was the first quarterback whose style ever reminded her of me," Graham said. "I ran a lot, threw on the run and all that stuff. Joe was a great athlete and I was a great athlete."

Graham first met Paul Brown when Brown was the head coach at Ohio State and Graham was a single-wing tailback for Northwestern. That was in 1942. Several years later, Brown called Graham and asked him if he'd like to be the first Cleveland Browns player.

"Paul was coaching at the Great Lakes Naval Training Center and I was a Navy air corps cadet just outside of Evanston, Ill.," Graham recalled. "He told me he would give me a $1,000 bonus if I would sign right away, a two-year contract worth $7,500 and also $250 a month starting immediately. As a cadet, I was making $75 a week, so $250 a month was like finding a gold mine. The war only lasted four or five more months, but it was a heck of a deal."

Graham's only experience in the T-formation was one year at the Chapel Hill Pre-Flight School in North Carolina. "We had copied the Chicago Bears' playbook that year," Graham said. "One of our assistants was a man named Bear Bryant. Of course, no one knew him from Adam back then. I basically learned the T-formation by looking at the playbook and teaching it to myself."

Brown wanted Graham as his quarterback based on one play he had seen the quarterback make against his Buckeyes in 1942. "I was the tailback in a single-wing offense," Graham said. "On one play, I ran around left end one time, stopped and threw the ball back to the right. Paul thought that took an awful lot of ability, so he liked that."

Graham always credited his success as a quarterback in the T-formation to his basketball experience. In 1945-46, Graham played for the champion Rochester Royals of the Nation-

al Basketball League (the forerunner of the NBA). When he won the AAFC title with the Browns in 1946, he became the only player to win championships in two different professional sports in the same year.

"I've always said the best athletes in the world are basketball players," Graham said. "I was lucky to be born with more coordination than most people."

"When you talk quarterbacks, give me Otto over anyone else," said right end Dante Lavelli. "Otto doesn't own one passing record today, but all he did was win championships."

The 1956 season, the Browns' first without Graham and last with Lavelli, was disastrous

FAMILIAR FORM: *After coming out of retirement in 1955, Graham soon returned to former greatness. Following a loss to Washington in the opener, Graham led the Browns to nine wins in 11 games, including this 41-10 defeat of the Green Bay Packers in October.*

George Ratterman
1952-56

for the quarterback position. Graham's old backup, George Ratterman, started the season, but injured a knee in the fourth game against the Redskins and was lost for the year. He later retired.

Vito "Babe" Parilli was next, lasting three games before separating a shoulder. In desperation, the Browns signed free agent and former Chicago Bear Tommy O'Connell.

Under O'Connell, a former Big Ten passing champion at Illinois, the Browns won three of their final six games, but a loss to the Chicago Cardinals on the final day of the season gave the Browns their first-ever losing record.

In 1957, the Browns wanted to draft Purdue quarterback and future Hall of Famer Len Dawson, but they lost a coin flip to the Steelers,

who selected Dawson. The Browns, shut out of quarterback choices in a first round that also included Paul Hornung and John Brodie, "settled" for a guy named Jim Brown.

Ironically, the Steelers and the Browns both had shots at another Hall-of-Fame quarterback, but both rejected the talents of a young former Louisville quarterback named Johnny Unitas.

The Steelers, who had drafted Unitas in 1955, released him before the start of the season, prompting Unitas to call Paul Brown for a tryout. But Brown now had Otto Graham for another year and didn't need one more backup. The tryout request was denied, although Brown invited him to camp for '56. By then, of course, Unitas had become a Baltimore Colt on his way to winning back-to-back NFL championships in 1958 and '59.

Dawson, meanwhile, did eventually make it to Cleveland in 1960-61, but as a backup to Milt Plum, the Browns' second choice in the '57 draft. Dawson threw 28 passes as a Brown, completing 15 for 109 yards, one touchdown and three interceptions. In 1962, he moved on to the AFL's Dallas Texans, who became the Kansas City Chiefs in '63. Eventually he led the Chiefs to victory over the Minnesota Vikings in Super Bowl IV.

With Plum and O'Connell in the fold, Paul Brown held a special three-day quarterback "school" in July of '57, prior to the opening of training camp in Hiram, Ohio. Also participating were John Borton of Ohio State, Bobby Freeman of Auburn, Joe Clarke of Santa Clara and Bobby Garrett of Stanford.

Garrett, the Browns' bonus pick in the 1954 draft, had been dealt to Green Bay before the '54 season, but now was returning for a second try after Brown reacquired him in a deal that sent, among others, Babe Parilli, Carlton Massey, John Petitbon and Sam Palumbo to the Packers. By the opening of the season, however, it was back to O'Connell, backed up by Plum and Freeman.

With the Browns' 1957 offense increasingly centered upon Jim Brown, Cleveland recaptured the Eastern Conference. But O'Connell

1957 Quarterback Candidates

Left to right: Joe Clarke, John Borton, Bob Garrett, Milt Plum, Bob Freeman, Tommy O'Connell

broke an ankle in late season and Plum pulled a hamstring prior to the title game in which the Browns were beaten by Detroit, 59-14.

O'Connell retired following the season and Plum assumed full-time duties in 1958, a position he held through 1961. Plum's backup in 1958-59, Jim Ninowski, was dealt to the Lions in '60, but then was traded back to the Browns in '62 for Plum. The deal also brought to the Browns longtime defensive end Bill Glass and the former Heisman Trophy winner from Ohio State, Howard "Hopalong" Cassady.

The maturing Ninowski was considered ready to assume the full-time role, but a dislocated shoulder and fractured collarbone suffered in Game 7 versus Pittsburgh opened the gate for Frank Ryan to take over.

Ryan, acquired from the Los Angeles Rams prior to the '62 season, remained the starter in 1963 and then came into his own in 1964 with the help of an outstanding offensive line, a legend named Jim Brown and receivers Gary Collins and rookie Paul Warfield.

By 1960, quarterbacks had to deal with defenses that had evolved from the six-man lines of the 1940s and early 1950s to the 4-3-4 defenses. With the nose guard becoming a more mobile middle linebacker, defensive players like Sam Huff and Joe Schmidt had begun to get as much attention as the offensive stars.

Ryan continued in the starting role through 1967. He was intelligent, too, holding a doctorate degree in mathematics and working as an assistant professor of mathematics at Case Western Reserve University during his playing days. In 1964, Ryan led the NFL with 25 touchdown passes and then threw three more to Collins as the Browns upset the heavily-favored Baltimore Colts, 27-0, in the NFL championship game.

"I'm sure Otto Graham and Brian Sipe have all the records, but Frank did a great job in his

Frank Ryan *1962-68*

Bill Nelsen *1968-72*

Mike Phipps *1970-76*

round in 1972 certainly did. San Diego State's Brian Sipe, who was 6-1 when he stood up straight, didn't throw a pass in a game until 1974, and wasn't given the starting job with the Browns until 1976.

But in 1980, Sipe became one of the most beloved athletes in Cleveland history. The year of the "Kardiac Kids" and their last-minute victories electrified the city and stunned the NFL. It also gave the Browns an 11-5 record and their first playoff appearance since 1972.

Sipe was at the center of it all, leading the Browns past the defending Super Bowl champion Steelers in the AFC Central Division. He completed 61 percent of his passes, throwing for a team-record 4,132 yards, a team-record 30 touchdowns and only 14 interceptions in 554 attempts. He won the NFL's MVP Award.

"Brian had that special charisma, that kind of presence that assured you things would be all right," said former Browns offensive tackle Doug Dieken. "When you were down by two touchdowns, he was the guy who would be loose. He was never uptight. He'd always say, 'We got them right where we want them.'

"He also was the guy who wasn't afraid to take the chance to make the play," Dieken added. "You know how Larry Bird would throw the pass that most people wouldn't throw because they didn't think they could? Well, Brian was that way in football."

Unfortunately for Sipe, his finest season ended against the Oakland Raiders in a gray way on a dismal, bitterly cold January 4, 1981,

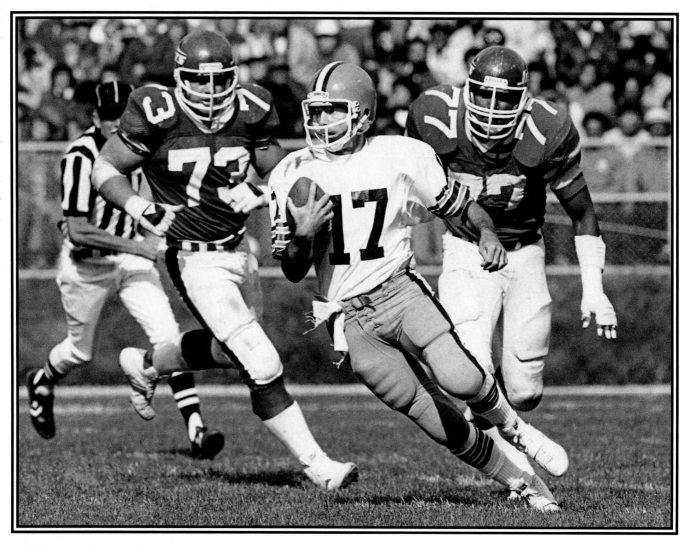

afternoon in Cleveland Stadium. It was the day the words "Red Right 88" became synonymous with the frustrations of a city and its football team. With the Browns trailing, 14-12, and well within field goal range during the playoff game's waning moments, a Sipe pass to tight end Ozzie Newsome was intercepted in the end zone by defensive back Mike Davis.

Sipe left the Browns for the United States Football League following the 1983 season. He took with him nearly every passing record in Cleveland history. In 1995, Sipe still held the Browns' NFL career records in, among many others, passing yardage (23,713), touchdowns (154), passes completed (1,944) and passes attempted (3,439).

Paul McDonald succeeded Sipe in 1984, but the Browns lost seven of their first eight and Head Coach Sam Rutigliano lost his job. McDonald lasted the season, but soon he was likewise on his way out.

That was because in 1985, Bernie Kosar Jr. basically dictated to the NFL which team he wanted to play for. And that team was the Browns, whom he had followed while growing up in nearby Boardman, Ohio.

On Jan. 15, 1985, Bernie Kosar Sr. called the NFL office for a clarification on the supplemental draft rules. On March 14, he called a news conference for his son to announce he was passing up the remaining two years of his college eligibility at the University of Miami.

On April 9, the Browns traded their first and third picks in the 1985 regular draft and their first and sixth picks the following year for Buffalo's first pick in the 1985 supplemental draft. On April 24, Kosar announced he would skip the regular draft, graduate from school early, and make himself available for the supplemental draft.

The Browns had their man. They signed him to a series of five one-year contracts, and then watched as the man who had won a national championship as a freshman at Miami helped lead them to five straight playoff appearances. The 1986, 1987 and 1989 teams all came within a game of the Super Bowl, losing to Denver each time.

The 1986 Browns team was Kosar's best. It finished at 12-4, the Browns' best mark in the NFL, as Kosar threw for 3,854 yards. A year later, he led the Browns back to the AFC championship game when he threw 22 touchdown passes and only nine interceptions as he completed an NFL-best 62 percent of his passes.

Kosar, 6-5, 215, was able to use his intelligence and excellent vision to overcome his physical deficiencies. He had slow foot speed and an awkward sidearm throwing motion. And making it tougher was the fact he played during an era in which the defensive players became both faster and bigger, as well as more specialized. Nickel and dime defensive backs, designated speed rushers and 300-pound tackles who ran sub-5.0 40-yard dashes were some of the obstacles Kosar had to overcome during his prime in Cleveland.

"Sipe and Kosar were a lot alike," said Dicken, who stepped into the radio booth as a color analyst the year after he retired in 1984. "Things happen real fast in football, but people like Brian and Bernie saw them a little slower. They were able to diagnose what people were doing. They're pretty sharp as to what was actually happening [on the field].

"If the defense was doing something unexpected, a Kosar or a Sipe could break it down, see what they were doing and do something else that worked."

Unfortunately, the end of Kosar's career in Cleveland was not as happy as the beginning. On Nov. 8, 1993, Head Coach Bill Belichick ended his rocky relationship with Kosar when he released the fan favorite.

Paul McDonald
1980-85

Kosar had lost his starting job to former college teammate and ex-Tampa Bay Buccaneer Vinny Testaverde earlier, but Testaverde was sidelined with a shoulder injury and the Browns were in first place with a 5-3 record at the time of the release. Thus for Browns fans, the timing of the release was difficult to comprehend.

"We made a move that had to be made," said Browns owner Art Modell. "I take a back-seat to nobody in my admiration for Bernie

Bernie Kosar *1985-93*

Eric Zeier *1995*

Vinny Testaverde
1993-95

Kosar. But it would have been a whole lot worse had we benched him and he sat there for the rest of the season."

The Sunday following Kosar's release, he started for the Dallas Cowboys in their 20-15 win over the Phoenix Cardinals. Troy Aikman, the Cowboys' regular starting quarterback, was sidelined with an injury.

Kosar picked up a Super Bowl ring as Aikman returned to health and led the Cowboys to the championship. Kosar then signed a two-year deal with Miami in 1994 and remained Dan Marino's backup in 1995.

After an 11-5 record in 1994 and their first playoff appearance in five years, the Browns remained committed to Testaverde for the 1995 season and provided him with ex-Falcons All-Pro wide receiver Andre Rison as a new target.

Testaverde, the 1986 Heisman Trophy winner, completed 207 of 376 (55.1) for 2,575 yards and 16 touchdowns in 1994. Dating back to '93, Testaverde had thrown at least one TD pass in 19 of his last 23 games. His most memorable performance was on Dec. 26, 1993, when he set an all-time NFL single-game record for completion percentage (91.3) when he went 21 for 23 in a 42-14 victory over the Los Angeles Rams.

Georgia's Eric Zeier, a third-round draft choice in '95, became Testaverde's backup after a productive preseason. Zeier joined the Browns as holder of 18 Southeast Conference and 67 Georgia passing records, including the SEC career mark of 11,153 yards passing, third highest all-time in the NCAA.

Training camp for the Cleveland Browns already had started by the time Jim Brown's red Corvette pulled into Hiram College in August 1957. It had been a long overnight drive from Chicago where Brown had played sparingly for a team of pass-happy ex-college seniors that lost to the defending NFL champion New York Giants in the College All-Star Game.

Running Backs

By Mark Craig

"I remember him looking more intimidating than any player I had ever seen," said Chuck Heaton, who covered the Browns for the *Cleveland Plain Dealer* at the time. "He wasn't happy that he hadn't been used much in the All-Star game, and he had driven all night to get to Hiram. Normally, the rookies were razzed a little bit by the veterans. I don't remember anyone picking on Jim when he got there."

Brown, of course, was special. And everyone could sense it from Day 1. "I had players come up to me and talk about Jim even early on in his career," said Ken Coleman, the former radio and television voice of the Browns. "They'd say, 'You know, I hope my grand kids believe me when I tell them one day that I played football with Jim Brown.'"

Brown didn't play much in his first exhibition game, a 20-10 loss in Detroit. But a week later in the Akron Rubber Bowl, Brown gave a preview of what was to come. With 26,669 fans looking on, he was spectacular in the Browns' 28-13 win.

In fact, after a dazzling 48-yard touchdown run, Head Coach Paul Brown, who always was reluctant to start first-year players, was overheard telling his rookie, "You're my fullback." Nine years later, Jim Brown stepped away from the game having never let another player start in his place.

Brown played in 118 straight games, carrying the ball 2,359 times for 12,312 yards (5.2 average) and 106 touchdowns. He also had 20 TDs receiving on 262 receptions.

Brown left the game with all of its major rushing and scoring records. He led the NFL in rushing eight of nine seasons, running for more than 1,200 yards seven times, and made the Pro Bowl all nine seasons. And at age 30, there was no doubt Brown could have continued. Coming off an NFL-MVP season in 1965 and a three-touchdown effort in the 1966 Pro Bowl, Brown retired July 14, 1966 while on the set of his movie "The Dirty Dozen" in England. Cleveland had tried to get him to report to training camp on time, but Brown would not be forced to leave the set early.

Even after his records began to be broken two and three decades later, many still consider him the greatest football player of all time. In 1979, several of the greatest running backs in history were surveyed on a variety of subjects. When asked to name the best ever, Chicago Bears Hall-of-Famer Gale Sayers said, "I've said many times, and I will always say, Jim Brown is the best — and he will still be the best long after all his records are broken."

Another Hall-of-Famer Paul Hornung of the Green Bay Packers, simply said, "…give me Jim Brown over anybody at anything."

The NFL had never seen anything like Brown. He was a powerfully built 6-foot-2, 228

THE BEST: *Jim Brown led the NFL in rushing eight of his nine seasons, gaining over 1,000 yards seven times. He led the league in touchdowns five times and recorded 58 100-yard games. He finished with 2,359 carries for 12,312 yards gained (5.2 average) and 106 rushing TDs in 118 games.*

Marion Motley *1946-53*

The Legacy of
Running
Backs

*A strong backfield has been a
Browns tradition for 50 years.
These four became Pro Football
Hall of Famers.*

Bobby Mitchell *1958-61*

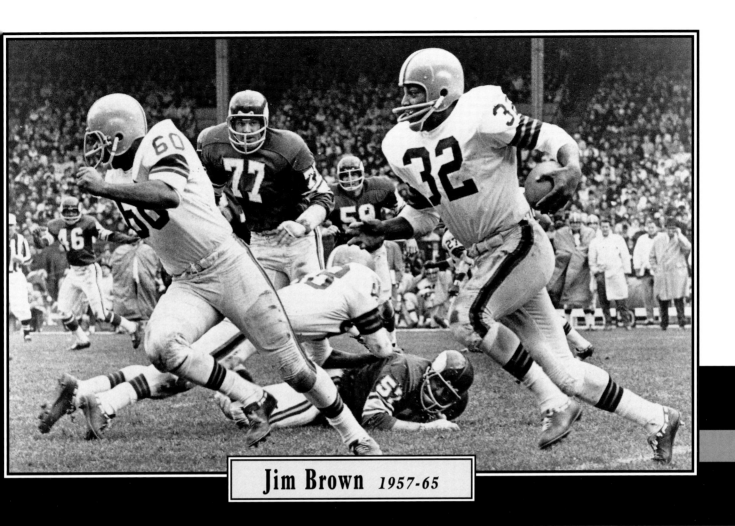

Jim Brown *1957-65*

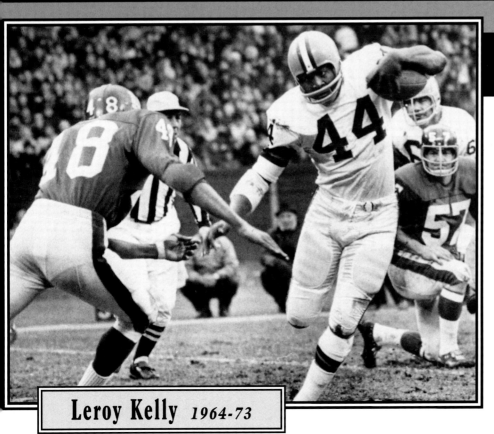

Leroy Kelly *1964-73*

football, saying he'd rather "play three straight days against the Giants, Bears and Packers than to get in the ring with those guys."

During his career, there were two things for which Brown was regularly criticized: that he was not a topflight blocker and that he did not practice hard. It upset Paul Brown, who later admitted he thought about trading Brown before the 1962 season because his attitude might have been hurting the team. Two years later, retired Browns quarterback Otto Graham said Brown should be traded because of his failure to block or fake. "The Browns will not win anything as long as Brown is in there," Graham said in the summer of 1964. "Now chew on that awhile."

The Browns, of course, went on to win the NFL title that year. They also went to the championship game in Brown's rookie season, 1957, losing to the Lions, and in his final season, 1965, losing to the Packers.

Years later, Brown answered his critics. "I was not a great blocker," he admitted. "But if I couldn't run the way I did, I would have been the best blocker going."

Brown, simply, was a devoted runner. "He would study films of the great runners, which I don't think a lot of people knew about," said Coleman, who hosted a television show with Brown during the 1960s. "I know he looked at the old Eagles running back, Steve Van Buren. And I believe he even looked at Red Grange. There were others, too, which he would look at to see what made them successful."

Rex Bumgardner
1950-52

Paul Brown wasn't looking for a fullback in that 1957 NFL draft. He wanted a quarterback. But when he lost a coin flip with Pittsburgh to determine who would make the fifth selection, Brown watched as the Steelers took their quarterback, Purdue's Len Dawson. At that point, Brown settled for the "best available" player: Jim Brown.

After Jim Brown was selected, Paul Brown signed him to a $12,000 contract and gave him a $3,000 bonus, which at the time was the most ever given to a Cleveland rookie. "He's worth it," Paul Brown said at the time.

From 1958-61, Jim Brown shared the backfield with another future Hall of Famer. Bobby Mitchell started 48 consecutive games at halfback for the Browns, scoring 38 touchdowns and gaining 2,297 yards rushing.

Also an outstanding kick returner and pass receiver, Mitchell was traded to Washington in 1962 in the deal that brought ex-Syracuse running back Ernie Davis to Cleveland. Mitchell's service duties had limited him to a game-day player only. Washington, meanwhile, was getting pressured to sign its first black player.

Davis never played a down in the NFL after learning during the week of the 1962 College All-Star game that he had leukemia. He died in May 1963. Mitchell's best years were in Washington where he played primarily as a receiver and returner through 1968. His 1,436 yards receiving in 1963 were an all-time Redskins record. Mitchell was elected to the Pro Football Hall of Fame in 1983.

the ball and got a full head of steam going."

Graham doesn't like to imagine what kind of player he would have been without Motley to block and keep defenses honest. Asked what he would have done without Motley, Graham said, "Nothing. I'd have been dead. He saved my life many times, which is good because I don't remember ever completing a pass lying flat on my back."

Brown saw what kind of player Motley was when Brown's Massillon teams played Motley's Canton McKinley teams in the 1930s. Brown's Tigers handed Motley's Bulldogs their only loss three straight seasons, but Brown developed a great admiration for Motley. Years later, with Motley in the service and Brown coaching at the Great Lakes Naval Training Center, their paths crossed again. Motley became the fullback on the team Brown used to beat Notre Dame, 39-7, in 1945.

"Marion just happened to be passing through Great Lakes one day," Horrigan said. "He had orders to go somewhere else, but Brown found out he was there and went to the commander and said he had to have Motley on his team. Motley was close to leaving. In fact, they literally went out and pulled his bags off the train."

Long after Brown retired from coaching, he called Motley the best running back he ever coached, and that included Jim Brown.

Motley's backfield mates during his eight-year Browns career included Edgar "Special Delivery" Jones, Ken Carpenter and Rex Bum-

Ernie Green *1962-68*

gardner. As Motley neared the end, Harry "Chick" Jagade saw increased playing time in 1952-53. After Motley's departure, the Browns' backfield remained in transition until Brown and Mitchell joined forces in 1958. Included in the 1954-57 mix were Billy Reynolds, Chet "the Jet" Hanulak, Maurice Bassett, Fred "Curly" Morrison, Lew Carpenter, Preston Carpenter, Ed Modzelewski and Milt Campbell.

Shortly before Jim Brown shocked the professional football world with the announcement of his retirement, he wrote Head Coach Blanton Collier a letter. It wasn't a farewell letter as much as it was a forecast of great things to come for Leroy Kelly, the Browns' third-year running back from Morgan State.

"I told Blanton he would not have to worry because he still had a great running back,"

Brown said. "Leroy was the man. He was ready."

Brown was correct. After two seasons performing as an outstanding kick returner and downfield tackler on the special teams, Kelly averaged 5.5 yards per carry as he rushed for 1,141 yards and a league-high 15 touchdowns. Only the Bears' Gale Sayers had more yards rushing that season.

Kelly followed that season with back-to-back NFL rushing titles and a league-high 120 points on 20 touchdowns in 1968. He rushed for 1,205 yards and a 5.1-yard average in 1967, followed by 1,239 yards and a 5.0-yard average in 1968. When he retired, the future Hall of Famer ranked fourth in career rushing behind

Cleo Miller
1975-82

Running behind the blocking of Joe DeLamielleure.

Mike Pruitt *1976-84*

Brown, Jim Taylor and Joe Perry. Kelly, a 6-foot, 205-pounder with the quick feet, slashing style and long strides, lasted 10 seasons and scored 90 touchdowns. He compiled 12,329 total yards and was a six-time Pro Bowler. His 7,274 rushing yards rank second to Brown on the Browns' all-time career list.

"Leroy was like a cat," said Ernie Green, the only man to start alongside both Brown and Kelly. "So was Jim, only a bigger cat. It's difficult to knock a cat off his feet. Jim and Leroy also were similar in that they had the same seriousness about their play."

After Green retired in 1968, Kelly's backfield mates included Reece Morrison, Bo Scott and Ken Brown. Not until the late 1970s would the Browns again feature a consistent running-back combination.

Kelly's three consecutive 1,100-yard seasons were even more impressive when considering he did them before the hash marks were moved in to 23 yards, one foot, nine inches in 1972. From 1966-68, only 10 NFL players broke the 1,000-yard mark and Kelly did it three times. In '72, the first year the hash marks were moved in, 10 players ran for more than 1,000 yards.

Greg Pruitt
1973-81

Kelly's career had run its course by 1973 as nagging knee problems limited his effectiveness. He was released the following year to make room for a speedy water bug-type runner named Greg Pruitt, a 1973 second-round pick from Oklahoma. Pruitt, however, didn't get

much of an opportunity to run the ball his first two years in Cleveland under Head Coach Nick Skorich.

"Nick thought I was too small," said Pruitt, whose playing size was 5-10, 190. "That was tough to take because I may have been small, but I looked down on Nick Skorich. Then when Forrest Gregg was hired in 1975, he called me at home and told me I would be getting the opportunity I had been crying for. He said be sure you're in shape, and I was."

Although the Browns went a combined 18-24 from 1975-77, "Do-It" Pruitt became one of the most exciting players in the National Football League. Before the NFL outlawed the tearaway jersey, Pruitt probably went through more No. 34 jerseys than any player in NFL history.

From 1975-77, Pruitt ran for 1,067, 1,000 and 1,086 yards.

At the height of Greg Pruitt's success, the Browns went after another Pruitt. Purdue's Mike Pruitt, no relation to Greg, was the team's first-round pick in 1976. For two-and-a-half years, Mike Pruitt was basically considered a first-round bust. "Forrest and Mike didn't see eye-to-eye," said former Browns offensive tackle Doug Dieken. "Forrest just didn't like Mike."

But Sam Rutigliano did. After taking over as head coach in 1978, he worked the 6-foot, 225-pound Pruitt into the workhorse role in a 41-20 win over Buffalo on Oct. 29, 1978. He ran for 173 yards, including a 71-yard TD run.

Prior to Pruitt-and-Pruitt, a variety of performers shared the backfield with Greg Pruitt

Kevin Mack *1985-93*

Gary Collins
WR • 1962-71

caught 85 touchdown passes and averaged 20.1 yards per catch during his career. The eight-time Pro Bowler had 427 receptions, but who knows how many he would have had if he had played in a passing offense. In Miami's 17-0 season, for instance, Warfield only caught 29 passes.

"In Super Bowl VII [a 14-7 win over Washington], we only threw the ball 11 times the whole game," Warfield said. "The next year, in Super Bowl VIII [a 24-7 win over Minnesota], we threw it only seven times and completed six. I caught five passes in those two Super Bowls, but it never bothered me. Winning was all that mattered back then."

Warfield always was a fantastic athlete. He set the Warren Harding (Ohio) High School record with a time of 9.7 seconds in the 100-yard dash. He long jumped 23 feet, nine inches and also set the state mark in the 180-yard low hurdles at 18.1. At Ohio State, he starred for three seasons at both halfback and defensive back. In track, he once leaped 26-2 and represented the United States in a meet against the Soviet Union.

While Warfield was flashy, 6-foot-4 Gary Collins was, as he likes to say, "the lunch pail guy who showed up and made all the crappy plays" from 1962-71. Collins did, however, manage to lead the Browns in receptions in 1963, 1965-66 and 1969.

"If I were playing today, I'd make a lot of money as the guy who would come in on third down and catch the football," Collins said. "I wasn't fast and I ran OK pass routes. But there

GREATEST GAME: *Gary Collins leaps for one of his three second-half touchdown catches in the 27-0 victory over the Baltimore Colts in the 1964 NFL title game in Cleveland Stadium. Although Collins enjoyed 10 productive seasons with the Browns, he says that one performance will be his epitaph.*

Johnny Brewer
TE-LB • 1961-67

the 1964 NFL championship game in Cleveland Stadium. Ryan and Collins hooked up for TDs of 18, 42 and 51 yards that afternoon.

"When I die, they'll say: 'Gary Collins, dead at whatever age.' And underneath, they'll say: 'Caught three touchdown passes in the 1964 championship game,'" Collins said. "I had a lot of great seasons after that game, and to tell you the truth, I wasn't that good in 1964. But at least I'll be remembered for something."

Collins also will be remembered by his teammates as the guy who predicted the Browns' upset of the Colts every day for two weeks leading up to the game. "I'd drive to work with some of my buddies like Dick Schafrath, and I'd say, 'You know what? I think we're going to kick those guys' butts,'" Collins laughed. "I told a guy from Channel 8, John Fitzgerald, the Thursday or Friday before the game the same thing. And I also said, 'Get me the ball, too.'"

Collins doesn't buy the argument that players from his generation couldn't play the game today because the athletes are bigger and stronger.

Said Collins: "Somebody said to me recently that I couldn't play in today's game. I said wait a minute, this guy couldn't play in my game in the 1960s. When I played, defensive guys would hit you all the way down the field.

"It didn't matter if you had the sprinter's speed of Bob Hayes, the elusiveness of Paul Warfield or my strength, that gave you problems. That's why I think it's so unfair to compare different eras."

was one thing I could do better than 99.9 percent of the people out there, and that was catch the football."

Something Collins could also do was make the "post-pattern" play a memorable feature of the Browns' offense in the mid-'60s. In the days when the goalposts still stood on the goal line, Collins would often break downfield and cut or "slant" behind the goalposts in time to catch a touchdown pass from quarterback Frank Ryan.

Heading into the 1995 season, Collins ranked second on the Browns' all-time reception list with 331. But even he realizes the three catches for which he will forever be remembered are the touchdown passes from Ryan in the Browns' 27-0 upset win over Baltimore in

Tight end Milt Morin arrived in 1966 and succeeded Johnny Brewer at the position when Brewer closed out his career in '66-67 as a linebacker. The Browns used their first-round pick to select the 6-4, 240-pounder from the University of Massachusetts. When healthy, Morin was a starting tight end for most of his 10-year Browns career. In 1995, Morin ranked eighth on the team's all-time receptions list with 271 catches for 4,208 yards. In 1968, his

Milt Morin TE·1966-75

Andre Rison WR•1995

Derrick Alexander
WR•1994-95

Brennan led the Browns in receptions in 1986 (55) and caught 315 passes from 1984-91, fourth on the all-time list.

In 1985, Reggie Langhorne of Elizabeth City College was uncovered in the seventh round. Though he never led the Browns in receptions, he became Kosar's favorite target on those hard-to-make, over-the-middle passes. After leaving the Browns via Plan B free agency, Langhorne did lead the AFC in receptions as a member of the Indianapolis Colts in 1993.

Webster Slaughter, a second-round pick from San Diego State in 1986, was the flashiest of the three. "Web-Star," as he was called, led the Browns in receiving from 1989-91. In 1989, he had 65 catches for a team-record 1,236 yards

and six touchdowns, including a 97-yarder versus the Chicago Bears.

In Modell's eyes, Slaughter's last year in Cleveland, 1991, may have marked the beginning of what the Browns' owner believes will become the best era in team history when it comes to wide receivers. Michael Jackson was selected in the sixth round in 1991 and Derrick Alexander was taken in the first round in 1994.

Then in 1995, Andre Rison arrived. After spending his rookie year in Indianapolis (1989), Rison joined the Atlanta Falcons and averaged 85 catches over five seasons. Only twice in Browns history has a receiver caught more than 80 in a season: Ozzie Newsome in 1983 and '84. The addition of Rison and the development of Jackson and Alexander gave Modell plenty of reasons for optimism in '95.

Michael Jackson *WR•1991-95*

Strength in the offensive line has been a trademark of the Browns throughout their 50-year history. In the early days, Paul Brown's offensive strategies required quality linemen to protect Otto Graham or open holes for Marion Motley. Later, Jim Brown and Leroy Kelly followed the lead of Gene Hickerson or John Wooten on many long runs. In the late '70s and early '80s, Doug Dieken, Tom

Offensive Linemen

By Mark Craig

DeLeone, Joe DeLamielleure and others gave Brian Sipe time to set Browns passing records during the Kardiac Kids era. Likewise, in the mid '80s, Mike Baab, Cody Risien and Dan Fike helped to keep Bernie Kosar in the pocket long enough to lead the Browns to three AFC championship games.

Two Browns linemen are Pro Football Hall of Famers: center Frank "Gunner" Gatski and right tackle Mike McCormack. Another, left tackle Lou Groza, is likewise enshrined, but primarily as a place-kicker.

Groza, however, is the beginning link to the greatest legacy of all in Browns offensive line history. Heading into Cleveland's 50th season in 1995, only Groza (1948-59), Dick Schafrath (1960-71), Doug Dieken (1971-84), Paul Farren (1985-90) and current starter Tony Jones (1991-

95) had anchored the starting left tackle position for longer than two seasons.

In 1971, Dieken was 22 years old and now admits he "didn't have a clue" when it came to playing left tackle in the NFL. Listed at 6-5, 236 as a University of Illinois tight end, Dieken gained 18 pounds between his senior season and the opening of the '71 campaign. Drafted by the Browns with the intention of converting him to tackle, the reality of the switch first hit home when an equipment manager handed him a jersey with the number 73 on it. "I knew right then I was doomed," Dieken recalled.

He was working his way into the lineup ahead of 34-year-old Dick Schafrath when the Browns hosted Atlanta on Halloween, 1971. It turned out to be a rather frightening experience because the Falcons' excellent pass rush was coming to Cleveland Stadium. "I remember looking up and seeing [defensive end] Claude Humphrey, in his prime," Dieken said. "At that point, I'm thinking to myself, 'Oh my God, what have I gotten myself into?'"

The Browns were crushed that day, 31-14, in Dieken's seventh game as a pro. Dieken did, however, survive to play in a team-record 203 consecutive games during a 14-year career that ended with his retirement after the '84 season.

How fitting that the person who brought Dieken and the Browns together was a man named Lou Groza. After watching Jim Daniell and Ernie Blandin handle the left tackle spot for the Browns' first two seasons, Groza moved in during the 1948 season and played the position until 1959. Signed by Paul Brown because of his abilities as a place-kicker, Lou "The Toe" Groza proved he was a pretty dominating tackle as well.

Scouts weren't exactly beating a path to Dieken's door, but Groza showed up and liked what he saw. He was working as part-time scout for the Browns and part-time insurance salesman. "I didn't come back and guarantee he could be the next left tackle for the Browns," Groza said. "I just said I think he could be a

Mike McCormack *T·1954-62*

"Gunner"
Frank Gatski
C · 1946-56

good blocker with capabilities to play that position. Doug was a tight end at the time, and he might get mad at me, but I think what hindered him there was his speed."

The Browns drafted Dieken in the sixth round with a selection they acquired from Chicago for wide receiver Eppie Barney. So thanks to Groza, the Browns had quietly extended their legacy at the left tackle spot into what would become a fifth decade.

In 1960, Groza's back problems forced him into a one-year retirement. When he returned in 1961 as a place-kicker only, Dick Schafrath was in his second full season as the starting left tackle. Groza said he saw a lot of himself in Schafrath, a fellow former Ohio State Buckeye.

"Dick was a very intense player who really hustled," Groza said. "There wasn't much difference between us. I just got old quicker."

In 1995, the left tackle position seemed to have fallen back into the hands of a player who will take it into the next century. Tony Jones, a 1988 free agent signee from Western Carolina University, was the only player to start every game at the same position since Bill Belichick was hired as head coach in 1991.

Groza, Dieken and Schafrath — "The Big Three" as Schafrath refers to them — smile when they look at Jones. He is the new-breed of tackle at 6-foot-5, 300 pounds.

"In my era, the line coach wanted guys with long arms, and he didn't want anybody who weighed over 260 pounds," said Dieken, whose playing weight remained in the 250-255-pound range. "If you were over 260 pounds, you were fined. Now in the 1990s, if you aren't 290, you're on a Greyhound bus out of town."

Groza's playing weight was listed at 250, but he says he played a lot of games at 235. Of course, as Groza points out, 235 pounds made for a rather large person in the '40s and '50s.

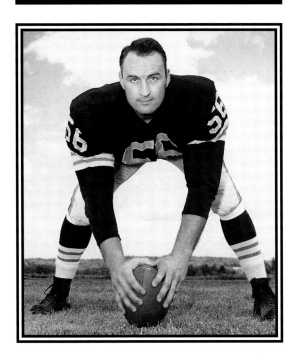

John Morrow C•1960-66

"It was important back when I played that the tackles and the offensive linemen could run," Groza said. "So much of the game was based on speed in those days. We had to pull out and lead sweeps a lot of the times, or you had to release from the weak side and get downfield in front of plays to the other side of the field."

The late Lin Houston, the Browns' right guard from 1946-53, said coaches didn't have to break down the running drills into groups for the linemen and skill players back when he played. "Our guards were faster than the backs in those days," said Houston, who Paul Brown used to call the fastest guard he ever coached. "Bill Willis and I played right guard on offense and middle guard on defense in the early days, and we'd always beat the backs. Paul wanted size and speed in his linemen, but if he had to choose one over the other, he took the speed."

As late as 1971, the NFL placed a greater need for speed at the tackle positions. "My rookie year, I was covering kickoffs and punts," Dieken said. "Today, you basically have your 11 hired guns to handle the special teams."

Size, however, became more of an important commodity for NFL offensive linemen when the league's defensive players began to get bigger, faster and more specialized during the 1970s. "I remember a scout by the name of Mike Nixon talking to us down at the Senior Bowl," Dieken said. "They were weighing us and measuring us, and I'll never forget him telling me to stand up straight because that extra inch probably would be worth an extra $1,000 dollars. Today, that extra inch is probably worth $100,000, if not more."

Midway through Dieken's career, he began to experience the dawning of a new era for NFL

Jim Ray Smith
G•1956-62

Quarterback Milt Plum's pass protection in 1961 included Smith (64) and Mike McCormack (74). All three were Pro Bowlers.

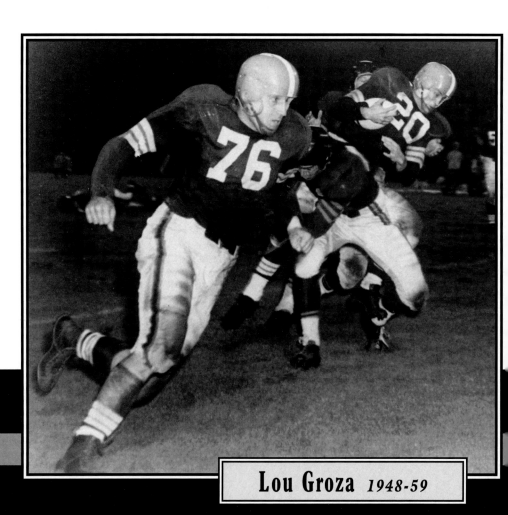

Lou Groza *1948-59*

The
Left Tackle
Legacy

Five players have been primarily in charge of this key quarterback-protection position. Beside their names are the years they started at left tackle.

Dick Schafrath *1960-71*

244

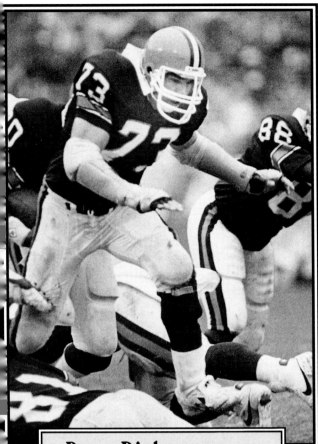

Doug Dieken *1971-84*

Paul Farren *1985-90*

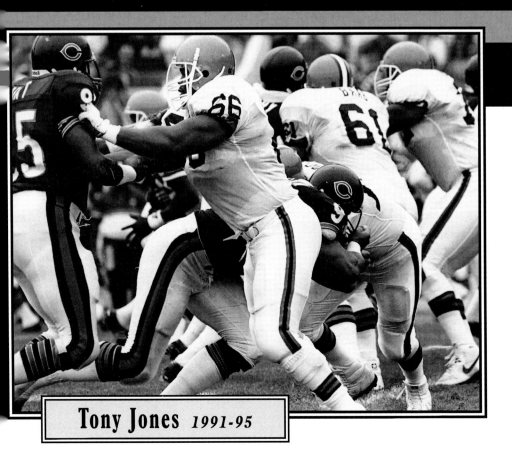

Tony Jones *1991-95*

Gene Hickerson
G • 1958-60, '62-73

Blocking for Ernie Green against the Packers.

defenses. "Because the passing picked up throughout the league, the defensive coaches wanted to increase the speed coming off the quarterback's blind side," Dieken said. "They started widening the ends, and it got to be a footrace to see whether they could get to the quarterback before the offensive tackles could get out there to get a piece of the guy.

"Fred Dean was one of the first guys I saw do that. Now, they draft players strictly for that purpose."

That's one reason left tackle became more of a glamour position in the 1990s. When free agency was unveiled in 1993, left tackles became instant millionaires because of the difficulty of playing the position and the importance of protecting the blind side of the era's high-profile, highly-paid quarterbacks. Jones earned $2 million in 1994 and was not the highest-paid left tackle in the league. "Today, I read in the papers where they always give special recognition to the left tackle," Groza said. "We never got that. No one even looked at us unless we got called for holding."

When the defenses got bigger and faster in the 1970s, the league began loosening the rules for offensive linemen out of safety for the quarterback and the desire to keep scoring high. By the mid-1980s, offensive linemen not only were allowed to extend their arms, they were allowed to open their hands and push the defensive player.

"Around 1986, they pretty much made it sumo wrestling," Dieken said.

"I see guys today put both hands on a defensive player, grab him and fall down, and they don't call it," Houston said. "In my day, you had to knock the guy out of the way using your shoulders. If we even put one hand on the guy, it was 15 yards."

The best offensive line in Browns history might have been the one in the late 1950s and early-to-mid '60s. In 1965, Jim Brown's final season, Cleveland led the NFL in team rushing with 2,331 yards. Then, in the first two years following the retirement of arguably the best running back in NFL history, the Browns still led the NFL in rushing with 2,166 yards in

1966 and 2,139 in 1967. Thirty years after his retirement, Brown still wondered why not one of the key linemen who blocked for the three Browns Hall of Fame running backs of that era — Brown (1957-65), Bobby Mitchell (1958-61) and Leroy Kelly (1964-73) — is not also in the Pro Football Hall of Fame.

"How in the world can you have three Hall-of-Fame runners and not have anybody in from the line?" Brown asked. "Two runners who started together. Two runners who played back-to-back. You got to go directly to the commonality those players had."

Left tackle Dick Schafrath, right guard Gene Hickerson, left guard John Wooten and

247

Joe DeLamielleure *G·1980-84*

Tom DeLeone C•1974-84

center John Morrow all started in front of Brown, Mitchell and Kelly. Together, they appeared in 16 Pro Bowls, led by Schafrath and Hickerson with six apiece. "We had the best downfield blocking in history," Brown said. "As I look at the game, there's no doubt in my mind I'd take Hickerson and Schafrath right now for my all-time team."

Regarding pass blocking, the 1980 team would be hard to top. It didn't set the team record for fewest sacks, but it did allow only 23 in 554 attempts. The only time the Browns ever attempted more passes was a year later when they threw the ball 567 times.

"When we had Brian Sipe, we were definitely in an era where we used the pass to set up the run," Dieken said. "You basically wanted offensive linemen who could keep the defense at arm's length from Brian. Now, it's more of a smash-mouth approach in football."

Playing with Dieken on that 1980 offensive line was Cody Risien at right tackle, Joe DeLamielleure at right guard, Tom DeLeone at center and Henry Sheppard at left guard. Except for DeLamielleure, who was picked up that season from Buffalo, the line had been together for a few years. Dieken, DeLamiel-

Robert E. Jackson
G•1975-85

leure and DeLeone were Pro Bowl selections.

Robert E. Jackson, who had gone to Duke University as a quarterback and converted to a guard, had been the starting right guard before DeLamielleure. Jackson moved back into the lineup in 1981 as a left guard and held the position through 1984.

Risien enjoyed one of the finer careers for a right tackle in Browns history. He played from 1979-83 and 1985-89. He did play some left guard, but he was the starting right tackle from 1980-83 and 1985-89.

Lou Rymkus (1946-51) and Monte Clark (1963-69) also were standouts at right tackle. Rymkus and Groza teamed at tackle from 1948-51, dubbing themselves "Lou the Heel" and

Dan Fike G-T • 1985-92

Cody Risien
T • 1979-83, '85-89

"Lou the Toe." The best right tackle of all, however, was Mike McCormack (1954-62). After a year as Bill Willis' successor at middle guard (1954), he played the balance of his career at right tackle, making the Pro Bowl five times. He was elected to the Hall of Fame in 1984.

Frank Gatski was an original member of the Browns in 1946. He became a starter at center in 1948 and held the position through 1956. He was a quiet man who never missed a game or a practice in 20 years of high school, college and pro ball. At 6-3, 240 pounds, Gatski was one of the strongest players on the team. He also was one of the toughest, having worked as a coal miner

in West Virginia before going to Marshall to play college football.

After Gatski was traded to the Lions in 1957, Art Hunter took over and held the position through 1959. He was selected for the Pro Bowl in his final season, but was dealt to the Los Angeles Rams in 1960 for another center, John Morrow, who played through 1966.

The Browns have remained solid at center since Fred Hoaglin succeeded Morrow in 1967. Since then, the primary starters have been Bob DeMarco from 1972-74; Tom DeLeone from 1975-82; Mike Baab from 1983-87 and 1990-91; and Steve Everitt from 1993-95.

At right guard, Lin Houston (1946-53) and Gene Hickerson (1958-60 and 1962-73) are the names of distinction. Houston, brother of former Browns linebacker Jim Houston, shared

Steve Everitt *C • 1993-95*

duties with Bill Willis through part of his career. Hickerson is best remembered as the familiar No. 66 leading Brown or Kelly around end on the Browns' sweeps of the '60s. In the 1990s, Bob Dahl has emerged as a solid force at right guard, having held the position since the 1993 season.

At left guard, Abe Gibron (1950-56) and Jim Ray Smith (1956-62) were Pro Bowlers four and five times, respectively. John Wooten (1959-67), made it twice. Wooten was a regular right guard for two seasons before succeeding Smith on the left in 1963 after Smith was traded to the Dallas Cowboys for Monte Clark.

Meanwhile, the course of Dieken's career, and the pipeline at left tackle, might have taken a different course had the Browns tried to play Dieken at tight end.

"There was only one tight end in rookie training camp in 1971, and I finally talked him into quitting," laughs Dieken, who in 1995 was

Bob Dahl
G • 1992-95

entering his 11th season as the Browns' radio color analyst. "I thought I had my chance, but they called up Milt Morin, one of the veterans, and he came into rookie training camp. I never got my chance."

And the Browns' legendary left tackle position was better because of it.

In 1995, the Browns appeared to be the most settled on the offensive line since the Bill Belichick era began in 1991. Starters included center Steve Everitt; tackles Tony Jones and Orlando Brown; and guards Bob Dahl and Wally Williams.

The long history of Cleveland's fabled football franchise is one of names steeped in tradition, nostalgia and on-field excellence, including 13 Pro Football Hall of Famers. Except for Paul Brown, Bill Willis and Len Ford, the other immortals are linked to the offense. However, regardless of being outnumbered, the Browns' defenders, no matter the era, have been a vital part of the

Defensive Linemen

By Jim Campbell

team's outstanding success over 50 years. Ford and Willis both played on the defensive line, Ford at end and Willis at middle guard. Willis would often drop back behind the line to take advantage of his speed and agility, enabling him to "go to the play" and thus creating a prototype of today's middle linebacker position.

"Dee-Fense" isn't new or unusual in Cleveland. The earliest Browns team knew that "the best offense is a good defense." Paul Brown went looking for skilled football players to start his team and many were great defenders. One of the early defenders was Tommy James, a halfback who played for Brown at Massillon and Ohio State. James, skilled as a two-way performer, found himself playing defensive halfback in Cleveland over an eight-year career (1948-55).

Said James: "Everyone was playing a seven-diamond in those days — seven defensive linemen, just a middle linebacker, two defensive halfbacks, and a single safety. Eventually, we got to a 6-2-2-1 and a 5-3-2-1. About the time my career was winding down, the 4-3 was firmly established."

When the Browns first took the field in 1946, their lineup was one that wouldn't necessarily strike fear in the hearts of their opposition, at least not from a size perspective in comparison to today's behemoths. However, the defense's skill level was as good or better than anything its opponents could field.

The ends were George Young of Georgia (6-3, 210), and John Yonakor of Notre Dame (6-5, 218). Tackles were Ernie Blandin of Tulane (6-3, 245), Chet Adams of Ohio U. (6-4, 228) and Lou Rymkus of Notre Dame (6-4, 230). The defensive guards were Eddie Ulinski of Marshall (5-11, 200) and Lin Houston of Ohio State (6-0, 205). Bill Willis of Ohio State (6-2, 206) was the middle guard who played nose to nose with the offensive center.

James further discussed tactics: "Our ends in the seven-diamond played somewhat like linebackers in that they were wide, outside of the offensive ends, and had to protect against short passes. Also, you should know that even with a lot of platooning we had to know both offensive and defensive plays. We had to be ready to play on either side of the ball."

This explains why Yonakor caught seven passes (two for TDs). Why Young caught three passes. Why Otto Graham had five interceptions in 1946. Why halfback Tommy Colella ran the ball 30 times and had 10 interceptions in the Browns' first season of play.

With further specialization, the seven-diamond quickly gave way to a five-man line, with Willis still in the middle. Willis' main attribute was his cat-like quickness. His reflexes were so quick that he often shot between a center's legs and grabbed a very surprised and bewildered quarterback before he could pull away with the snap from center. Early Browns press books stated, "Photographers need to set their shutter speed at 1/600th of a second to stop the action on Willis."

Because there is no such thing as a defensive guard in the NFL today, (even the nose tackle in the 3-4 doesn't quite fit the description), Willis is sometimes listed and thought of as a linebacker. True, he often played behind the line as defensive sets changed. But anyone who played against him, or saw him play very much, remembers him more as a middle guard, playing squarely on the nose of the opposing team's center.

Offensive centers remember Willis as well as, if not better than, the many ball carriers he tracked down. Hall-of-Fame center Clyde "Bulldog" Turner of the Chicago Bears said, "The first guy to convince me that I couldn't handle anybody I ever met was Bill Willis. He was skinny and didn't look like he should be playing middle guard, but he would jump right over you. The only way I could block him was to remain low in a squat after I snapped the ball, and when he tried to jump over me, I'd come up and catch him. That Willis was a warhorse, I'll tell you that."

Mike "Mo" Scarry, a center on the Browns and later a longtime Don Shula assistant in Miami, may have been the first pro to witness Willis' speed and quickness firsthand. Scarry had played with the Cleveland Rams in 1944 and 1945, but elected to jump to the AAFC Browns in 1946 rather than go with the Rams to Los Angeles. He, too, was known for his quickness and was reputed to have "the fastest hands in football."

In Willis' first preseason scrimmage, he played head up on Scarry. This was kind of a tryout in that Willis wasn't yet under contract. On four successive plays, Willis blew by, over, or through Scarry and tackled Graham before the play could start. Finally, an unbelieving Scarry yelled, "Hey, check the offsides. Check this guy for offsides!"

Paul Brown had Blanton Collier, then an assistant, check. Everything was legal. Willis,

Bill Willis
MG•1946-53

who had made All-America as a tackle for the Buckeyes, was just too quick. Willis later told author Myron Cope in *The Game That Was*, "What I had been doing, you see, was concentrating on the ball. The split second the ball moved, or Scarry's hand tightened, I charged. And I charged in a different way every time. I would go under him, then over him. I would bang off his left shoulder, then bang off his right shoulder. I caught Graham every time, usually before he had even begun to pull away from center."

After the practice, which P.B. called off early, Willis was summoned by the head coach. He said, "Paul offered me a four-thousand dollar contract." That's how the "color line" was broken in the AAFC. A few days later, Marion

Len Ford
E • 1950-57

Pulling down Redskins quarterback Eddie LeBaron.

Motley also became a member of the Browns. The careers of the two Hall of Famers were intertwined — Willis and Motley, Motley and Willis.

The first big change in the Browns' defensive line from a personnel standpoint was in 1950. When the Browns were folded into the NFL that year, several key players came from the defunct AAFC teams. None bigger, literally as well as figuratively, than the 6-5, 260 Len Ford. Brown was familiar with Ford from his days at the University of Michigan. A fine two-way end with the Los Angeles Dons in 1948 and '49, Ford caught 31 passes in 1948 for 598 yards and seven touchdowns. The next year he gathered 36 for 577 yards.

Brown saw Ford in a different light. He would be exclusively a defensive end. Ford, a Washington, D.C., native, never saw a down of offense with the Browns, but did he play defense! He played it so well that he, too, was inducted into the Pro Football Hall of Fame in 1976, although, sadly, four years after his death at age 46 in 1972.

Ford's ability allowed the Browns to adjust their defense at the time. Stationing linebackers behind the defensive ends, Ford could move even closer to the ball, "crash" — as the pass rush was called then, and apply pressure to the quarterback. Ford may well have been the prototype for the Rams' Deacon Jones a generation later in the 1960s. Ford's old AAFC coach Jimmy Phelan said, "Len can become the best all-around end in history, he has everything."

John Kissell *T·1950-52, '54-56*

Don Colo
T·1953-58·

Ford epitomized Paul Brown's "you play like you practice" theory. Lou Groza, who often lined up opposite Ford in practice, said, "He was always 'hell-bent for leather' anytime he stepped on a football field." Especially, if the "leather" was in the hands of a passer. Ford, like the Bears' Doug Atkins later, often leap-frogged blocks to nail an unsuspecting and unlucky quarterback.

In his first season in Cleveland, in the leather helmet era before face masks were common, Ford caught Chicago Cardinals fullback Pat Harder's well-placed, well-timed elbow right in the face. The damage report: several missing teeth, two fractured cheekbones and a broken nose. Plastic surgery was needed and it looked unlikely that Ford would play again that 1950 season. However, a specially-con-structed helmet with a protec-tive device allowed him to play in the championship game against the Los Angeles Rams. Ford's all-out play was a factor in the stunning 30-28 victory in Cleve-land Stadium.

Title games seemed to bring out the best in Ford. In the 1954 championship, 56-10 over the Lions, Ford made two interceptions. More than just a one dimensional pass rusher, Ford was solid against the run. He also recovered 20 fum-bles in his relatively short Browns career.

Paul Wiggin, a youngster in Ford's final years, summed up what most feel about Ford, "He was a man among men." Ford, not entirely boastful, often said, "There is no one in this league who can take me on alone."

LINE OF DISTINCTION: *The defensive line of the Browns' 1955 NFL champions included (left to right) E Len Ford, T Don Colo, MG Bob Gain, T John Kissell and E Carlton Massey.*

Joining Ford in Cleveland for the 1950 season, via the defunct AAFC Buffalo Bills, was defensive tackle John Kissell of Boston College. Kissell, one of several from a New England family to play pro ball, was familiar to Paul Brown for two years. Like Ford, he filled a specific need on the team. His 247-pound bulk presented a formidable obstacle for teams to overcome. Much like tackle Art Donovan later allowed end Gino Marchetti of the Colts to freelance more as a pass rusher, Kissell gave Ford greater latitude in his play.

Forrest "Chubby" Grigg, not to be confused with latter-day Browns head coach Forrest Gregg, joined in 1948 after playing with the 1946 Buffalo Bisons and 1947 Chicago Rockets (the "Bisons" became the "Bills" in '47). Grigg provided 280 pounds of roadblock at tackle on the side away from Ford and Kissell.

Don Colo, who came from the Colts in a quality-for-quantity trade in 1953 that also brought Mike McCormack, established himself at right tackle after one season on the left. Colo, from Brown University, was a hard-bitten World War II veteran who represented the evolving player. He stood 6-3 and weighed 260 — more in keeping with today's dimensions and proving out Tommy James' theory that "about every three years the players seemed to get an inch or two taller and ten or twenty pounds heavier." Colo was a good "hand fighter." He had the bulk and technique to battle

blockers at the line of scrimmage and then "slide" to the point of attack.

During the 1950s, the Browns were unusually well stocked with outstanding defensive linemen. Len Ford and Bill Willis, of course, became Hall of Famers while wearing brown and orange. Four others, however, had Hall-of-Fame careers after leaving Cleveland. One can't help but speculate on how much better the Browns would have been if these linemen could have worked long-term into the Browns' defensive system.

Doug Atkins (1953-54), Henry Jordan (1957-58) and Willie Davis (1958-59) were all dealt at various times as Paul Brown felt he had a surplus of line talent. Art Donovan, a rookie in 1951, was traded to the New York Yanks as Brown elected to retain the more experienced Chubby Grigg at tackle.

Atkins played 12 seasons with the Bears, including the 1963 NFL championship team, and three with the New Orleans Saints, while Jordan and Davis anchored Vince Lombardi's Green Bay Packers defense of the '60s. Donovan became a key member of the Baltimore Colts' defense that helped win back-to-back NFL championships in 1958 and '59.

Around the same time Don Colo arrived, another longtime Browns defender also came to

Bob Gain
MG-T·1952,'54-64

Cleveland. Bob Gain, a native of Akron, Ohio, had been a consensus All-America tackle at Kentucky under the legend-in-the-making, Paul "Bear" Bryant. As a rookie in 1952, Gain (6-3, 250) started at left tackle. He then left the team to fulfill a military obligation in 1953, but was back in uniform in 1954. This time he was a swingman at both middle guard and left tackle, backing up Kissell, Colo and McCormack.

McCormack, who served in the military in 1952 and 1953 after an All-America career at Kansas and an early NFL career with the New York Yanks, was a middle guard, replacing the recently-retired Willis. In his own way, McCormack was every bit the "handful" that Willis was. Perhaps not quite as quick, but at 6-4, 248,

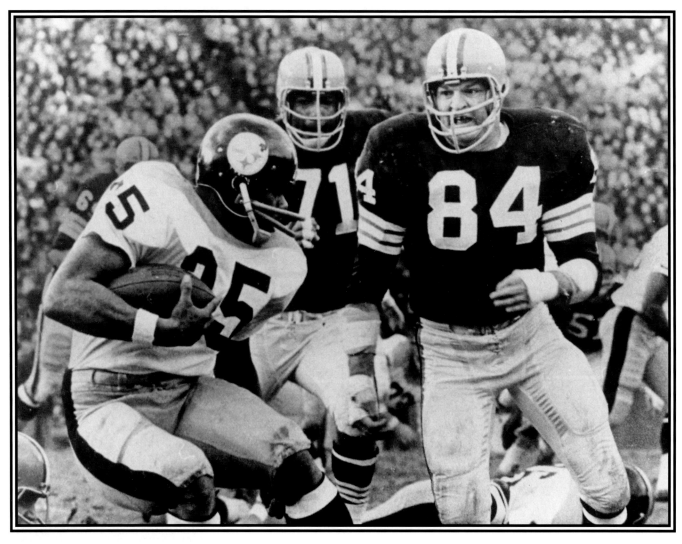

Paul Wiggin
E • 1957-67

With Walter Johnson (71), stopping Steeler Don Shy.

bulkier. McCormack was a strong force in the 5-3 defensive front.

Howard Brinker, a Browns assistant from 1952-73, said of McCormack, "No one took liberties in the middle with Mike when we turned him loose on a pass rush. He just crushed the middle with Kissell and Ford coming from the outside."

McCormack remembers this time: "The five-three was evolving into the four-three. About thirty percent of the time, we'd hit and back out. The rest of the time, you stayed in and played as a lineman."

According to Chuck Noll, a Browns teammate of McCormack for six seasons before moving on to his long coaching career, "McCormack was fast for his size. He could really get around in that five-three. He made the Hall of Fame as an offensive tackle, but he could have gotten there on defense. This was at a time when you tended to put your best players on offense. You wouldn't do that now."

Gain was another who could stand his ground while reading the offensive play and moving along the line of scrimmage. As Noll said, "He and Colo could 'parallel' and read." Eventually, added to technique was the tactic of penetrating across the line first and then "reading and reacting."

The surrounding cast on the defensive line would change during Gain's career. He broke in playing beside left end George Young, a link to the team's origins in 1946. He finished playing

next to Paul Wiggin, who retired in 1967. During his career, Gain was a five-time Pro Bowler.

Gain remained in the '60s, but new faces began to appear. The 4-3 was now in vogue and ends were primarily pass rushers. Wiggin and Bill Glass gave the Browns solidarity at the ends when Glass came over from Detroit in 1962 for Milt Plum in a deal that also brought the Browns quarterback Jim Ninowski. In 1995, Glass still owned the Browns records for most quarterback sacks in a season (14.5 in 1965) and most consecutive games with a sack (seven in 1966). He was a member of four Pro Bowl teams from 1962-67.

Through most of the '60s, Glass held forth on the field, and from the pulpit off the field.

The Baylor All-America was also an ordained Baptist minister, active in the Fellowship of Christian Athletes, and to this day carries on a Christian evangelical crusade. In 1965, Glass wrote a book, *Get in the Game*, that showed how it was possible to excel in pro football's violent world while maintaining an abiding sense of God's presence in everyday life.

Wiggin also was a multi-year Pro Bowler (twice). In fact, Paul Brown said, "The three greatest defensive ends in my time with the Browns were John Yonakor, Len Ford and Paul Wiggin." Both Wiggin and Glass could rush the passer and stop the run. Joining them at tackle in the 1964 championship season were old pro

Bill Glass
E • 1962-68

Leaping in the path of Steelers quarterback Bill Nelsen.

Jim Kanicki T·1963-69

Walter Johnson
T·1965-76

Wrapping up Redskins quarterback Sonny Jurgensen.

Dick "Mo" Modzelewski, a battle-tested veteran from the New York Giants and second-year man Jim Kanicki, a 270-pounder. The pair gave the Browns a solid middle in the middle '60s — very tough against the run.

Modzelewski talked about his technique: "If you just fired off the ball, the play could be a cross-block or trap, so you had to think what you were doing or you simply would have gotten beaten all the time."

By 1966, Walter Johnson, a former fullback from Taft High School in Cincinnati, who grew to a 270-pound defensive tackle at Cal State-Los Angeles, had supplanted Modzelewski as the starting left tackle.

Ray Mansfield, longtime Steelers center, remembers Johnson as a force. "He was big and strong and I don't think he got the credit he deserved. I know I didn't look forward to playing him. Bruce Van Dyke [a Steeler guard] and I often double-teamed him, but he was a load. Once I really hit him a cheap shot and he got up looking around to see who did it. I didn't want him mad at me, so I rushed over to Van Dyke and said, 'Way to go, Bruce.' I don't know how long it took Van Dyke to completely forgive me."

Jack Gregory would arrive at defensive end in the late '60s and play as well as anyone in the league. He made the Pro Bowl before being traded to the New York Giants in 1972. Gregory's forte was rushing the passer. His departure coincided with Jerry Sherk's arrival. At 253,

Jerry Sherk *T·1970-81*

Between Super Bowl flights with the Denver Broncos and Los Angeles Raiders, end Lyle Alzado had a three-year layover in Cleveland, adding experience and leadership to the defense of the "Kardiac Kids." Never one to underestimate himself, he once said, "If me and King Kong went into an alley, only one of us would come out — and it wouldn't be the monkey."

When Alzado arrived in 1979, time and nagging knee injuries were taking a toll on Sherk. Then a staph infection suffered in Game 10 settled in a knee, nearly took his life and caused him to miss the rest of '79 and most of '80. He returned for one last try in 1981, but mostly as a backup in the new three-man front.

The most unselfish position in football is the nose tackle in a 3-4. The position takes such a constant pounding that most teams use two or more players on a rotating basis. Using humor as an illustration, someone once said "being a nose tackle in a three-four is like being left to guard the camp during a rhinoceros stampede." The dubious honor of handling the job alone first belonged to Henry Bradley, a compact 260-pounder from Alcorn State. By 1982 Bradley was sharing the job with Cleveland native Bob Golic.

Golic, one of the true characters of the NFL who would blossom into a full-blown celebrity later as a Raider, took over the nose position in 1983 and held it through 1988. In 1989, the Browns went back to a 4-3. Golic came into the NFL in 1979 with the Patriots as a 240-pound linebacker out of Notre Dame.

The Pats would waive the young linebacker in 1982. At the peak of his career, Golic weighed 265. His best year was 1986. He was elected to the Pro Bowl squad, but a broken arm prevented him from playing. He was also elected in 1985 and '87.

A great wrestler at Cleveland's St. Joseph's High School and at Notre Dame, Golic used grappling techniques to neutralize opposing centers and guards.

Sherk seemed light for a tackle, but he was active, quick and very tenacious. This last attribute won him the Mack Truck Bulldog Award as the AFC Defensive Player of the Year. During his prime in the mid '70s, Sherk was generally conceded to be "the game's best interior defensive lineman," if not the most decorated. In 1975, though, those who know (the NFL Players Association) voted him the best defender in the NFL.

Sherk's reputation outside of the Cleveland area suffered because a portion of his career was played when the Browns were in a rare "valley" as opposed to on a "peak." His talents were often overlooked by the national media.

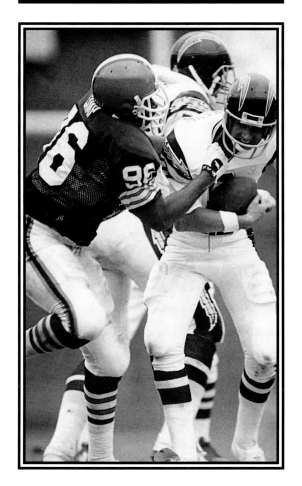

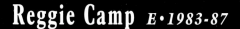

Reggie Camp E•1983-87

Always quick with one-liners, Golic said of the demanding position he played, "To play nose tackle you have to be either unemployed or crazy. So, I guess I was half qualified." He also said, "Contrary to popular belief, if I'd ever win the Ohio state lottery, I'd keep playing — until I got yelled at the first time. Then I'd buy the team and fire the coach who yelled at me."

Perhaps teammate Doug Dieken spoke best for Golic and the men in the trenches, saying, "Being a nose tackle is like being a fire hydrant at a dog show."

Golic continued in a more serious vain about his position, "Sometimes coaches say you win or do your job just getting a standoff, and you're not supposed to make the tackle. But then there are plays when you fight through all

those bodies and make a big hit, and that's pretty wild. It's an awfully tough position."

With only three men on the line, larger defensive ends were needed. Reggie Camp, Keith Baldwin and Elvis Franks all were in the 265-270 range. The Browns even got several solid seasons from longtime Eagles defensive end Carl "Big Daddy" Hairston. Although Hairston's well-traveled body may not have been built by Soloflex, Head Coach Sam Rutigliano put it in perspective: "Carl is living proof that you don't have to have a body that resembles a Greek statue. I've seen a lot of guys

Michael Dean Perry *T·1988-94*

Rob Burnett E·1990-95

like that working on the turnpike." Hairston was a solid force on the defensive line during the Browns' five straight playoff appearances in the '80s, first at right end in the 3-4 from 1985-88 and then at left tackle in 1989 after the Browns returned to the 4-3.

Added to Golic and Hairston during the playoff run were ends Sam Clancy, Reggie Camp and Al "Bubba" Baker. Also moving into the lineup in the '89 4-3 alignment was second-year tackle Michael Dean Perry, the most-recent perennial Browns All-Pro lineman.

Perry arrived in 1988 as a second-round draft choice and garnered about every rookie honor one could. He led the team in sacks even though he wasn't a starter. Perry would later annex AFC and NFL honors for his spectacular play that season.

From the start, many NFL insiders thought that Michael Dean was a much larger talent, if not a much larger body, than his big brother William "the Refrigerator" Perry. Said Nick Saban, his defensive coordinator, "He tried to play within the scheme and a lot of people paid special attention to him. It helped some of the other guys to play better football."

Rob Burnett and Anthony Pleasant, a pair of 280-pounders drafted in 1990, provided the Browns solid play at end in the '90s. But after free agents Perry and James Jones departed for Denver, the Browns opened '95 with new tackles: three-year veteran Dan Footman and Tim Goad, a free agent signee from New England.

Anthony Pleasant
E·1990-95

On the trail of Bengals quarterback David Klingler.

From the day there was just one in the seven-diamond, through the days of a troika in the 4-3, to a quartet in the 3-4, linebackers have been vital to a pro football team. They are the second line of defense, and in most alignments they should, and do, make the majority of a team's tackles.

Ahmad Rashad, the former wide receiver and current sportscaster, got tangled up with a few Browns linebackers in his NFL career. He had this to say about the men who play the position: "They're people who just plain love to run into things. They'll hit you as you go by them the way other people shake hands."

When the Browns moved to the 5-3, it featured a middle guard and three linebackers. Bill Willis was the nose man along with two tackles and two ends. The linebackers, Tony Adamle and Tommy Thompson on the outside, and Weldon Humble and Alex Agase splitting time on the inside, were formidable.

Strangely enough, the Browns' most devastating runner could have been their most devastating tackler, too: Marion Motley. Early in his career, he remained a part of the team's goal line defense. It was his skill at linebacking and fullbacking in his early days that led Paul Zimmerman, *Sports Illustrated's* Dr. Z, to proclaim in his *Thinking Man's Guide to Pro Football*, that

Linebackers

By Jim Campbell

Some of today's biggest names and biggest hitters are linebackers. Throughout the years, the Browns have had their share of men who policed the football field sideline to sideline. Certainly, few in recent years did it as long and as well as Clay Matthews. Jim Houston stood out among his contemporaries for a long while, and Tony Adamle and Walt Michaels had runners wishing they had never met in their time. In 1994, Pepper Johnson sparked a strong defense that led the Browns to their first playoff appearance of the decade.

In the late '40s, unlike some teams, the Browns didn't linger too long with the seven-diamond defense. But before abandoning the old-fashioned way, Lou Saban, a much-traveled coach in later life, distinguished himself as the only linebacker on the field.

Motley was "the greatest player" in the history of professional football.

No one disputes Motley's great offensive ability, blocking and running, but Zimmerman remembers his defense, too: "He backed up the line and I can still see him on one play, reaching out with one hand and grabbing Buddy Young by the seat of the pants and holding him up in the air for the crowd to see." In the same book, after giving it some thought years later, former Browns assistant coach Weeb Ewbank mused, "He [Motley] just might have been the greatest at that."

Tony Adamle is an interesting player. Like Willis, he played at Ohio State, then became a physician after he retired. Unlike latter-day players who attended medical school between seasons, Adamle waited until he retired to seri-

ously pursue his medical career. He also attained a renewed celebrity when his son Mike became an NFL running back before finding his way to the broadcast booth. Dr. Tony, a rugged tackler, was, not surprisingly, a keen diagnostician of plays.

The other linebacker in the early years was Tommy Thompson of William & Mary (not to be confused with the Eagles' one-eyed quarterback of the same name and era). Thompson's career was relatively short (1949-1953) due to a combination of an injury and a business opportunity that was just too good to pass up.

Former Browns assistant Dick Gallagher shared the rest of the league's high opinion of him: "Tommy Thompson... Now there was a football player. He was a rugged blond guy, good lookin' son of gun. But tough as nails —

also very smart. I was not surprised to see him so successful in business. He had a great mind for anything he did."

No matter who was playing in the middle, Humble or Agase, it was difficult making any headway through the center of the Browns' defense. Willis was right on the line and hard to get by, but if you did, Humble or Agase was right there to fill the hole.

Later, Willis would play off the line like a linebacker. His quickness and reactions gave him great range. Willis roamed far and wide in running down ball carriers. He could stay step for step with the fastest in the game, regardless of position. A Lions scouting report had this to

Clay Matthews
1978-93

Stripping the ball from Colts quarterback Jeff George.

say about Willis: "Pulls back very often and goes to the right 'hook' zone. Makes tackles all over the field."

Willis played eight seasons with the Browns (1946-53). He remained close to Paul Brown after retiring. In fact, knowledgeable fans would often pick him out sharing Paul Brown's owners box at Cincinnati Bengals games in the '70s and '80s (even if network sportscasters did not know who was on their screens).

In 1952, a new face appeared on the outside: Walt Michaels, a rough and tough guy from Pennsylvania's Anthracite Coal Region (Swoyersville), who would play long and well for Cleveland through 1961. After a rookie season

in Green Bay, he became a four-time Pro Bowl player, finishing with the 1963 New York Jets before embarking on a coaching career.

Michaels was such a student of the game and a motivator of men that he got the Jets to several playoffs, but was unable to duplicate Weeb Ewbank's success in getting the team to a Super Bowl. As bright as Michaels was, Mike McCormack remembers him for his toughness as well: "When Walter stopped them, they were stopped — period!"

Hal Herring (1950-52) was another intellectual player. He earned a doctorate and his doctoral dissertation was on "Defensive Tactics and Techniques in Professional Football."

Also in the 1950s, Tom Catlin brought his Oklahoma All-America credentials with him to man another outside position. If Michaels was

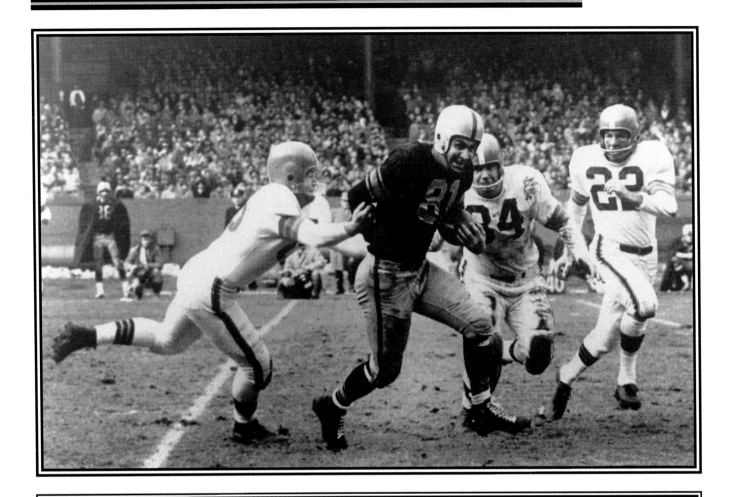

Chuck Noll *1953-59* • Walt Michaels *1952-61*

a student of the game, Catlin was a full professor. Again, McCormack: "Catlin, I think, was the most intelligent linebacker I have ever seen. He just studied and analyzed everything. He wasn't too big — about 190 or 195 and he had to fight to get up to 200 — but he was tough. He just knew where to be, knew his defenses and knew his coverages."

Buddy Parker, head coach of the Detroit Lions when the Browns and Lions were getting ready to do battle in the 1953 championship game, said, "He's a little guy, but he is quick and slips between blockers rather than play through them." Sounds like a pretty smart linebacker to avoid those head-on collisions.

Catlin was so impressive in his knowledge of football that he would follow Chuck Knox for the better part of two decades, eschewing

many head coaching opportunities to remain the architect and defensive coordinator of three division-winning playoff teams: the Rams, Bills and Seahawks. When Catlin and crew played, defenses were quite simple compared to today — three or four alignments up front and two or three coverages in the secondary. Pass defense was mainly man to man, but with some zone.

Chuck Noll, a graduate of Benedictine High School in Cleveland, came to the Browns unheralded in 1953 as a 20th-round draft choice from Dayton. He spent his first two seasons as a "messenger" guard, but then crossed the line of scrimmage to play outside linebacker through 1957 before returning to the

Noll (left), Michaels (34) and defensive back Ken Konz (22) surround Pittsburgh receiver Elbie Nickel.

Vince Costello
1957-66

"Next time we played I found him before the game and said, 'I just want to apologize for what happened in Philly,' and stuck out my hand. Noll got up to me, face to face, and just said 'Bull!' I was stunned and started walking away. He grabbed me and said, 'Okay, I accept,' but after that we just kinda stayed out of each other's way."

Galen Fiss, a Kansas Jayhawker, was a steady, heady linebacker in his era (1956-66). Fiss wasn't big at 6-0, 220, but he was a tough, analytical linebacker with a special knack for the big play. Jim Houston, a pretty good linebacker himself, said this of Fiss: "In the 1964 championship game with the Colts, Galen hit Lenny Moore something fierce and knocked him down. He hit [Johnny] Unitas, too."

Houston explained the significance: "That kind of thing determines how the defense will play; it was a spark. You see someone hitting a guy and all of a sudden, 'Hey, I wanna make sure I get my share.' Then your offense sees it and they wanna be a part of it, too."

Vince Costello's Browns career (1957-66) almost paralleled that of Fiss. Costello delayed his football career to take a whack at professional baseball after leaving Ohio University. He played in the middle and Fiss on the left or right, from 1958-65. They were teamed first with Michaels and then with Houston.

Like Catlin and Michaels, Costello also became a coach, most notably as Paul Brown's linebackers coach on the early Cincinnati Bengals teams of 1969-73.

In 1962, young Mike Lucci hit town and nearly everything else that moved. A Western Pennsylvania type, Lucci began at the University of Pittsburgh and finished at Tennessee. He gained real notoriety with the Lions, but before leaving for Motown in the 1965 three-team trade that brought the Browns defensive back Erich Barnes, Lucci played solid football for Cleveland.

In the short time he was a member of the Browns, Lucci impressed, among others, Green

offensive line in 1958 and '59. Noll was extremely intelligent and absorbed much of what Paul Brown had to offer as a teacher. Do you see a pattern developing in Browns players? They were tough with great character, skilled, but almost always highly intelligent. It's no coincidence. To be successful and productive in Brown's classroom approach to the game, a healthy intellect was required.

Smart as he was, Chuck Bednarik, the Philadelphia Eagles' Hall-of-Fame iron man center-linebacker, remembers a Noll who was also tough: "I got clobbered by a forearm while snapping for a punt. I got the number, 65. And I told the SOB I'd get him. Next year I did, on a kick return. He got up and told me he'd find me after the game.

"Sure enough, after the final gun, he comes over looking for me — helmet off. He started to say something and I just hit him cold-flush with a shot to the face. I mean, I powdered him. Only thing, [commissioner] Bert Bell was in the stands, saw it and fined me. Not only that, he told me to apologize to Chuck."

Galen Fiss *1956-66*

Jim Houston
1960-72

Nailing Cowboys quarterback Don Meredith.

destined to play in Cleveland. He is the younger brother of Lin Houston. He played at Massillon where the Paul Brown influence exists to this day. He played at Ohio State on an All-America level and as a youngster visited the Browns' camp with Lin. He met "Otto Graham, Mac Speedie, John Yonakor, Horace Gillom and all the greats the Browns had in those days."

The Browns never showed much attention toward Houston — maybe they didn't have to. But they did draft him No. 1 in 1960, right before the 49ers, who did show a great interest in him. Houston was very big for a linebacker in his day, even if he was stationed on the left or "strong" side. In fact, for probably the only time in history, when he lined up behind tackle Dick Modzelewski, it was a case of the linebacker (243) outweighing the defensive tackle (239).

Because of Jim Brown, Leroy Kelly, Frank Ryan, Paul Warfield and Gary Collins, the Browns' defense of the '60s probably didn't get the respect it deserved. When it did get some attention, it would come in the form of a left-handed compliment. The media dubbed the unit "the rubber band defense" — it stretched, but didn't snap. True, the Browns did give up yards, but were relatively stingy with points.

Regardless, it bothered Houston and his mates: "We didn't like to think of it in that sense. If a team runs the ball down your throat and continues to pile up yardage, well fine, so long as they don't score: that's their objective. Ours is to keep them from scoring."

Houston, who played defensive end when he first arrived, was very durable, playing 13 straight seasons. He trails only Clay Matthews (16), Doug Dieken (14) and Lou Groza (14) for consecutive seasons in a Browns uniform.

However, Houston recalls an odd incident leading to stretched knee ligaments, "It happened on a flare pass the year Jack Lemmon made the film 'The Fortune Cookie,' which used Cleveland Stadium as a backdrop. It was against Minnesota and I was concentrating so much I could see the laces on the ball. I

Bay Packers quarterback Bart Starr, who said of Lucci's Browns days, "He was strong, had good reactions and speed, and showed leadership potential, although sometimes his temper got him in trouble."

Lucci had an early awareness of the requirements of linebacking, saying, "The primary responsibility of a linebacker is to get to the ball and make the tackle. I've got to move and be there, wherever it is." Not a bad job description for an aspiring linebacker.

Jim Houston was another linebacker to impact the Browns' defense. Although he never thought much about it until he was about to play for the Browns, Houston was almost prethought, 'You got to be crazy to throw out there — it's mine.' Well, just about the time the ball is getting to Bill Brown [the Vikings' fullback], Red Phillips [a Vikings receiver] blocked back on me just as I planted my foot. I felt the knee go, and that's all there was to it. I played one more play and then hobbled off."

In 1966, Johnny Brewer, a tough old vet from Ole Miss, came over from tight end to play outside linebacker, and did quite well for two years. Brewer was part of a late-'60s transition period during which the Browns made room for new linebackers Dale Lindsey, Bob Matheson, John Garlington and Billy Andrews. While this was going on, Houston sometimes found himself starting in the middle. Regardless of his position, Houston played at a Pro Bowl level or above for a number of years.

One of the new faces, Matheson, was in the traditional Paul Brown mold: intelligent and tough. A No. 1 draft choice in 1967 from Duke, Matheson was what scouts call a "tweener" — his size (6-4, 240) was between that which is ideal for a defensive end, but a little bigger than what is needed for linebacker. With the Browns, however, he played primarily as a linebacker.

After four seasons with the Browns, Matheson was traded to Miami, where he really blossomed. Head Coach Don Shula named a defense, the "53," after Matheson's jersey number and deployed him in a way that had him function as a defensive end in some sets and a linebacker in others. He was quite a weapon in that opponents never knew what he was going to do and where he was going to do it.

D ale Lindsey, from Western Kentucky, played mostly in the middle from 1965-72, but also spent some time on the outside during Matheson's tenure. After a final year with the Saints in 1973, he joined the Browns' coaching staff in 1974. He absorbed well all the organization had to offer in the form of football knowledge and has been an NFL assistant for most of the past 20 years. In 1995, Lindsey is

Bob Babich
1973-78

passing along his know-how to Junior Seau and others as the AFC-champion San Diego Chargers' linebackers coach. His tactics work, since Bill Belichick said this of Seau: "Junior is the best defensive player we've faced, I'd say, by a wide margin. He does it all."

Billy Andrews was primarily a right linebacker from 1967-74, but also played occasionally in the middle as the Browns tried various combinations of Andrews, Houston, Garlington, Matheson and Lindsey in the late '60s and early '70s. Andrews, somewhat undersized at 6-0, 225, was known for 110-percent effort.

Joining the mix in 1971 was Charlie Hall, a third-round draft choice. Hall was a quiet star. The Texan from Houston just did his job with

Dick Ambrose *1975-83*

little fanfare for a decade. He played strong on the "strong" side.

Bob Babich returned to Ohio via San Diego in 1973 and remained a force for six seasons. He had a fine career at Miami University (of Ohio) from which he was drafted in the first round by the Chargers in 1969. At the NFL draft meeting, a linebacker from a Mid-American Conference school going in the first round raised a few eyebrows, but Jack Butler of the BLESTO-V scouting combine said, "Don't worry, he's the real deal."

Babich, playing in the middle, allowed Houston to retire gracefully in 1972. Although missing out as a Pro Bowl choice to Pittsburgh's Jack Lambert, Babich was a topflight

middle linebacker for the Browns in the '70s.

As Babich was moving into his "life's work," Dick Ambrose arrived in town. At 6-0, 235, Ambrose was a classic overachiever. Drafted 12th out of Virginia in 1975, he had one thing in mind that summer: "I went to camp prepared. I was determined to work as hard as I could and let the coaches make the decisions."

Ambrose, a strong silent type, was given the nickname "Bam Bam," because of the force of his hits (he literally broke his shoulder pads with the zealousness of his tackles) and the fact that his tackling was the only sound he made on the field. A couple of years later, Ambrose fought off the challenge of Robert L. Jackson,

Tom Cousineau
1982-85

Eddie Johnson
1981-90

Stopping Raiders running back Marcus Allen.

an All-America No. 1 draftee from Texas A&M. Jackson later became Ambrose's inside linebacking mate when the Browns switched to the 3-4 alignment in 1980 during the "Kardiac Kids" era.

Said Ambrose about his football philosophy: "People aren't all that unequal. Anybody can do almost anything if he puts time and effort into it. Sooner or later, he'll get results."

When Clay Matthews left sunny Southern California for Lake Erie in 1978, the Browns were still a 4-3 team. After a one-year apprenticeship, Matthews, a No. 1 draft choice from the University of Southern California, moved into a regular position at right outside line-

backer in 1979. He remained there through most of the '80s as the team went to a 3-4 in 1980. Except for a two-year stint on the left side (1989-90) when the Browns returned to the 4-3, Matthews was the team's right outside linebacker through 1993.

Matthews came from a pro football family. Father Clay Sr. was a defensive end with the 49ers in the early '50s and brother Bruce was a perennial All-Pro interior lineman with the Oilers, in the '80s and '90s.

As durable as he was skilled, Matthews owns the Browns' record for most games played (232) and his 16 seasons with the team ranks second only to Lou Groza's 21. Entering the 1995 season, his career wasn't over. He moved on to Atlanta in 1994 via free-agency. Regardless of how long Matthews plays, he has already

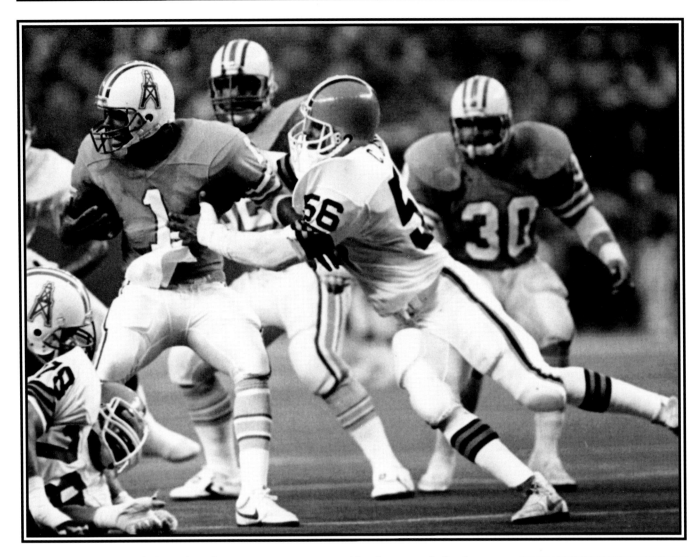

passed a milestone. He has played more games at linebacker that anyone in the history of the NFL. He is a worthy candidate for eventual enshrinement in the Hall of Fame.

Bill Muir, a longtime NFL assistant who was once the offensive line coach of the Baltimore Colts, said, "I'll tell you, when the Browns were in that 3-4, Matthews was as good as you get. Lawrence Taylor and a couple of others got the attention of the media, but Matthews got the attention of his peers. I know we wanted to know exactly where he was on every play. He was the complete package, the consummate linebacker. He was tough against the run, tough against the pass — just tough on every play. When Chip Banks was also on top of his game, Matthews and Banks were the best outside combination anyone had, maybe ever had."

A typical performance by Matthews was a 1986 win, 34-3, over the Bengals. He led a defense that limited 1,000-yard rusher James Brooks to 43 yards on 12 attempts. A scouting report on Matthews before the playoffs that season read: "Matthews has played very well and because of his smarts and experience is never out of position." Matthews again proved the above when in the 1989 playoffs he made a game-clinching interception in a 34-30 victory over Buffalo.

In the middle '80s, paired with Matthews, Chip Banks, another blue-chipper from USC,

Chip Banks
1982-86

Sacking Oilers quarterback Warren Moon.

Mike Johnson *1986-93*

gave the Browns as good a tandem at outside linebacker as any team in the league. Although traded after the 1986 season, Banks was a Pro Bowl selection in four of his five years with the team. There are those inside the NFL who, at the time, would have told you just as Bill Muir previously said, "Banks is among the best in the game at his position: in a class with LT [Lawrence Taylor]."

While in the 3-4 mode through the 1988 season, the Browns had several solid inside linebackers complementing Matthews and Banks. Prodigal Tom Cousineau, from Lakewood's St. Edward High School and Ohio State, returned from a trip to the Canadian Football League and played four seasons (1982-85).

Eddie Johnson of Louisville held down an inside position in the mid-'80s. Mike Johnson, an ex-Hokey from Virginia Tech, emerged as a force in 1987. Johnson started at both right and left inside early in his career, but became a fixture in the middle after the Browns returned to the 4-3 in 1989.

With Matthews and Mike Johnson forming two-thirds of the new alignment in '89, the Browns tried a variety of candidates for the remaining spot through 1992. Included were David Grayson (son of All-Time All-AFL safety Dave Grayson), Van Waiters and David Brandon.

In 1993, Bill Belichick went back to his New York roots, signed ex-Giants linebacker Pepper Johnson and brought him back to his Ohio roots: he had been Defensive Player of the Game 16 times in his Ohio State career.

Johnson, whose first name is Thomas, was nicknamed "Pepper" after sprinkling the spice on his cereal as a youngster. A rookie with the Giants in 1986, he became a star in 1987 and remained so throughout his Giants career. He played in Super Bowl XXI and was All-Pro in 1990 on the Super Bowl XXV champions.

Large at 255, Johnson was always a big hitter. The reputation as such followed him to Cleveland. Belichick said about him shortly after his arrival, "He is by far the best linebacker on the team." Johnson not only

Pepper Johnson
1993-95

responded on the field, but by 1994 was considered the motivational leader of the defense.

Also in 1994, Belichick again returned to his New York experience and signed ex-Giants linebacker Carl Banks, who had moved on to the Redskins for a year. Although 32 years old in '94, Banks was still regarded by most NFL personnel men as "the strongest outside linebacker in the NFL." The reunion of Johnson in the middle and Banks on the left outside seemed to rejuvenate each of them. They were instrumental in the Browns' playoff drive.

In 1995, the Browns again turned to Ohio State for linebacking help when they drafted Craig Powell, a lifelong Browns fan from Youngstown, Ohio, in the first round.

They're called "the last line of defense." If a defensive back makes a mistake, the result can be a quick-strike touchdown for the other guys. Fortunately for the Browns — from Tommy James, Warren Lahr and Cliff Lewis, through Hanford Dixon and Frank Minnifield, to the recent cast headed by Antonio Langham, Stevon Moore and Eric Turner — the tertiary (the third line)

Defensive Backs

By Jim Campbell

has usually been a strong one. One of the key factors in the Browns' playoff-bound resurgence of the mid '90s has been the play of Turner at free safety, Moore at strong safety, and Langham and Don Griffin at the corners.

By his fourth season, 1994, Turner was firmly established as one of the the NFL's best young safeties. No one had more interceptions (9) in the NFL than Turner in 1994. Perhaps his most memorable play, though, was the game-saving hit he put on Dallas' Jay Novacek inches from the goal line as time was running out in the dramatic 19-14 victory in Texas Stadium on Dec. 10.

Turner was simply fulfilling a prediction of a survey of coaches and personnel men who said of him, "Definitely playing at an All-Pro level. He can really sting and he likes the atten-

tion that comes with making big hits." When Turner was a rookie in 1991, his first hit was a "big" one — he bent Cincinnati Bengal running back James Brooks' face mask on his first official tackle in the NFL.

Langham, taken ninth overall in the 1994 draft out of Alabama, where he was the Crimson Tide's all-time interceptions leader, earned a starting job and won All-Rookie Team honors. Langham made the NFL sit up and take notice with his outstanding "cover" work. He consistently drew the opposition's best receiver and neutralized him. From day one, reports called him "fearless and aggressive."

In the beginning, the secondary was a three-man gang. While some teams put a gridiron version of the Three Stooges on the field, the Browns had some of the AAFC's very best in the lineup.

Tommy Colella, while seeing considerable action as an offensive halfback, made 10 interceptions in 1946. No one in pro football — AAFC and NFL — made more. It is still a Browns single-season record, although tied by Thom Darden in 1978. Cliff Lewis and Don Greenwood were other early secondary standouts. And remember, Otto Graham also contributed five interceptions that first year.

Because of the seven-diamond alignment, the secondary deployed as two "defensive halfbacks" and one "safety." In 1948, the Browns were infused with two future greats — Tommy James and Warren Lahr. They would give the team a solid set of defensive halfbacks.

James, of course, played for Paul Brown at Massillon and Ohio State. Lahr was from Western Reserve. James played for the Lions in 1947 and "welcomed the change" in coming to Cleveland. Through 1951, the Browns' trio was James and Lahr at the corners and Cliff Lewis at safety. No one took many liberties with this combo.

James reflected on the time: "We were all young and quick. Warren [Lahr] was quick and heady. He knew where to be and how to play

Eric Turner *FS-SS•1991-95*

Tommy James *CB • 1948-55*

the receiver. Same for Cliff [Lewis]. He was a quarterback at Duke — he could think, tackle and cover."

As to tactics, James said, "We used zone and man to man, and some combinations. But you had to be careful not to tip your hand. If you were in 'combo,' you had to disguise it. A quarterback didn't need to be an Otto Graham to figure out where the 'man' coverage was and go to that receiver — eventually, he'd be open. We had good personnel and were well-schooled."

As the '50s progressed, so did NFL defenses. The 5-3 evolved into the 4-3 and gave rise to a four-man secondary. After the 1951 season, Lewis retired and the Browns entered a transition period in both personnel and formation. Lahr and James continued at the corners in 1952, but rookie Bert Rechichar succeeded Lewis at safety. In addition, second-year man Don Shula saw limited playing time in James' position.

Then in 1953, Paul Brown engineered the largest trade in NFL history, a 10-for-five swap with Baltimore that sent, among the 10, both Rechichar and Shula to the Baltimore Colts. This, combined with the Browns switching to a four-man secondary in '53, left the team with two major holes.

They were filled by a pair of Kens: Ken Gorgal, a second-year man from Purdue, and Ken Konz, a rookie from Louisiana State. Konz, James and Lahr each had five interceptions in 1953's inaugural season of the four-man secondary. James had three in one game, on Nov. 1 in a 27-3 win over Washington.

Before the 1953 title game with the Detroit Lions, Head Coach Buddy Parker's scouting report included these quotes:

Ken Gorgal: "He is really a hard-nosed kid. Good tough tackler. He and Lahr work well together."

Warren Lahr: "Very good defensive halfback. Comes up fast on runs. Have to be careful throwing in his zone — he lays back on purpose trying to get you to throw in his area so he can intercept. You can throw on his side, but I think he is much tougher than the other side."

Ken Konz *S•1953-59*

Don Paul
CB • 1954-58

Tommy James: "Very good tackler. Comes up real fast on running plays. Good on pass defense. He will play [Cloyce] Box for the deep one. We should flank Box way out and 'hook' him until James comes up."

Parker wasn't quite as laudatory of Konz, but remember that he was a rookie and went on to play later in the Pro Bowl. Konz remained a starter through 1958 and was the yearly leader, or tied for the lead, in Browns interceptions five times. He also punted and returned punts during his Browns career. Gorgal, meanwhile, moved on to the Chicago Bears in '55.

Don Paul, sometimes confused with a villainous Rams linebacker of the same name and vintage, joined the mix in 1954 and allowed

James to move to safety where his savvy was still valuable. Paul was a free spirit obtained from the Chicago Cardinals. Former Browns assistant coach Dick Gallagher recalled how Paul would break the tedium at practice, if not endear himself to the staid Paul Brown: "He was really a character. One of the things he would do before practice on rainy days was to 'hit a home run.' He'd stand where home plate was on the infield part of the Stadium, knock an imaginary ball over the wall and then slide into each base as he shouted the play-by-play. He'd be covered with mud before we even started practice. It really cracked up the players, but I don't think P.B. appreciated it all that much."

But as long as Don Paul made the Pro Bowl (1957-59), Paul Brown put up with his antics. Later, a Browns publication rated Paul "the

Browns' greatest defensive back in the short term." In the long run, Lahr earned "the greatest" label.

Ex-Notre Damer John Petitbon moved in at right safety in 1956 before being traded to the Packers in '57. Not to worry — Lowe "Junior" Wren, a second-year man from Missouri, took over and started for three seasons before being dealt to the Steelers.

Lahr, "as heady a player as I've ever seen," according to James, moved to safety in 1959, his final season. That was the year two newcomers joined the starting secondary: corners Bernie Parrish and Jim Shofner.

Parrish was not only an All-America from Florida, but also a talented baseball player. At the time, baseball paid more and Parrish signed a $30,000 bonus contract with the Cincinnati Reds. But after two years of long, tiring bus rides in the minors, Parrish wanted to compete at a major league level, even if in a different sport.

He wrote a "bread & butter" letter to Paul Brown saying, "Being drafted by the Browns [No. 9 in 1958] was the greatest honor I ever received in football." Although an offensive standout, Parrish told P.B., "I like running the ball, but I think my best position may be defensive back." He was right. Parrish played in a couple of Pro Bowls and set an interception return record of 92 yards in 1960 that lasted until Najee Mustafaa went 97 in 1993.

To say Parrish was outspoken is to say Jim Brown could run with the football. Parrish was a leader of the players union and a burr under management's saddle. He also had many suggestions for his defensive coaches, but he was instrumental in the Browns' 1964 championship defense.

Threatening to retire in 1966, Head Coach Blanton Collier made Parrish a player-coach that year, saying, "Bernie knows as much or more about football than any other player in the NFL, and this year he will be coaching the defensive backs as well as playing with them." But Parrish said he seldom had any coaching input. If getting even for the slight was on Par-

rish's mind, he did to some extent. In 1971, he authored a controversial book, *They Call It A Game*. Some looked at him as an ingrate; others as a visionary. The book was billed as "an indictment of the pro football establishment," and did ruffle more than one feather, especially in the Cleveland area.

Jim Shofner
CB • 1958-63

During the seven seasons (1959-65) that Parrish started at left cornerback, he was paired for the first five on the right with Texas Christian's Jim Shofner. A running back at TCU, Shofner led the Southwest Conference in rushing his senior season and was drafted No. 1 by the Browns in '58. Converted to cornerback by

Ross Fichtner
S • 1960-67

his short time he made quite an impression. He went to Florida from Shadyside, Ohio, a mill town not too far from Groza's Martins Ferry. He began his Gators career as a 180-pound two-way end, but made his reputation as a receiver.

Drafted in the 28th round by the Chicago Cardinals in 1959 with a year of eligibility remaining, Fleming didn't give pro football much thought and was going to give baseball a shot. However, his Florida roommate, Parrish, convinced the Browns he could be a good defensive back and they traded for his rights.

Fleming didn't disappoint. He became a starter immediately. In his first pro game in 1960, he intercepted Norm Van Brocklin twice — it was the season the Dutchman led the Eagles to their last NFL crown. Parrish likened Fleming to Pro Football Hall of Famer Larry Wilson in size and temperament: "Don was angular and lean like Wilson and a relentless hitter. He was a good student of the game."

Paul Brown agreed: "Don Fleming will be one of the stars of this game." But tragedy struck on June 4, 1963. Working on a construction project (both Fleming and Parrish were building construction majors in college), the young defensive back was electrocuted.

Bobby Franklin of Ole Miss was another 1960 addition. He had been a fine quarterback in college, but like many offensive stars of the two-way era in college, he found himself learning how to back-pedal and knock down passes in the pros.

Paul Brown, Shofner adapted so successfully that he tied Bobby Franklin for the team lead in interceptions in 1960 with eight. He still utilized his running skills, however, as he returned punts for portions of his Browns career (1958-63).

Shofner later coached at TCU in the '60s and '70s. He returned to the Browns for two separate assistant coaching stints, 1978-80, and in 1990, the latter of which resulted in his serving as interim head coach after Bud Carson was fired with eight games remaining.

The Browns have retired just five jersey numbers over the years. Graham's and Groza's are obvious. One that may not be so, outside of Browns followers, is No. 46, Don Fleming's. He was a safety with the Browns from 1960-62. In

Franklin and rookie Lowell Caylor of Miami University (Ohio) were starting right safeties in a very young Browns secondary in the 1964 championship season. Second-year men Larry Benz and Walter Beach were the primary left safety and right cornerback, respectively. Benz moved in following an injury to fifth-year man Ross Fichtner. Parrish, at left corner, had the most NFL experience.

In an era when the NFL looked down its collective nose at the AFL, Beach caused a stir. He was cut by the AFL's Boston Patriots, one of

Erich Barnes *CB-S • 1965-71*

Ernie Kellermann *S·1966-71*

Mike Howell CB-S · 1965-72

Ben Davis
CB · 1967-68, '70-73

the rival league's weaker teams, and became a starter for the Browns. Go figure!

Cornerback Erich Barnes arrived in 1965 as part of a three-team deal involving the Browns, Giants and Lions. The Browns traded linebacker Mike Lucci to Detroit, who shipped quarterback Earl Morrall to New York. The Giants then sent guard Darrell Dess to Detroit and Barnes to Cleveland. Barnes was the prototype for today's bigger defensive back: 6-3, 198, fast and tough. It was said that Barnes was "good at pushing and shoving before the bump-and-run was used." He began his Browns career at right corner. Then, after Parrish retired, he moved to the left for five years before finishing his career at right safety in 1971.

Ernie Kellermann, who produced big yards as a quarterback at Miami University (of Ohio),

joined the Browns in 1966 and played safety with distinction. The baby-faced assassin gave the Browns quality service through 1971 and then moved on to Paul Brown's Cincinnati Bengals.

Mike Howell of Grambling played both corner and safety from the mid '60s through 1972. He led the Browns in interceptions in 1966 with eight (tied with Ross Fichtner) and in 1969 with six.

Cornerback Ben Davis joined the team in 1967. He became a starter almost immediately and, with the exception of missing the 1969 season due to injury, provided steady play through 1973. In his second season, 1968, he set a team

Clarence Scott
CB-SS-FS • 1971-83

record for most consecutive games with an interception: seven.

He did it between Oct. 20 and Dec. 1, 1968 for a streak of seven games as the Browns finished the season with a 10-4 record and the Eastern Conference title. He had eight interceptions in the regular season and one against the Dallas Cowboys in the conference championship game.

Davis' rise to NFL stardom was meteoric. Born in Alabama, he went to high school in Fair Lawn, N.J., via sponsorship by the Quakers. It wasn't to play football, but to play the cornet in the Fair Lawn High School band.

He spent a post-graduate year at Bridgton (Maine) Academy. Bridgton had no band, so Davis joined the football team. He attended

Defiance College, an NCAA Division III school in northwestern Ohio, where he gained 1,815 yards on 288 carries (6.3 yards a carry) and scored 23 touchdowns.

In his first season with the Browns, Davis led the NFL in punt return average (12.7 yards per return) and returned kickoffs (26.2 average, seventh in the league). When he retired after the 1973 season he had 17 career interceptions.

Walt Sumner of Florida State was another versatile defensive back. From 1969-74, he logged playing time at safety and corner.

At Kansas State, Clarence Scott played well enough to warrant being the Browns' No. 1 pick in 1971. All he did after that was give the Browns 13 solid seasons in the secondary. As knowledge replaced speed as his number one asset, Scott moved from cornerback to strong

Ron Bolton CB • 1976-82

Thom Darden FS • 1972-74, '76-81

safety to free safety, but the important thing is that for more than a decade, he played at a level that allowed him to remain in the starting line-up longer than any defensive back in Browns history.

Thom Darden left Michigan in 1972 as a No. 1 draft choice and brought great range to the free safety position through 1981. He had actually been a "Wolfman," or roving line-backer for the Wolverines. By this time, zones were prevalent and right safeties were "free" to roam and play the ball. Darden played "center-field," as it was called, as well as anyone in the game at the time.

Darden led or tied the Browns in intercep-tions six times. Approaching 1995, his 10 inter-ceptions in 1978 and 45 in his career were both team records.

Darden and Scott manned the two safety slots for Sam Rutigliano's 1980 Kardiac Kids, while Ron Bolton and Clinton Burrell were the cor-nerbacks. Said Sam Rutigliano: "For a team to be successful, it must have a solid core of veter-ans to provide leadership. We were fortunate to have had a guy like Thom Darden. He was a leader and a winner."

Darden prepared for success after football by getting corporate and business experience during his playing days. He said, "If I had my druthers, I would play the rest of my life. But there's no way I can physically or mentally."

Hanford Dixon of Southern Mississippi arrived in 1981 as a No. 1 draft choice and immediately impressed NFL observers. But it

Hanford Dixon *CB·1981-89*

Stevon Moore *SS • 1992-95*

Antonio Langham
CB • 1994-95

wasn't until Frank Minnifield came over from the ill-fated United States Football League in 1984 that the Browns had a dominant young pair of cornerbacks for their playoff run of five straight seasons (1985-89).

The originator of the "Dawg" moniker that soon became the "Dawg Defense" and the "Dawg Pound," Dixon was a three-time Pro Bowl selection in his nine-year career (1981-89). Minnifield played through 1992 and was a four-time Pro Bowl pick.

For too short of a time (1984-85), they were augmented by Don Rogers, an All-America from UCLA and first-round draft choice. Tragically, Rogers died of a drug overdose.

Felix Wright, a free safety from Drake, moved into the starting lineup in 1987 and proceeded to lead or tie for the team interceptions crown four consecutive seasons, including an NFL high of nine in 1989.

The eventual departures of Dixon, Minnifield and Wright left Head Coach Bill Belichick with a secondary in transition when he assumed duties in 1991. A variety of names began to appear, and disappear, including Randy Hilliard, Steven Braggs, Harlon Barnett, Vince Newsome, Terry Taylor, Najee Mustafaa and Everson Walls.

But by 1995, the quartet of Don Griffin and Antonio Langham at the corners, and Stevon Moore and Eric Turner at the safeties, appeared set for several seasons. Once again, the Browns appeared to have a last line of defense that is first class.

When the Browns first started playing in 1946, little emphasis was placed on what was then very loosely defined as "the kicking game." Kicking, returning, covering kicks — now known as special teams — just weren't that special. It was simply a case of who was on the field rather than utilizing specialists for particular phases of the game. Once again, however,

Kickers & Punters

By Jim Campbell

Paul Brown showed the way. The precision place-kicking of Lou Groza and the cloud-seeding punting of Horace Gillom (despite what one writer called "the worst form and the best punts in pro football") gave the Browns a couple of early specialists before most teams even thought of such luxuries.

In the first years of the AAFC, Groza and Gillom really weren't luxuries. Groza was a regular left offensive tackle — good enough to start at the position in six Pro Bowls during his career — in addition to doing all the place-kicking.

After 1946, the punting was left to Gillom, who was used as an offensive and defensive end. In his career (1947-1956), he caught 74 passes for 1,083 yards, but only five receptions in his last three years. He backed up both

Dante Lavelli and Mac Speedie, leading Paul Brown to remark, after the Browns were admitted to the National Football League in 1950, that Gillom could be a starter with the other NFL teams.

Tommy James, a fine defensive back of the late '40s and '50s, and Groza's longtime holder, said: "If we didn't have Lavelli and Speedie, Horace would have been a starting offensive end — and a good one."

Groza would remain an All-Pro tackle until a back injury reduced him to kicking specialist only, after sitting out the 1960 season. Like the offensive left tackle spot (which featured Groza, Dick Schafrath and Doug Dieken from 1947-1984), the history of the Browns' kicking game can nearly be told by simply detailing the careers of Groza and his two primary successors — Don Cockroft and Matt Bahr, along with present day kicker Matt Stover.

Former Browns assistant coach Dick Gallagher shed some light on why the Browns were unique with one primary kicker and punter when many other teams took a committee approach: "Remember that in 1946 a lot of players were products of the old single-wing where the tailback was a 'triple threat' — run, pass, kick. We had players like Tommy Colella, Mac Speedie and Dippy Evans, who could kick and punt pretty well — but none like Groza and Gillom. Other teams weren't lucky. It was not uncommon to see a half-dozen or so different players figure in another team's season stats."

He continued, "Without specialists, it was just a case of who was in the game when the occasion arose."

Even the Browns practiced a little kicking by committee in 1946. Groza took 47 extra-point attempts (making 45) while two-way end John Rokisky and Speedie were good on each of their only attempts. By 1948 Groza was the man. He took every PAT and field goal attempt.

Like many of the Browns, Groza had played for Paul Brown at Ohio State, but only as a freshman. World War II interrupted and Groza served three years in the South Pacific, including on Okinawa. It was said that Groza kept his kicking skills sharp by kicking coconuts over palm tree goalposts. An amusing story, but one that wilted under closer scrutiny. However, between military duties, Groza did get some kicking time in, using balls and shoes sent to him by Brown.

Asked if he thought Brown singled him out for his kicking potential, the Hall of Famer replied, "No mention was made. I felt he signed me as a football player. You have to remember there was no real specialization then. In those days, kicking was incidental to playing. Horace Gillom was an end and his punting was incidental, too. But he did it well and helped our football team to win."

Groza was very innovative in his kicking methods. He and Don Greenwood, one of his first holders, devised a six-foot length of tape with a crosspiece for a "spot" — from where the ball was to be kicked to where Groza stood — to help him align himself and take the proper steps. Later he incorporated the guiding strip into an actual tee. It worked marvelously well, but was banned by the NFL before the Browns joined the league in 1950.

He still considers his last-minute 16-yard field goal, the margin of victory over the Rams in the 1950 title game, "my biggest thrill in pro football."

Sitting out the 1960 season with a back injury, Groza returned in 1961 to kick seven more years. He was exclusively a kicker by then, but still among the game's best. Including Groza's AAFC totals, "the Toe" scored 1,608 points.

Although his field goal kicking percentage (55%) is not as lofty as today's kickers, several things need to be kept in mind. First and foremost, the goalposts were on the goal line at the time, not the end line (10 yards further back) as they are today. If the Browns had the ball on their opponent's 40 yard line or closer, Groza could try a 47-yard kick. If he made it, three points. If he missed, the opponent got the ball at their 20. No big deal! Today, it would come out to the 40 on a miss — a nice bonus for the opposition. The philosophy seemed to be then: cross midfield and we'll try a field goal from anywhere we bog down. Thus, while the kicks today may actually be longer in relation to the

scrimmage line and goalposts, the penalty for a miss is now greater. Consequently, many coaches are reluctant to try a kick from far out. No longer can NFL teams automatically think "three points" as soon as midfield is crossed. A more realistic place to try a field goal today is from the 20 or 25 yard line on in. Only in desperate situations, such as time running out or behind in the score, are teams likely to take anything other than a "chip shot." This helps modern percentages.

Another thing to keep in mind is that work on sophisticated blocking schemes — protection for the kicker — was not intense in Groza's day. There was a larger chance of a "leaker" sifting through to block an attempted kick. An

CLASSIC STYLE: *Groza displays an early version of his straight-on kicking form in this field goal versus the New York Yankees in 1947. Otto Graham is the holder in the 26-17 win.*

295

incident where a 6-6 Big Daddy Lipscomb would hoist a 6-4 Don Burroughs on his shoulders to block a kick attempt would no longer be allowed by today's rules.

Today's kickers benefit from closer hash marks, too. Groza and his contemporaries had a much more difficult angle when kicking from the hashes. All this doesn't mean Groza could not match today's kickers at times. In 1953 he boomed 23 of 26 field goal attempts through the pipes, 88.5%, the best season in Browns his-

STAYING STRAIGHT: *Groza and holder Tommy James practice in 1948 with the six-foot guide tape designed to keep the Browns' kicker properly aligned. The tape was later ruled illegal by the NFL before the Browns joined the league in 1950.*

tory until Matt Stover broke the mark with 26 of 28 (92.8%) in 1994.

Late in Groza's career he had to contend with a new phenomenon, the kamikaze. By the mid 1960s in the NFL, rookies and hellbent-for-leather younger players were assigned to kick-coverage and return teams, where they just streaked downfield on kickoffs and tried to tackle the returner, separating him from the ball if possible, if not separating his head from his shoulders.

Ike Kelley, a linebacker for the Philadelphia Eagles at the time, took it a step further.

As part of the kick-return team, he wasn't as interested in blocking for the return man as he was in taking out Groza, the kicker. He would seek out Groza, who by this point in his career was not so intent on getting downfield to make a tackle, and try to wipe him out. Usually, the younger man prevailed, but Groza never shied away from the confrontation. Ironically, Kelley was a fellow Buckeye, having played at Ohio State for Woody Hayes.

Despite being a pioneer specialist, Groza still kicked over 50% of his field goals when the norm was closer to 30%. Ben Agajanian, a man who kicked for many years for many teams in many leagues, said of Groza, "Lou was the best of the olden days kickers. He kicked better under pressure than anyone I know. I can't remember him missing a clutch field goal."

Paul Brown said it simply, succinctly and best: "Lou Groza shortened the football field for us — from one-hundred yards to sixty yards."

As for Groza, he is very philosophical about the pressures of kicking. "If I missed," he said with a chuckle, "I just blamed the center or the holder and looked forward to the next kick." Groza seldom had to blame the center or the holder.

The year Groza sat (1960), Sam Baker filled in capably. Baker, a player who did nothing to dispel the image of kickers as flakes, led the NFL in PAT attempts and PATs made (46 and 44). The journeyman kicker was also good on 12 of 20 field goals. For good measure, the eccentric Baker did the Browns' punting and compiled a 42-yard average.

The Browns were indeed fortunate in maintaining continuity in their kicking game. Groza retired after the 1967 season. In 1968, after a year of learning and observing on the taxi squad, Don Cockroft took over. As a rookie, he converted 46 of 48 PATs and 18 of 24 field goal attempts. The ex-Adams State kicker was also the Browns' punter. He continued to go against the flow of NFL mainstream thinking and do both, saving the team a valuable roster spot, through 1976.

In his 13-year career, Cockroft kicked 432 of 458 PATs and 216 of 328 field goals. This added up to 1,080 points, No. 2 on the Browns' all-time NFL-only list behind Groza's 1,349. In his nine seasons as a punter, Cockroft kicked 651 times, averaging 40.3 yards per kick.

By the time Cockroft came on the scene, no other team had the same person as their front line kicker *and* punter.

Cockroft, a man whose 13 consecutive seasons with the Browns is third behind Clay Matthews' 16 and Groza's and Doug Dieken's 14, represented a dinosaur in another way, too. He was a straight-on kicker. And by the end of his career, he would be a true throwback as the sidewinding soccer-style kickers had made irreversible inroads in the NFL.

A superbly coordinated athlete, Cockroft had great power in his well-used leg, especially for a 190-pound straightaway kicker. His 57-yard field goal versus Denver in 1972 trails only Steve Cox's 60- and 58-yarders in the Browns' record book. Cox, primarily a thunder-footed punter, was occasionally called on for long distance field goals. At least twice he delivered.

When Cockroft reached the end of his very productive career in 1980, the team recycled former Steelers kicker Matt Bahr via a mid-season trade with the 49ers. Bahr, a soccer player for his father, Walter, at Penn State, was the Browns' first soccer-style kicker when he came on board.

Like his brother, Chris, also a Penn Stater who enjoyed a fine and lengthy career with the Bengals and Raiders, Matt had played pro soccer before graduating from Penn State. NCAA rules allow a student-athlete to retain his or her amateur standing in a particular sport, even in light of signing a professional contract, as long as the sport in which the athlete "turned pro" is

TOP FORM: *Groza cleans his familiar high-top shoes in one of his best-ever seasons: 1957. He led the NFL in scoring with 77 points on a league-high 15 field goals on 22 attempts and a perfect 32-for-32 on PATs.*

not the same one in which he or she attempts to still compete in college.

The smallish Bahr (5-10, 175) led the Browns in scoring eight times in nine seasons from 1981-89. Bahr's theory on kicking was simple: "Pressure is what you put on yourself. What's important is how you handle it. One thing you have to do as a kicker is to want to go out and kick. You live for the clutch situations. If you miss, you have to want to get out and try again."

However, during Bahr's tenure, injuries prevented him from always playing week after week. One who took up the slack was longtime Redskin Mark Moseley, the last of the straight-on place-kickers who was vital in the late-sea-

The Legacy of Kickers

In the Browns' 50-year history, the majority of place-kicking has been done by these four players.

Lou Groza *1946-59, '61-67*

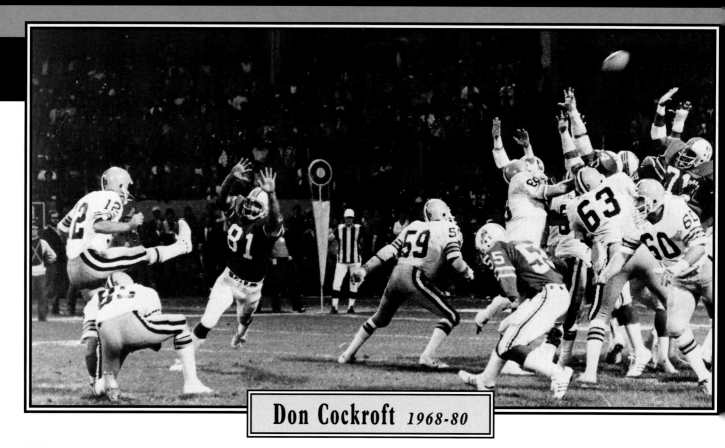

Don Cockroft *1968-80*

Matt Bahr *1981-89*

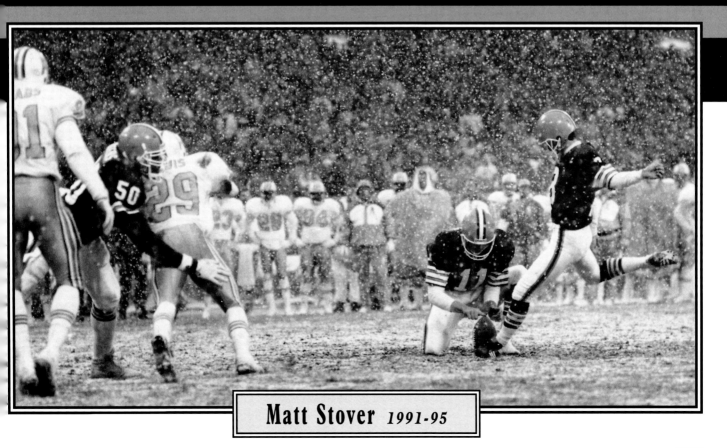

Matt Stover *1991-95*

Sam Baker P-K • 1960-61

BETWEEN TOES: *Sam Baker performed kicking duties in 1960 during Lou Groza's one-year retirement. Baker also punted in 1960-61. Above, his blocker (left) and holder (right) is safety Bobby Franklin.*

son drive of 1986, especially his winning field goal in the double overtime playoff win over the New York Jets.

Nevertheless, Bahr eventually became the Browns' most accurate field goal percentage kicker during his tenure. He converted 143 of 193 attempts for a 74.1 percentage. As was the case with Groza and Cockroft, the longevity factor also applies to Bahr. Entering the 1995 season with the New England Patriots, Bahr looked forward to his 17th NFL season.

Two years after Bahr departed and a year after Jerry Kauric held kicking duties in 1990, the Browns settled on Matt Stover, a refugee from the Giants' injured reserve list, in 1991.

The Louisiana Tech graduate has proven to be an increasingly productive and accurate kicker. It was his fourth and final field goal of the game (a 45-yarder with :04 on the clock) that beat the Bengals in the third week of the 1991 season.

Stover entered 1995 as the new Browns record holder for field goal accuracy. He surpassed Bahr during the 1994 season when he kicked 26 of 28 and raised his career percentage to 78.2%. He has converted 79 of 101 attempts through 1994, including 20 straight to close out the '94 season, a new team record.

Although Horace Gillom would become a great punter with the Browns for a number of years, he didn't join the team until he left the University of Nevada in 1947. Gillom was no stranger to Paul Brown. He played for him at Massillon's Washington High School before Brown went to Ohio State.

Until Gillom's arrival, the Browns passed the punting duties around. In their first season, Tommy Colella was the main punter — 47 kicks for a 40.3 average, but Fred "Dippy" Evans and Mac Speedie punted eight and three times for a 38- and 28-yard average, respectively. From 1947 on, it was mainly Gillom's job, although Ermal Allen, Cliff Lewis and Warren Lahr would occasionally put instep to leather from punt formation.

Gillom brought a different style of punting to the game. He was the first to kick for height and distance. His 80- and 75-yard punts are still in the Browns' record book. Gillom was a proponent of "hang time" long before the term gained widespread usage. Gillom also stood

duties from 1956-61. Baker, filling in for Groza as a place-kicker when Lou was injured in 1960, stayed on to punt only in 1961 and had another fine season with a 43.3 yard average.

Rookie No. 1 draft choice Gary Collins took over in 1962. Again, good fortune or good planning favored the Browns. Collins, a consensus All-America at the University of Maryland, was also a starting wide receiver and a good one. In addition to burning various and sundry corner-

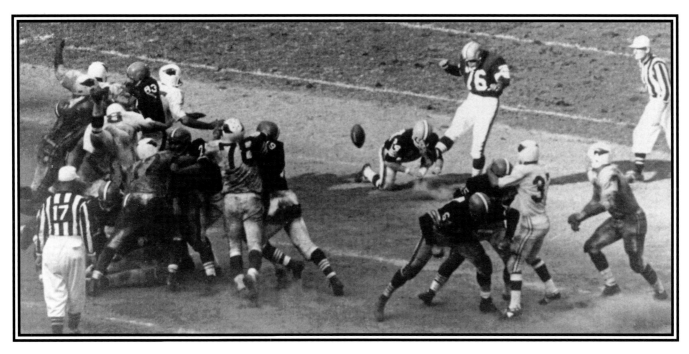

much deeper than the average punter of his era. This cut down on the possibility of any of his punts being blocked. He took a 15-yard drop, while many others still kicked from 10 or 12 yards behind the line of scrimmage.

In addition, Paul Brown was beginning to spread the punting formation. Rather than bunching up to protect the kicker, Brown felt if Gillom would drop deeper the Browns could spread themselves a little thinner along the line. This allowed the cover men — mostly the ends at the time — to get downfield more quickly. That Gillom could be so deep and still average 45.5 or 45.7 in some seasons tells you just how much thunder there was in his foot.

When Gillom's career ended, Fred "Curly" Morrison, Ken Konz, Dick Deschaine, Lowe "Junior" Wren and Sam Baker handled the

OLD RELIABLE: *After a one-year retirement due to a back injury, Groza returns in 1961 to kick the winning field goal in a 20-17 victory over the St. Louis Cardinals in Game Two. His second retirement would not come until age 43 in 1967.*

backs on his seemingly patented "post-pattern" pass routes, Collins was the Browns' punter through 1967.

Collins always posed a threat to run or pass from punt formation. But mainly he was a strong kicker. His 46.7 yard average in 1965 led the NFL by a substantial margin. Keep in mind that Collins would often be called on to punt after running downfield on a pass pattern on the previous down.

The Browns often benefited from having a specialist who was more than a specialist. The kicking phase of Browns history is filled with

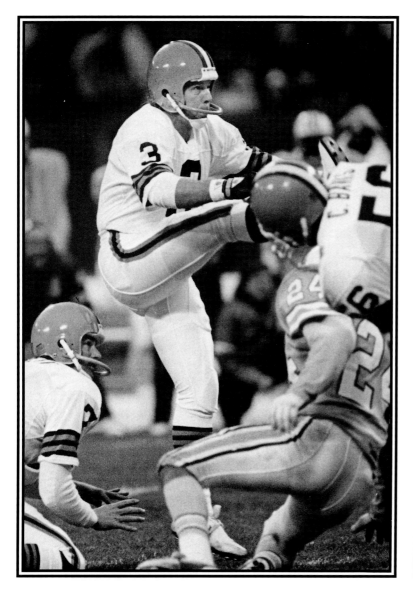

Steve Cox *P-K • 1981-84*

Mark Moseley
K • 1986

names of players with multiple duties: Groza, tackle-kicker; Cockroft, kicker-punter; Fred "Curly" Morrison, fullback-punter; Collins, receiver-punter; Junior Wren, defensive back-punter; and Johnny Evans, quarterback-punter. Even the 1994-95 punter, Tom Tupa, has played QB.

Cockroft took over from Collins in 1968 and held the job through 1976. Then in '77, the punting parade featured Greg Coleman, who would later have a successful career with the Vikings, followed by Johnny Evans (1978-80).

Steve Cox, whose strong leg often overshadowed the fact that he could place the ball out of bounds when needed, was the regular in 1981-82 and '84. Jeff Gossett was the choice in 1983 and 1985-87. He was followed by Max Runager

(1988), Bryan Wagner (1989-90), Brian Hansen (1991-93) and finally Tupa (1994-95).

Tupa, once the Cardinals' starting quarterback, also became the Browns' holder on placekicks. Many punters end up as holders by default. Teams feel that they may as well do something useful at practice other than just stand around when not working on punting. Holding seems to be a logical move. They have a chance to get to know the place-kicker much better than a "position" player would and can establish a better rapport, which is very important in creating a smooth-working snapper-holder-kicker relationship.

Tupa is destined to become the answer to a trivia question: Who was the first NFL player to score on a two-point conversion? He did it in 1994 when the rule was first instituted.

Jeff Gossett *P·1983,'85-87*

Brian Hansen
P·1991-93

In addition to punters, quarterbacks have been frequently utilized as holders, although in the '90s era of high-salaried quarterbacks, the risk of injury to a "franchise" player is usually too great to make a starting QB the holder. Quarterback holders for the Browns have included Otto Graham, Bobby Freeman, Jim Ninowski and Paul McDonald.

A rule that also affected punting averages, as well as punt return averages, is the one keeping cover men on the line until the ball is actually punted — earlier rules allowed the kicking team to send their kamikazes flying downfield at the snap.

Special teams are sometimes taught to leave at the thud of the kick — although more sophisticated coaching has the cover guys leaving on a certain count, knowing just how long after the snap the ball will be kicked. This is all well and good on a perfect snap, but if the ball in bobbled, an illegal procedure (leaving before the ball is kicked) penalty is almost automatic.

Each team now has several specialists who are important parts of the punting team in that they are the widely-placed cover men who attempt to get downfield in a hurry and down the ball, keep it from going into the end zone, or tackle the returner, whichever the case may be. Kick return teams counter by assigning two men, usually, to hold up the fleet "bomb squadders." As with other aspects of the game, for every new move by one unit a counter move is usually made — and made quickly — by the other unit.

Those who cover professional football have been known to remark of an electrifying performer, "He can change your field position quicker than anyone on the football field other than the referee." As often as not, the player they're talking about is a kick returner. There's no more dramatic example of this, nor of his value to the ball club, than what Eric Metcalf did on Oct. 24, 1993 before 78,118 in Cleveland Stadium. In a 28-23 victory over the Steelers, Metcalf turned the game on two monster plays.

His 91-yard punt return helped stake the Browns to a 14-10 lead. And with the Steelers leading, 23-21, at the midway point of the final

Returners

By Jim Campbell

quarter, the 190-pound "lightning bolt in a bottle" ripped through the Steelers' coverage, streaked down the right sideline, cut back, and scored on a 75-yard punt return to seal the victory for Cleveland. Speaking at a time when the World Series was won by Toronto on a dramatic seventh-game home run, Metcalf said, "I kinda feel like Joe Carter." (the Blue Jays' outfielder who hit the winning shot.)

Statistically, the Steelers had the better of the game, by far. But only one statistic really counts, the final score, and Metcalf put the Browns on the long end. It wasn't the only time the son of one-time St. Louis Cardinals "franchise" Terry Metcalf had done that for the Browns.

Metcalf's 91-yarder was the longest punt return in Browns history, eclipsing the previous

mark of 84 yards, set by Gerald McNeil in 1986. Four Browns have broken the 100-yard barrier on kickoff returns: Carl Ward (104) in 1967, Leroy Bolden (102) in 1958, Metcalf (101) in 1990 and McNeil (100) in 1986.

The emphasis placed on today's kick and punt return game is in dramatic contrast to professional football of the 1940s, when the Browns made their debut in the All-America Football Conference. Dick Gallagher, a Browns assistant coach from 1947-49 and 1955-59 said, "Returning kicks was no big deal when we first started. If you were on the field, you did it."

A look at the figures proves the accuracy of Gallagher's statement. No less than seven different Browns players returned punts in 1946. Nearly double that number returned kickoffs. Who were the primary guys? A couple of Hall of Famers who did OK in other phases of the game: Otto Graham and Marion Motley. Sound incredible?

Who would risk injury to a legendary quarterback today by having him perform what is arguably the most dangerous job in football? Certainly, the 49ers never even thought of asking Joe Montana to return punts. How many other rushing-leader, 240-pound fullbacks can you name who also led the team in kickoff returns as Motley did? All of this just adds to what Gallagher said about it being "no big deal" in the days before specialization.

It was 1948 before Cliff Lewis took over for Graham as the front-line punt returner. However, Graham continued to return some punts a while longer. By the time the Browns had joined the NFL, Motley, too, had turned over the return chores to others.

In the 1950s, teams began using younger runners for return duties, both punts and kickoffs. For the Browns it was players such as Ken Carpenter, Don "Dopey" Phelps, Bob Smith,

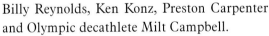

Billy Reynolds, Ken Konz, Preston Carpenter and Olympic decathlete Milt Campbell.

By 1954, most teams used twin rather than single safeties. Two players were deep, but either could, and did, return the kicks. An example was Reynolds and Chet "the Jet" Hanulak. Reynolds returned 25 punts and 14 kickoffs that year; Hanulak 27 punts and nine kickoffs. Interestingly, the Browns returned only 30 kickoffs all year. It was the days of kicking off from the 40-yard line when touchbacks were more the norm than the exception.

In the late '50s, Bobby Mitchell brought his special brand of magic to the game. Not only did he lead the Browns in punt and/or kickoff returns from 1958-1961, he ran like blazes from scrimmage and caught passes, too. During the time frame, Mitchell scored at least one touch-

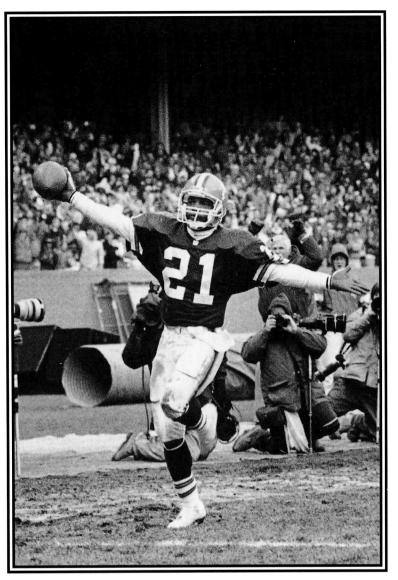

CHANGING TIMES: *Return specialists did not exist in the '40s when 6-1, 238-pound Browns fullback Marion Motley (left) returned kicks. In the '90s, however, the Browns and all NFL teams knew that a speed burner like 5-10, 190-pound Eric Metcalf (right) can make the game-breaking difference in the score.*

down on a punt or kickoff return each year, usually in the 90-yard category.

There are those who will tell you that Mitchell made the Pro Football Hall of Fame on his numbers as a prolific receiver with the Washington Redskins, but very few of them live in the Cleveland area. Paul Warfield, who knows about these things, said of Mitchell, "He really terrified defenders."

After Mitchell departed, the Browns utilized Howard "Hopalong" Cassady and Jim Shorter as punt returners in 1962 and '63,

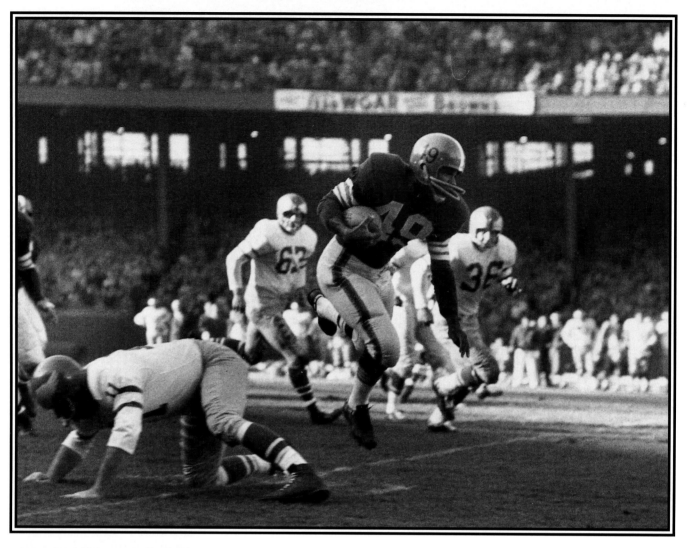

Bobby Mitchell
1958-61

respectively. The Browns' primary kickoff returners were Tom Wilson in 1962 and Charley Scales in '63. Then came three of the best seasons in Browns return-man history. From 1964-66, it was Leroy Kelly returning the punts and Walter "the Flea" Roberts returning the kicks. They formed arguably the best tandem in team history until Metcalf and Randy Baldwin shared duties in the 1990s.

Roberts is generally recognized as the Browns' first true return specialist: "The Flea" was a 160-pound flyer from San Jose State. He led the team in kickoff returns in each of his three seasons with the team (1964-66) before being taken by the Saints in the 1967 expansion draft. Roberts' 25.9-yard return average ranks

second behind Greg Pruitt (26.3) in the Browns record book.

At about the time that Roberts and Kelly emerged, the trend was for teams to use different players for punts and kickoffs. The jobs evolved to where different skills were needed for each task.

Tommy James, who did both for the Browns in the early years, said, "For kickoffs, you could almost get by on speed alone. The field was more open and the tacklers weren't right on top of you. Punt returning is different. Speed helps, but you gotta make sure you have the ball first, make the catch — even with a lot of people breathing down your neck. You just find yourself in congested traffic a lot sooner on punts."

With Jim Brown still in the backfield, about all Leroy Kelly could do to get noticed was

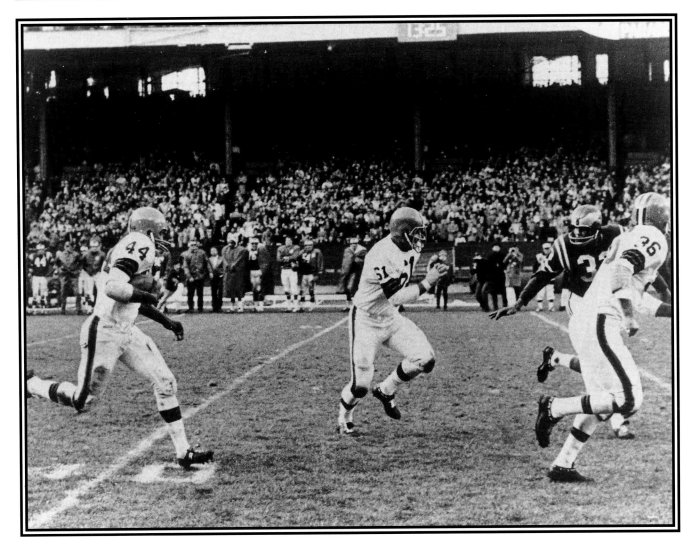

return punts. For the future Hall of Famer's first three seasons (1964-66) he led the team in punt returns, and when needed again in 1971, he turned in team-leading numbers, saying, "I'm willing to do whatever I can to help the team." Kelly led the NFL in 1965 with a sterling 15.6 yard average. That included two returns for touchdowns.

Jim Garrett, who would later become a Browns assistant, foresaw Kelly's greatness while the Morgan State youngster was still confined to return duties. Said Garrett at the time of Jim Brown's retirement, "Leroy Kelly will pick up where Jim Brown left off and not miss a beat."

Kelly proved the knowledgeable Garrett a great prophet. In his first year as a full-time runner after Brown's departure for the silver screen in 1966, Kelly rushed for 1,141 yards, with a league-leading 5.5 yards-per-carry average, a league-long 70-yard scrimmage run and 15 touchdowns, an NFL high for the season.

Leroy Kelly
1964-73

With Roberts gone and Kelly in the backfield, the Browns turned to a variety of return men in the late '60s and early '70s. Cornerback Ben Davis handled both kickoff and punt returns in 1967, as did running back Charley Leigh in '68. Afterward, the jobs fell to a long list of performers, including Reece Morrison, Walt Sumner, Bo Scott, Ken Brown, Homer Jones and Bobby Majors. Then in 1973, the list shortened dramatically.

While waiting to become a 1,000-yard rusher, Greg Pruitt, a water bug running back from

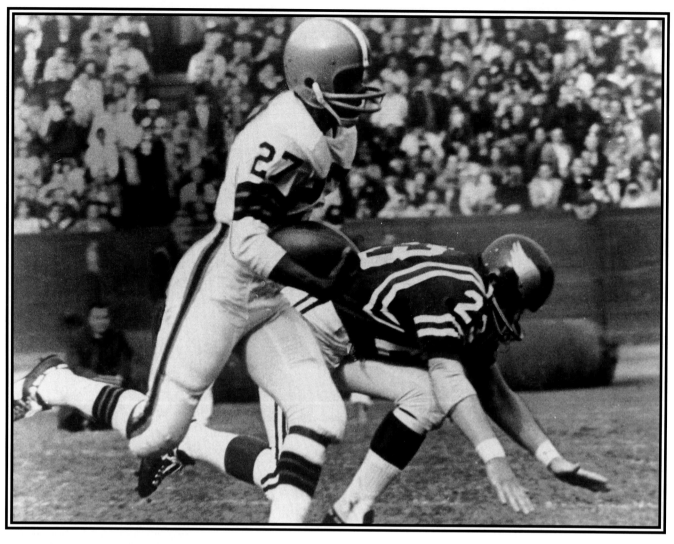

Oklahoma, became the primary Browns return man. His talent defied the conventional wisdom of the day that you couldn't do both — return punts and kickoffs. In 1973-75, Pruitt led the team in both categories each year, ranking at or near the top in NFL and AFC totals.

Helping Pruitt at this time was an all-out returner named Billy Lefear, who had no fear. When not laying the first block for Pruitt, Lefear returned kicks for well over 1,000 yards in his brief stay (1972-75).

Diminutive Dino Hall was the Browns' next established returner, and again proving the wisdom of the special teams coaches in the selection process, handled both jobs effectively from 1979-83. He led the Browns in kickoff and punt returns three times each. The 5-7, 165-pounder from Glassboro State was fearless and durable. Once after a brilliant day with Mr. and Mrs. Hall in the stands, teammate Dave Graf said, "I bet Dino's folks feel *five* feet tall."

During the time that 300-pound-plus William "the Refrigerator" Perry became a national folk hero, Gerald McNeil brought his 140 pounds to the game. When looking for a suitable nickname in keeping with the appliance theme established by Perry, "the Ice Cube" seemed appropriate for the tiny, slippery McNeil. He led the NFL in kickoff returns in 1986 and punt returns in 1989. In Pittsburgh, they still grumble about a 100-

yarder that defeated the Pittsburgh Steelers on Oct. 5, 1986. Many observers still wonder how the Baylor mite did it on the NFL level. "Never giving them too much of a target," is how he explained his survival and effectiveness.

Between McNeil and Metcalf, the return positions were filled primarily by Stefon Adams, Webster Slaughter and Glen Young.

Metcalf first returned kicks in 1989. Initially, he was used more on kickoffs than punts, but in 1992 he handled both and became the NFL leader with 44 punt returns for an AFC-leading 429 yards.

In 1990, Metcalf had his best season as a Browns kickoff returner, handling 52 for 1,052 yards and two touchdowns: 98 yards versus the New York Jets on Sept. 16 and 101 against the Houston Oilers on Dec. 9.

Randy Baldwin, a running back from Mississippi, took over for Metcalf as the primary kickoff man in 1992 and 1993 as the Browns worked Metcalf more into the regular offense, but Metcalf continued to return punts.

Ben Davis
1967-68, '70-73

In 1994, it was Metcalf (punts) and Baldwin (kickoffs) again setting the pace for the Browns. Baldwin's 26.9-yard average was best in the AFC. But after the season, Metcalf was traded to Atlanta and Baldwin signed a free agent deal with the expansion Carolina Panthers, thus leaving the Browns' special teams with two pairs of shoes to fill in 1995.

During times when two roster spots were taken by two returners — one for punts and one for kickoffs, the Browns have been fortunate to

Dino Hall *1979-83*

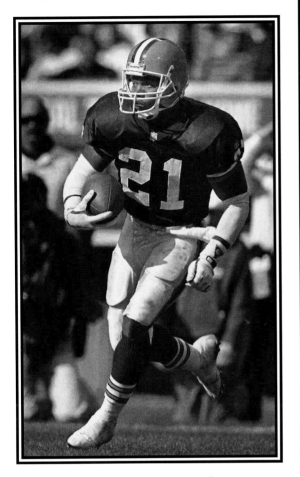

Eric Metcalf *1989-94*

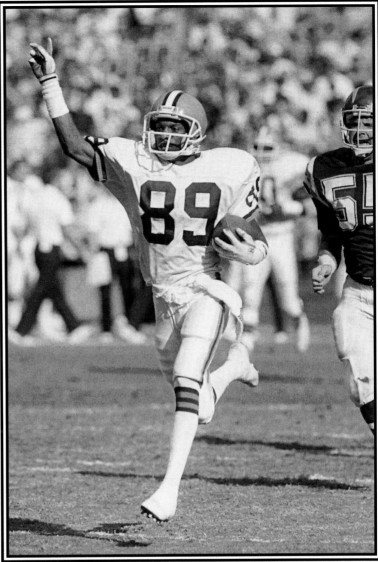

"The Ice Cube"
Gerald McNeil
1986-89

have the Greg Pruitts, the Dino Halls and the Gerald McNeils to do both and give the team the opportunity to keep another player. Even special teams got special, but the Browns proved to be a step ahead of some NFL teams.

What players are accomplishing in the 1990s is truly amazing. Sure, the athletes returning kickoffs and punts are probably more skilled than their forbearers, and the coaching is a little more sophisticated than it once was, but remember this: the same holds true for those covering kicks. Coaches realize now that special teams play can — and usually does — win a couple of games a year just by itself. Case in point: Metcalf's two-TD performance against the Steelers in 1993.

For each hour spent by the Browns' various special teams in preparing for kickoff and punt returns, every other team in the NFL is likely putting in just as much time. Their athletes are just as hungry, just as fast and just as dedicated. But hopefully for Browns fans, they may be a little less skilled or opportunistic overall.

At first, Pro Bowl selections included no return specialists, but Gerald McNeil was selected in 1988, as returners gradually were voted the honor. And, most recently, a special teams "bomb squadder" or cover man is now included. Special teams have become special and for every move today there seems to be a corresponding counter move.

J. Brown

Graham

Willis

P. Brown

Motley

Ford

McCormack

Groza

Browns
Hall of Fame
Gallery

Author/artist Bob Carroll created these illustrations of the 13 Browns Hall of Famers. Carroll is director of the Professional Football Researchers Association and the writer of numerous books on pro football history. His illustrations appear regularly in Pro Football Weekly.

Kelly

Lavelli

Mitchell

Warfield

Gatski

Jim Brown

Running Back • Inducted in 1971

Otto Graham

Quarterback • Inducted in 1965

Mike McCormack

Offensive Tackle • Inducted in 1984

Frank Gatski

Center • Inducted in 1985

Bill Willis

Middle Guard • Inducted in 1977

Bobby Mitchell

Running Back • Inducted in 1983

Lou Groza

OT-Kicker • Inducted in 1974

315

Marion Motley

Running Back • Inducted in 1968

Paul Brown

Head Coach • Inducted in 1967

Len Ford

Defensive End • Inducted in 1976

Paul Warfield

Wide Receiver • Inducted in 1983

Dante Lavelli

End • Inducted in 1975

Leroy Kelly

Running Back • Inducted in 1994

Cleveland Browns Records & Statistics

All-America Football Conference

Year	Conference	Division	W-L-T	Finish
1946	----------	Western	12-2	First
1947	----------	Western	12-1-1	First
1948	----------	Western	14-0	First
1949	---------- *	----------	9-1-2	First

National Football League

Year	Conference	Division	W-L-T	Finish
1950	American	----------	10-2	First-tie
1951	American	----------	11-1	First
1952	American	----------	8-4	First
1953	Eastern	----------	11-1	First
1954	Eastern	----------	9-3	First
1955	Eastern	----------	9-2-1	First
1956	Eastern	----------	5-7	Fourth-tie
1957	Eastern	----------	9-2-1	First
1958	Eastern	----------	9-3	First-tie
1959	Eastern	----------	7-5	Second-tie
1960	Eastern	----------	8-3-1	Second
1961	Eastern	----------	8-5-1	Third
1962	Eastern	----------	7-6-1	Third
1963	Eastern	----------	10-4	Second
1964	Eastern	----------	10-3-1	First
1965	Eastern	----------	11-3	First
1966	Eastern	----------	9-5	Second-tie
1967	Eastern	Century	9-5	First
1968	Eastern	Century	10-4	First
1969	Eastern	Century	10-3-1	First
1970	American	Central	7-7	Second
1971	American	Central	9-5	First
1972	American	Central	10-4	Second
1973	American	Central	7-5-2	Third
1974	American	Central	4-10	Fourth
1975	American	Central	3-11	Fourth
1976	American	Central	9-5	Third
1977	American	Central	6-8	Fourth
1978	American	Central	8-8	Third
1979	American	Central	9-7	Third
1980	American	Central	11-5	First
1981	American	Central	5-11	Fourth
1982	American	----------**	4-5	Eighth
1983	American	Central	9-7	Second
1984	American	Central	5-11	Third
1985	American	Central	8-8	First
1986	American	Central	12-4	First
1987	American	Central	10-5	First
1988	American	Central	10-6	Second
1989	American	Central	9-6-1	First
1990	American	Central	3-13	Fourth
1991	American	Central	6-10	Third
1992	American	Central	7-9	Third
1993	American	Central	7-9	Third
1994	American	Central	11-5	Second

* AAFC played as one league with no divisions.
** NFL played without divisions in strike-shortened season.

League Championship Results

Year	League	Score				Date/Location
1946	AAFC	Browns	14	Yankees	9	12-22-46, Cleve.
1947	AAFC	Browns	14	Yankees	3	12-14-47, N.Y.
1948	AAFC	Browns	49	Bills	7	12-19-48, Cleve.
1949	AAFC	Browns	21	49ers	7	12-11-49, Cleve.
1950	NFL	Browns	30	Rams	28	12-24-50, Cleve.
1951	NFL	Rams	24	Browns	17	12-23-51, L.A.
1952	NFL	Lions	17	Browns	7	12-28-52, Cleve.
1953	NFL	Lions	17	Browns	16	12-27-53, Det.
1954	NFL	Browns	56	Lions	10	12-26-54, Cleve.
1955	NFL	Browns	38	Rams	14	12-26-55, L.A.
1957	NFL	Lions	59	Browns	14	12-29-57, Det.
1964	NFL	Browns	27	Colts	0	12-27-64, Cleve.
1965	NFL	Packers	23	Browns	12	01-02-66, G.B.
1968	NFL	Colts	34	Browns	0	12-29-68, Cleve.
1969	NFL	Vikings	27	Browns	7	01-04-70, Minn.

Conference Championship Results

Year	Conf.	Score				Date/Location
1950	American	Browns	8	Giants	3	12-17-50, Cleve.
1958	Eastern	Giants	10	Browns	0	12-21-58, N.Y.
1967	Eastern	Cowboys	52	Browns	14	12-24-67, Dal.
1968	Eastern	Browns	31	Cowboys	20	12-21-68, Cleve.
1969	Eastern	Browns	38	Cowboys	14	12-28-69, Dal.
1986	American	Broncos	23	Browns	20	01-11-87, Cleve.
1987	American	Broncos	38	Browns	33	01-17-88, Den.
1989	American	Broncos	37	Browns	21	01-14-90, Den.

Additional Playoff Results

Year	League	Score				Date/Location
1949	AAFC	Browns	31	Bills	21	12-04-49, Cleve.
1971	NFL	Colts	20	Browns	3	12-26-71, Cleve.
1972	NFL	Dolphins	20	Browns	14	12-24-72, Miami
1980	NFL	Raiders	14	Browns	12	01-04-81, Cleve.
1982	NFL	Raiders	27	Browns	10	01-08-83, L.A.
1985	NFL	Dolphins	24	Browns	21	01-04-86, Miami
1986	NFL	Browns	23	Jets	20	01-03-87, Cleve.
1987	NFL	Browns	38	Colts	21	01-09-88, Cleve.
1988	NFL	Oilers	24	Browns	23	12-24-88, Cleve.
1989	NFL	Browns	34	Bills	30	01-06-90, Cleve.
1994	NFL	Browns	20	Patriots	13	01-01-95, Cleve.
1994	NFL	Steelers	29	Browns	9	01-07-95, Pitts.

Browns Head Coaches

Coach	Years	Record
Paul Brown	1946-1962	167-53-8 (.759)
Blanton Collier	1963-1970	79-38-2 (.675)
Nick Skorich	1971-1974	30-26-2 (.536)
Forrest Gregg	1975-1977	18-23-0 (.439)
Dick Modzelewski	1977 (interim)	0-1-0 (.000)
Sam Rutigliano	1978-1984	47-51-0 (.480)
Marty Schottenheimer	1984-1988	46-31-0 (.597)
Bud Carson	1989-1990	12-14-1 (.463)
Jim Shofner	1990 (interim)	1-6-0 (.143)
Bill Belichick	1991-1994	32-34-0 (.485)

Team Records: NFL

Total Points
Season 415 (1964)
Game 62 (12-6-53 vs. Giants)
62 (11-7-54 vs. Redskins)

Touchdowns
Season 54 (1966)
Game 8 (12-6-53 vs. Giants)
8 (11-7-54 vs. Redskins)

Extra Points
Season 52 (1966)
Game 8 (12-6-53 vs. Giants)
8 (11-7-54 vs. Redskins)

Field Goals
Season 26 (1986, 1994)
Game 5 (10-19-75 vs. Broncos)

Combined Net Yards
Season 5,915 (1981)
Game 562 (10-25-81 vs. Colts)

Rushing Attempts
Season 559 (1978)
Game 60 (10-2-55 vs. 49ers)

Rushing Yardage
Season 2,639 (1963)
Game 338 (10-29-50 vs. Steelers)

Passing Attempts
Season 624 (1981)
Game 57 (9-7-81 vs. Chargers)

Passing Completions
Season 348 (1981)
Game 33 (12-5-82 vs. Chargers)

Passing Yardage
Season 4,339 (1981)
Game 444 (10-25-81 vs. Colts)

Interceptions
Season 32 (1968)
Game 7 (12-11-60 vs. Bears)

Punt Returns
Season 61 (1954)
Game 8 (11-7-54 vs. Redskins)
8 (11-28-54 vs. Giants)
8 (11-18-56 vs. Eagles)

Kickoff Returns
Season 75 (1979)
Game 9 (10-17-54 vs. Steelers)
9 (10-7-79 vs. Steelers)

Quarterback Sacks
Season 48 (1992, 1993)
Game 11 (11-18-84 vs. Falcons)

First Downs
Season 364 (1981)
Game 35 (11-23-86 vs. Steelers)

Fumbles
Season 50 (1978)
Game 9 (12-20-81 vs. Seahawks)
9 (12-23-90 vs. Steelers)

Penalties
Season 128 (1978, 1989)
Game 21 (11-25-51 vs. Bears)

Punts
Season 97 (1989)
Game 12 (12-3-50 vs. Eagles)
12 (11-19-88 vs. Chiefs)

Individual Records: NFL

Longest Plays

Running 90 Bobby Mitchell (11-15-59 vs. Redskins)
Passing 97 Kosar-Slaughter (10-23-89 vs. Bears)
Punt Ret. 92 Eric Metcalf (9-4-94 vs. Bengals)
Kick Ret. 104 Carl Ward (11-26-67 vs. Redskins)
Int. Ret. 97 Najee Mustafaa (10-10-93 vs. Dolphins)
Fmb. Ret. 89 Don Paul (11-10-57 vs. Steelers)
Punt 80 Horace Gillom (11-28-54 vs. Giants)
Field Goal 60 Steve Cox (10-21-84 vs. Bengals)

Scoring

Total Points
Career 1,349 Lou Groza (1950-59, '61-67)
Season 126 Jim Brown (1965)
Game 36 Dub Jones (11-25-51 vs. Bears)

Touchdowns
Career 126 Jim Brown (1957-65)
Season 21 Jim Brown (1965)
Game 6 Dub Jones (11-25-51 vs. Bears)

Extra Points
Career 641 Lou Groza (1950-59, '61-67)
Season 51 Lou Groza (1966)
Game 8 Lou Groza (12-6-53 vs. Giants)

Field Goals
Career 234 Lou Groza (1950-59, '61-67)
Season 26 Matt Stover (1994)
Game 5 Don Cockroft (10-19-75 vs. Broncos)

Combined Net Yards

Attempts
Career 2,650 Jim Brown (1957-65)
Season 353 Jim Brown (1961)
Game 39 Jim Brown (10-4-59 vs. Cardinals)
39 Mike Pruitt (12-3-81 vs. Oilers)

Yardage
Career 15,459 Jim Brown (1957-65)
Season 2,131 Jim Brown (1963)
Game 313 Jim Brown (11-19-61 vs. Eagles)

Rushing

Attempts
Career 2,359 Jim Brown (1957-65)
Season 305 Jim Brown (1961)
Game 37 Jim Brown (10-4-59 vs. Cardinals)

Yardage
Career 12,312 Jim Brown (1957-65)
Season 1,863 Jim Brown (1963)
Game 237 Jim Brown (11-24-57 vs. Rams)
237 Jim Brown (11-19-61 vs. Eagles)

Touchdowns
Career 106 Jim Brown (1957-65)
Season 17 Jim Brown (1958, 1965)
Game 5 Jim Brown (11-1-59 vs. Colts)

Receiving

Receptions
Career 662 Ozzie Newsome (1978-90)
Season 89 Ozzie Newsome (1983, 1984)
Game 14 Ozzie Newsome (10-14-84 vs. Jets)

Yardage
Career 7,980 Ozzie Newsome (1978-90)
Season 1,236 Webster Slaughter (1989)
Game 191 Ozzie Newsome (10-14-84 vs. Jets)

Touchdowns
Career 70 Gary Collins (1962-71)
Season 13 Gary Collins (1963)
Game 3 Eight times, most recent by
Eric Metcalf (9-20-92 vs. Raiders)

Passing

Attempts
Career 3,439 Brian Sipe (1974-83)
Season 567 Brian Sipe (1981)
Game 57 Brian Sipe (9-7-81 vs. Chargers)

Completions
Career 1,944 Brian Sipe (1974-83)
Season 337 Brian Sipe (1980)
Game 33 Brian Sipe (12-5-82 vs. Chargers)

Yardage
Career 23,713 Brian Sipe (1974-83)
Season 4,132 Brian Sipe (1980)
Game 444 Brian Sipe (10-25-81 vs. Colts)

Touchdowns
Career 154 Brian Sipe (1974-83)
Season 30 Brian Sipe (1980)
Game 5 Frank Ryan (12-12-64 vs. Giants)
5 Bill Nelsen (11-2-69 vs. Cowboys)
5 Brian Sipe (10-7-79 vs. Steelers)

Interceptions

Number
Career 45 Thom Darden (1972-74, '76-81)
Season 10 Thom Darden (1978)
Game 3 Eight times, most recent by
Frank Minnifield, 11-22-87 vs. Oilers)

Yardage
Career 820 Thom Darden (1972-74, '76-81)
Season 238 Bernie Parrish (1960)
Game 115 Bernie Parrish (12-11-60 vs. Bears)

Touchdowns
Career 5 Warren Lahr (1950-59)
Season 2 Five times, most recent by
Thane Gash (1989)
Game 2 Bobby Franklin (12-11-60 vs. Bears)

Punt Returns

Number
Career 161 Gerald McNeil (1986-89)
Season 49 Gerald McNeil (1989)
Game 7 Six times, most recent by
Eric Metcalf (11-8-92 vs. Oilers)

Yardage
Career 1,545 Gerald McNeil (1986-89)
Season 496 Gerald McNeil (1989)
Game 166 Eric Metcalf (10-24-93 vs. Steelers)

Touchdowns
Career 5 Eric Metcalf (1989-94)
Season 2 Leroy Kelly (1965)
2 Eric Metcalf (1993, 1994)
Game 2 Eric Metcalf (10-24-93 vs. Steelers)

Kickoff Returns

Number
Career 151 Dino Hall (1979-83)
Season 52 Eric Metcalf (1990)
Game 9 Dino Hall (10-7-79 vs. Steelers)

Yardage
Career 3,185 Dino Hall (1979-83)
Season 1,052 Eric Metcalf (1990)
Game 172 Dino Hall (10-7-79 vs. Steelers)

Touchdowns
Career 3 Bobby Mitchell (1958-61)
Season 2 Eric Metcalf (1990)
Game 1 11 times, most recent by
Randy Baldwin (9-4-94 vs. Bengals)

Quarterback Sacks

Number
Career 76.5 Clay Matthews (1978-93)
Season 14.5 Bill Glass (1965)
Game 4 Jerry Sherk (11-14-76 vs. Eagles)
4 Mack Mitchell (11-20-77 vs. Giants)

BIBLIOGRAPHY

Books

Brown, Jim, with Myron Cope. *Off My Chest*. Doubleday, 1964.

Brown, Paul, with Jack Clary. *P.B.: The Paul Brown Story*. Atheneum, 1979.

Campbell, Jim. *Golden Years of Pro Football*. Crescent. 1993.

Cerbaro, Varo. *Twenty Years with the Cleveland Browns*. Varo Cerbaro, 1966.

Clary, Jack. *Great Teams, Great Years: Cleveland Browns*. Macmillan Publishing Co., 1973.

Clary, Jack. *Pro Football's Great Moments*. Sammis Publishing Corp., 1983.

Collett, Ritter. *Super Stripes*. Landfall Press, 1982.

Cope, Myron. *The Game That Was*. The World Publishing Co., 1970.

DeLuca, Sam. *The NFL Playbook*. Jonathan David Publications, 1972.

Eckhouse, Morris. *Day by Day in Cleveland Browns History*. Leisure Press, 1984.

Glass, Bill. *Get in the Game!*. Word Books, 1965.

Grosshandler, Stanley. *The Mighty Ones*. Vantage, 1969.

Huff, Sam, with Leonard Shapiro. *Tough Stuff*. St. Martin's Press, 1988.

King, Peter. *Football. A History of the Professional Game*. Oxmoor House, 1993.

King, Peter. *Inside the Helmet*. Simon & Schuster, 1993.

Kowet, Don. *Golden Toes*. St. Martin's Press, 1972.

Leuthner, Stuart. *Ironmen*. Doubleday, 1988.

Levy, Bill. *Return to Glory, The Story of the Cleveland Browns*. The World Publishing Co., 1965.

Levy, Bill. *Sam, Sipe and Company*. J.T. Zubal and P.D. Dole, 1981.

McGuire, Dan. *San Francisco 49ers*. Coward-McCann, 1960.

Owen, Steve. *My Kind of Football*. David McKay, 1952.

Parker, Raymond "Buddy." *We Play to Win*. Prentice-Hall, 1955.

Parrish, Bernie. *They Call It A Game*. Dial Press, 1971.

Rutigliano, Sam. *Pressure*. Oliver Nelson, 1988.

Riffenburgh, Beau and Jack Clary. *The Official History of Pro Football*. Crescent Books, 1990.

Schneider, Russell. *Cleveland Browns Memories*. Russell Schneider, 1990.

Slone, Kay Collier. *Football's Gentle Giant: The Blanton Collier Story*. Life Force Press, 1985.

Whittingham, Richard. *Giants in Their Own Words*. Contemporary Books, 1992.

Zimmerman, Paul. *A Thinking Man's Guide to Pro Football*. E.P. Dutton, 1970.

Record Books & Guides

AAFC Record Manual. All-America Football Conference, 1947-49.

Cleveland Browns Media Guide. Cleveland Browns, selected years, 1946-95.

Neft, David S. and Richard M. Cohen, *Sports Encyclopedia: Pro Football*. Sports Products, Inc., 1987.

Riffenburgh, Beau. *The Official NFL Encyclopedia*. New American Library, 1986.

The NFL's Official Encyclopedic History of Professional Football. Macmillan Publishing Co., 1973.

The Official National Football League 1995 Record & Fact Book. National Football League and Workman Publishing, 1995.

The NFL Official Record Manual. National Football League, selected years.

Treat, Roger. *The Encyclopedia of Football*. A.S. Barnes, 1952 & 1974.

Publications

Kable, F.T., *Pro Football Illustrated*. Elbak Publications, 1946-50.

PRO! NFL Properties, selected issues.

Pro Football Weekly. Pro Football Weekly, selected issues.

Street & Smith's Pro Football Annual. Street & Smith's, selected years.

ILLUSTRATIONS

Bob Carroll: pages 8, 15, 26, 38, 49, 60, 67, 80, 94, 125, 312, 313, 314, 315, 316, 317.

PHOTO CREDITS

Legend: T=top, B=bottom, L=left, R=right, TL=top left, TR=top right, BL=bottom left, BR=bottom right

AP/Wide World Photos: pages 29, 37, 111, 208 T.

Browns News/Illustrated: pages 7, 41, 46 R, 52 L, 61, 64 TL-TR-BL-BR, 66, 68, 69, 70, 71, 72 L-R, 73, 75 TL-TR-B, 76 T-BL-BR, 77 L-R, 79, 81 L-R, 82, 83, 84, 85, 86 T-BL-BR, 87 L-R, 90, 91 TL-TR-B, 92, 93, 95, 96, 97 TL-TR-BL-BR, 98 TL-TR-B, 99, 100, 101 L-R, 102, 103 L-R, 132, 140, 142 T-BL-BR, 143, 144, 145 T-BL-BR, 147, 149, 151, 152, 153, 154, 155, 156, 157, 158 T-BL-BR, 159 T-B, 160 T-B, 161 B, 162 TL-TR-B, 163 T-B, 164 TL-TR-B, 168, 170, 171, 172, 173, 182, 183, 184 L-R, 185, 187, 189 R, 190, 196 L-R, 197, 199 L-R, 200, 201, 202, 203 L-R, 207, 209 T, 213 L-R, 215 L-R, 216, 217, 218, 219, 220, 221 L-R, 222, 227, 228, 229, 232, 233, 234 L-R, 235, 236, 237 L-R, 238 L-R, 239, 241, 242 L-R, 243 L, 244 B, 245 TL-TR-B, 248, 249 L-R, 250 L-R, 251 L-R, 253, 255 R, 256, 257 L-R, 260 R, 261, 262, 263 L-R, 264, 265 L-R, 267, 270, 271, 273, 274, 275, 276, 277, 278, 279, 281, 282, 285, 286, 287, 288, 289 R, 290, 291 R, 292, 293 L-R, 298 T-B, 299 T-B, 300 R, 302 L-R, 303 L-R, 305 R, 310, 311 L-R.

Cleveland State University Archives/*The Cleveland Press* Collection: front & back end sheets; pages 9, 12, 13, 16, 20, 23, 27, 32, 34 BL-BR, 35 T-B, 45, 46 L, 48, 50, 54, 55, 56, 58 L, 110, 112, 113, 137 BR, 139, 141 T-BL-BR, 180, 188, 198, 208 B, 211 L-R, 214, 230, 244 T, 246, 247, 255 L, 268, 269, 289 L, 300 L, 301, 307, 308. Frank Aleksandrowicz: 47 L-R, 138 T, 259. Fred Bottomer: back end sheet, 34 T, 40 R, 116, 117, 136, 137 BL, 177, 212, 225 R, 283, 284. Byron Filkins: front end sheet, 166-67, 193, 254. Daniel Ho: 291 L. Larry Lambert: 74. John Nash: 25 T, 176, 295. Ted R. Schneider Jr.: 309. Paul Tepley: 58 R, 59, 62 R, 63, 65, 181, 258, 260 L, 272.

The Dallas Morning News: Louis DeLuca, page 131.

The Dayton Daily News: page 127.

The Ohio State University Photo Archives: pages 10 L-R, 11.

PRO-file Collection: pages 18, 205, 206.

Transcendental Graphics: pages 39, 40 L, 42, 43, 51, 138 BL-BR, 178, 179, 194, 195, 224, 231, 243 R, 297.

UPI/Bettmann Newsphotos: pages 1, 14, 17, 19, 21, 22, 24, 25 B, 28, 30, 31, 33, 36, 44, 52 R, 53, 57, 62 L, 78, 88, 89, 107, 108, 114, 119, 120, 122 T-B, 123, 129, 134, 135, 137 T, 148, 161 T, 175, 192, 209 B, 210, 225 L, 226, 296, 305 L, 306.